Advance Praise for *Homeschooling Your Struggling Learner*

"A wonderful resource for anyone who is new to home education, home educators new to special needs, and veteran home schoolers with a special needs child looking for fresh ideas."
— **Kim Ashby,** founder and president of the board of directors of GIFTSNC, Inc.; homeschooling mom to three special learners.

———————————□———————————

"Told in a straightforward, practical, and sometimes witty style, this book will be useful to parents, teachers, and health care professionals who want to develop a successful home schooling program based on the knowledge of people with direct experience."
— **Robert Hendren, D.O.,** Professor of Psychiatry; Executive Director, M.I.N.D. Institute; Chief, Child and Adolescent Psychiatry, UC Davis.

———————————□———————————

"Just when you think you've read everything that can be said on the subject of children with learning and attention problems, a book like Homeschooling Your Struggling Learner *comes along and makes you sit up and take notice.*

"Extensively researched, carefully documented, and well organized, Homeschooling Your Struggling Learner *is a veritable treasure trove of up-to-the-minute information, guidelines, and suggestions for helping children who flounder in traditional academic settings. Don't be fooled by the title: anyone who lives or works with a struggling learner—parent, educator, or mental health professional—will find many a valuable nugget to aid in their work with these children.*
— **Barbara D. Ingersoll, Ph.D.,** author of *Your Hyperactive Child.*

"Kathy Kuhl provides parents with a compass and a roadmap for this challenging journey. This readable and complete book explores the issues and obstacles faced by parents who choose to homeschool their struggling children. Kathy deals with all aspects of a child's development—academic, social, emotional and recreational. Kathy's experience, wisdom and knowledgeable advice will be of immeasurable assistance and comfort for you."
— **Richard D. Lavoie, M.Ed., M.A.,** author of *It's So Much Work To Be Your Friend* and *Motivation Breakthrough*; producer of *The F.A.T. City Video.*

"Kathy Kuhl has written a volume that ought to be an essential reference for the parents of children who are being homeschooled. Her suggestions will go far to ensure that these students are receiving an education that is enriching at the same time that it is customized to meet their needs as individuals. Don't homeschool your child without absorbing the wisdom in this well-written and extremely helpful guide."
— **Mel Levine, M.D.,** author of *A Mind at a Time.*

"Kathy Kuhl has complied a wealth of information; a must-read for most, if not all, homeschooling parents. She can talk the talk because she has walked the walk. Don't homeschool without this book."
— **Theresa Powell,** veteran special education teacher and retired homeschool parent.

"When parents conclude that their child might do better in a home schooling program than in their public school or in a private school, they are faced with major questions and concerns. Did I make the correct decision? What do I need to know about my child's educational needs as well as any other needs? How do I start? Where do I go for help?

"Kathy Kuhl's scope of knowledge, sensitivity to the questions and needs of parents who home school, and list of resources are invaluable to any parent who home schools their child."
— **Larry B. Silver, M.D.,** author of *The Misunderstood Child.*

HOMESCHOOLING *your* STRUGGLING LEARNER

Kathy Kuhl

LEARN DIFFERENTLY

Herndon, Virginia

Printed in the United States of America.

First Edition

Published by Learn Differently LLC, P.O. Box 711241, Herndon, Virginia 20171
For individual orders, visit www.LearnDifferently.com.
For wholesale orders, write info@LearnDifferently.com or write Learn Differently at the address above.

Scripture quotations are from The Holy Bible, English Standard Version®, © 2001 by Crossway Bibles, a publishing ministry of Good News Publishers. Used by permission.
All rights reserved.

Disclaimer

Information in this book is based on the author's research, interviews, and experience as a parent seeking services for a child with special needs. It should not replace seeking advice from certified professionals; nor should any part of this book should be construed as medical or legal advice.

Publisher's Cataloging-in-Publication
(Provided by Quality Books, Inc.)

Kuhl, Kathy.
Homeschooling your struggling learner / Kathy Kuhl.
 -- 1st ed.
  p. cm.
  Includes bibliographical references and index.
  LCCN 2008910456
  ISBN-13: 9780981938905
  ISBN-10: 0981938906

  1. Learning disabled children--Education. 2. Home schooling. I. Title.

 LC4704.K84 2009   371.9
        QBI08-600338

Book design and cover design by Martha Leone.
Cover photographs © 2008 Frederick Kuhl.

———□———

To my three favorite men:

My creative, insightful, and persevering son,

My father:
encourager, research assistant,
and chairman of the history department
of the Kuhl Academy,

and
My husband for his love, support,
tolerance, humor, and wisdom.

———□———

I can no other answer make, but thanks,
and thanks, and ever thanks.

William Shakespeare, Twelfth Night

Acknowledgements

I am indebted to many people for their contributions to this work.
First and foremost, thanks to the sixty-four homeschooling parents across
North America who I interviewed. Their gifts of their time and insights
strengthened this book tremendously.

Next, thanks to Dr. Elliot Blumenstein, pediatric occupational
therapist Laurie Chuba, Dr. John Umhau, and Marilyn Zecher, C.A.L.T.,
for their interviews. Thanks to Amy Antler, M.A., CCC-SLP, Lynn
Kuitems Henk, Nancy Holmes, Dr. Barbara Ingersoll, and Diana L.
Thomas for answering questions.

Thanks to many kind friends and relatives who read drafts of this
book. First, thanks to Janet Barker, Theresa Powell, and Gene Weithoner
for reading the complete manuscript. Thanks to readers Rebecca Bowman,
Tammy Breene, Laurie Chuba, Betsy DeMarco, Kathy Haber, Fred Kuhl,
Stephen Kuhl, Rachel Nagy, Russell Ottaviano, and Tammy Wyman.

Thanks to Janet Barker, Margaret Cranor, Diane Kwiatkowski, and
Betty Statnick of HSLDA, who gave me support and encouragement to
begin homeschooling.

Thanks to the following for encouragement and support:
Dr. Barbara Ingersoll, Dana and Theresa Powell, Tara Taylor, and
Betty Weithoner. Thanks to two talented friends: my copy editor,
Sarah Hamaker, and Martha Leone, my book designer. Thanks to the

members of Capital Christian Writers Group, and to two great support groups for homeschoolers with special needs children: GiftsNC and our local branch, GiftsNVA.

Despite all this generous help from so many, mistakes remain, but they are my responsibility and no reflection on anyone else.

Finally, thanks to my son for letting me tell our story, and to my husband for supporting, helping, encouraging, and challenging me in this endeavor.

Table of Contents

Introduction

I wrote this book as a comprehensive introduction to homeschooling children who struggle to learn. I intend to help parents new to homeschooling, homeschoolers just beginning to learn about their children's learning difficulties, and homeschoolers long familiar with their children's special needs, who need encouragement, ideas, and resources.

You cannot do everything

Homeschooling Your Struggling Learner includes many resources and strategies—more than any one family can or should do. Think of this book as a smorgasbord; I hope every reader will find enough useful ideas and insights to make a good meal.

How to use this book

If you are just beginning to homeschool or have not yet begun, start with chapter 1. If you already homeschool and are beginning to suspect learning problems, start at chapter 4. Everyone should read chapter 5. For the remaining chapters, read the introduction and the "In this chapter" box, to see which chapters and sections you need.

Every family and every homeschool is different

I homeschooled my son for grades four through twelve, but I wanted
to draw on the experience of others as well. I interviewed sixty-four
homeschooling parents across North America whose children have a
wide range of problems that make learning difficult: children diagnosed
with learning disabilities, attention deficit disorder, autism spectrum
disorders, or a combination of these, and many other co-existing
conditions. Some of these struggling learners also are gifted. Unless last
names are included, I have changed the names of all parents and children
to preserve their privacy.

Who are "struggling learners"?

After all, don't we all struggle to learn some things? My hope is that this
book will help many families. But there is a limit to my experience and to
the range of my interviews. I have interviewed few families homeschooling
children with serious physical difficulties or with mental retardation. Those
children certainly also are struggling learners. I have had the privilege of
working with and knowing children and adults with multiple sclerosis,
muscular dystrophy, cerebral palsy, and mental retardation. I have seen
them make heroic efforts. Nothing in this book or its title is meant to
suggest that they do not struggle or cannot learn.

For help homeschooling children with needs beyond the scope of this
book, I would refer the reader to NATHHAN, the National Challenged
Homeschoolers Associated Network (www.nathhan.com); to GIFTSNC,
Giving and Getting Information for Teaching Special Needs Children
(giftsnc.com; also see their group at groups.yahoo.com); to Sharon
Hensley's *Home Schooling Children with Special Needs*, and to Joe and
Connie Sutton's *Strategies for Struggling Learners*; see the end of chapter 10.

What about those abbreviations?

At this writing, the American Psychiatric Association abbreviates Attention
Deficit/Hyperactivity Disorder AD/HD, meaning attention deficit disorder

with or without hyperactivity. But some parents tell me, "My child has ADD, not AD/HD." When I mean both with or without hyperactivity, I use ADD/ADHD.

Though also known as pervasive developmental delays (PDD), ASD (autism spectrum disorders) is the abbreviation I use to refer to all disorders on the autism spectrum.

He or she?

Because struggling learners can be girls or boys, women or men, I have alternated between male and female pronouns. In the odd-numbered chapters, I write as if your child was a girl; in the even chapters as if your struggling learner was a boy.

Disclaimer

Information in this book is based on my research, interviews, and experience as a parent seeking services for a child with special needs. It should not replace seeking advice from certified professionals; nor should any part of this book should be construed as medical or legal advice.

For which of you, desiring to build a tower,
does not first sit down and count the cost,
whether he has enough to complete it?

Luke 14:28

Part I

Deciding Whether to Homeschool a Struggling Learner

1

Is School Working
for Your Child?

Do you need to pull your child out of school?

Homeschooling can be a frightening thought. Fourteen years ago, it intimidated me. Though my child struggled with schoolwork in first and second grades, I never thought I had the energy or the patience needed to teach him at home. Getting him and his homework out the door on school mornings was hard enough. I did not want to take on his education.

My son was a bit of a shock, coming nearly three years after his conscientious, attentive big sister. My son Pete[1] always was thinking of new activities to try, involving hazards I had never thought to prohibit. Many adventures ended with the same conversation:

"What do you learn from this, dear?"

"Not to."

Our boy had many strengths. He loved to talk to anyone. His bad moods usually lasted only a few minutes. But there was an odd combination of intelligence and slowness. He was still trying to master the alphabet song in second grade—was it "emma, emma, pea"? In third grade, he still could not count to sixty. At home, he often would forget instructions. He liked to please his parents and was clearly frustrated by his lapses.

All in all, dealing with my sweet, charming, and highly distractible little boy took plenty of my attention and energy before and after school. I certainly did not want to homeschool him.

1. Unless first and last names are given, names of homeschoolers and their children have been changed to preserve their privacy.

Yet I did, for nine years.

Many who homeschool were reluctant at first but decided it was the best option for their struggling learners. What makes some parents and guardians move from saying, "Not me!" to taking the plunge?

In this chapter:
- Struggling in the classroom and at home
- Is public school a good fit for your child
- Alternatives to the classroom

Struggling in the Classroom and at Home

For some children, learning is fun and rewarding. For others, it is a struggle, a chore to be overcome. Children can struggle different ways:

- Carl cannot sit still even though he is fourteen.
- Jessica daydreams constantly.
- Anna knows the answers, but her handwriting is not only painfully slow, it is illegible.
- For Michelle, the buzzing of the overhead fluorescent lights is intolerable.
- Sam has trouble reading, but remembers details and asks great questions.

These children have at least average intelligence, but they perform below their ability. When your children struggle, you devote many hours to helping them succeed in school. You meet with the school staff regularly. They may write an Individualized Educational Plan (IEP), guaranteeing some special help for your child. They may disagree among themselves about the best approach and behave inconsistently with your child, to her confusion. Your school staff may be difficult for you to work with. You may be battling the school system, because either they are not providing the services promised in the IEP, or the services promised are inadequate. But even if your school staff is professional and helpful—as was everyone at my son's school—you spend hours keeping in touch with teachers; studying special education laws, regulations, and acronyms; attending seminars; and trading information with other parents.

Every night you help your child slog through homework. Don, a teacher in Illinois, remembered life before he started homeschooling his daughter with high-functioning autism:

She had struggled with homework from the beginning. It always took her much longer than it would take other kids. As she got into higher elementary grades, we were spending two, three, four hours a night on homework. [By seventh grade] homework was sucking up all our time.

Your child may sense your anxiety over her future. She may be a perfectionist, furious with herself because of each small error. Or she may rush carelessly on, not expecting to learn. When the homework is done, you want to help her in her areas of need, but she has no energy left for tutoring—and neither do you.

Perhaps she often comes home from school tired, angry, or tearful. For a variety of reasons, she may have social problems, missing the cues that other kids pick up. If she has an Autism Spectrum Disorder (ASD)[2], she needs help recognizing the point of view of others and responding appropriately. If she is distractible, she needs training in awareness and self-control. My son's second grade teacher described a typical scene: Pete goes to the pencil sharpener, accidentally bumping a classmate's chair. She complains, but Pete does not hear. On the return trip, his mind still elsewhere, he does not notice that he jiggles her desk again. Five minutes later, Pete gets up to throw away some trash, and squeezing through, jars her again. So she yells at him. He has no idea why, so he gets mad, as well.

The brighter the child, the more frustrated the parents can be as they contrast their child's ability with her difficulty in school. And the brighter the child, the more frustrated the child can become. Even the brightest children may conclude: "School isn't that hard for most people. I must be stupid."

Apart from school work, your child's difficulties create strains at home. Learning difficulties may make it hard for kids to hear, understand, or respond when Mom or Dad give instructions, causing tension and misunderstandings. My son once wrote what goes on in his head. (I have left out two-thirds of it.)

2. Autism Spectrum Disorders (ASD) are a range of complex developmental disabilities that usually appear in the first three years of life. They affect development in the areas of social interaction and communication skills. Source: Autism Society of America, "Defining Autism." www.autism-society.org, accessed January 17, 2008.

Oh, Wow! Look at the clouds out there. I wonder if it's going to rain. I should have looked at the newspaper this morning at breakfast. What kept me from looking? I dunno. Those eggs were good. Wait, Mom said something to me. What did she say? Oh, I remember: to do the dishes.

So when you said, "Do the dishes," did you mean you want me to clean the dishes? With what? Is there enough soap in the wash basin? Oh, yes, and how old is that water? Do I need to dump it out and get new water? And I have to remember to ask Mom about the weather once I am done with the dishes. Oh, dear! Am I still standing here, not answering what Mom said? Why do I think like this?

Meanwhile, back out on planet earth, Mom is thinking, "Come on. Look at me when I talk to you. I asked you a simple question: Will you please do the dishes?"

Children's difficulties can affect home life in different ways. Parents of children with ASD work daily and intensively on communication and social skills, coaching for situations which the average child could handle easily. They also may be trying to modify quirky repetitive behaviors, which can isolate the child further. All children forget chores, but children with Attention Deficit Disorder[3] (ADD/ADHD) forget all the time. Their parents spend years teaching basic organization skills. It seems they have replaced so many lost hats, sweatshirts, and books that they could have outfitted another child.

Medical concerns may complicate schooling. You may be trying to squeeze time for medical appointments or therapies into your school week. Perhaps your child is prone to frequent illnesses. Is a sleep disorder the reason she cannot pay attention in class? Are her stomach aches caused by stress, irritable bowel syndrome, or something else?

Perhaps your child needs medication for seizures, allergies, or other conditions. You may be trying medication, alternative treatments, or special diets. If so, you are trying to make sure the regimen is followed at school. Before and after school daily, you are evaluating your child's mood and

3. ADD/ADHD is used in this book to refer to AD/HD, Attention Deficit/Hyperactivity Disorder, which, despite the "H," can occur with or without hyperactivity. Some parents interviewed for this book have children with different kinds of ADD/ADHD: inattentive, hyperactive, distractible, impulsive, or combined.

behavior, which is complex and variable. But you don't see your child's performance at school—you must rely on brief reports from a busy teacher. You wish there was litmus paper you could slip in your daughter's mouth: "Yes, blue! She's paying attention today." But why? Maybe the teacher was just more interesting today, or there were fewer distractions. Trying to figure it out takes even more time.

Helping your struggling learner may take its toll in another way. Trying to help a child with learning difficulties succeed in a traditional school setting may make you start to think of your child not just as different, but defective. You can forget that your child is a growing person, with her own gifts. You can start to neglect the strengths that are the seeds of her success in adulthood. Wrapped up in your worry about her future, you can forget to enjoy your child.

Is Public School a Good Fit for Your Child?

Schools face a difficult job, serving hundreds or thousands of students. Teachers must adopt methods that help a majority, so many teachers lecture and expect children to sit still and listen. Beginning around fourth grade, teachers also expect students to learn from textbooks. Schools set schedules that enable them to teach large groups efficiently. This can be hard for some struggling learners. Moving from classroom to classroom befuddles some children. Teachers may have to announce details and changes quickly, which some children have trouble absorbing. For many students, these are just inconveniences. For your student, they may be disastrous.

I have supported public schools for years. I received a good education in public schools. I taught junior high public school with dedicated professionals who gave and gave to help their students. When my children started at our wonderful public school, I volunteered as a tutor, classroom aide, and PTA newsletter editor. I respect public school teachers and staff.

But, for some of our children, public school is not the best fit. Some kids fall between the cracks. Their needs are often outweighed by the needs of others, and the help they get is limited by budget crunches and classroom sizes. Every year, schools are told to meet more mandates and improve test scores. Schools have many children to serve, with a wide range of needs and abilities. And teachers have only so much time.

Donna, who homeschools three boys in Maryland, explained about why she first brought her oldest son home:

> *In the classroom, there was too much chaos, disruption, and distraction. There was not enough one-on-one or personal attention, and… his reading and writing were behind his peers. Too much in the classroom was learning through reading and writing. And it's very hard to learn though your weak areas.*

Anna recalled when her son was seven:

> *We met with all the specialists who had tested Brendan. I kept hearing the same thing over and over, like a chorus, that Brendan, one-on-one, could produce much more than he could produce in the classroom setting. [But] Brendan did not qualify for any special help.*

Alternatives to the Classroom

When public school began to seem inadequate for my child, I looked at private schools, hoping smaller classes and special accommodations would do the job. But finding the right school isn't easy, even if you can afford it. Private schools may not provide the accommodations your child needs.

Some private schools would have been a poor fit for my son. I observed classes and decided that merely having seventeen classmates instead of twenty-seven would not make much difference for him. At one school, the rooms were more crowded than in public school, so his classmates would be even more distracting. Another school boasted individualized instruction, but it was all by computer. My son loves people, and I knew he needed teachers, not software. A third school offered a self-contained program for students with language-based learning disabilities, but the plodding pace set by the teacher and her hypnotic, slow speech would have driven my son crazy.

I was fortunate to live near a city with several schools specifically for struggling learners. I visited them and was impressed with their excellent programs, with experienced, wise professionals. The best private school option for us was an hour's drive away and cost more than fourteen thousand dollars a year at the time. (Today it is more than twenty thousand.) Along with the cost of tuition, I also considered how two hours of commuting would affect my son, who hates long drives.

After her son failed first grade at a small private school, Sarita, a mother in Georgia, was at a loss:

> *I just absolutely despaired: "What am I going to do with this child because I can't put him in public school, and he can't function in private school." I didn't really think of homeschooling as an option even though I was already a stay-at-home mom.*

Although some people homeschool from the beginning out of personal conviction, others I interviewed, like Sarita, switch to homeschooling out of necessity. She began in 2005 and enjoys the freedom to customize their homeschool to her son's needs and interests. Below, Marcia describes why she removed her son from private school. He has learning disabilities and ADD/ADHD:

> *Number one, he needed the distractions of the classroom removed. Number two, we were doing most work at home as homework, anyway. Number three, there was a lot of ridicule. Kids are kids, and they picked up on the fact that he was a struggling learner, and they could be pretty unkind. And then I found that the private services I needed him to have were very difficult to get. Everyone was trying to get those before- or after-school hours. My child was exhausted after school, and not quite plugged in before school. And then, to have to turn around [after early morning tutoring] and go to school! Life was getting extremely complicated, trying to give him everything he needed, the way he needed it.*

Another option we considered was keeping Pete in school and hiring a tutor to help with reading, writing, math, and homework. A good tutor can help. But it would have made life busier without removing our son from the tense school situation. And the tutor would have had only the dregs of our son's energy and attention after school, just as we did helping our son with homework.

My husband and I saw four options:

- keep our son where he was, a great school, but one where he was "emotionally exhausted," as one teacher said,
- enroll him in a private school,
- hire a tutor to help with schoolwork,
- homeschool him.

We decided our best option was for me to stay home and teach our son myself. But we only reached that decision slowly, as we learned more about homeschooling.

2

Misconceptions
About Homeschooling

As you look at homeschooling, you may have questions and doubts. In this chapter, we will look at some common misconceptions about homeschooling.

In this chapter:
- Myth #1: I don't have the patience to homeschool.
- Myth #2: Homeschooled children are isolated and do not learn how to socialize with others.
- Myth #3: I cannot homeschool because I am not trained as a teacher.
- Myth #4: A special needs child should have a special education teacher.
- Myth #5: Homeschooling will solve all my struggling learner's problems.

Only a decade ago, complete strangers would sometimes express concern when they learned I homeschooled. Today, when people learn my son was homeschooled, they are more likely to tell me they have a friend or relative who homeschools or who was homeschooled. Homeschooling has become more acceptable as it has become more popular.

Statistics indicate that homeschooling is growing. In 2003, the U.S. Department of Education estimated that, out of approximately fifty million children in kindergarten through grade twelve in the United States, 1.1 million children were homeschooled. These homeschooled students represent a twenty-nine percent increase in four years.[1] The non-profit National Home Education Research Institute (NHERI) estimated even more homeschooling was taking place: that between 1.7 and 2.1 million children were homeschooled in 2003. NHERI reported that homeschooling was increasing seven percent per year from 1999 to 2003.[2] In Canada, in 2001, an estimated fifty to ninety-five thousand children were homeschooled.[3]

Despite the growing popularity of homeschooling, confusion remains. In this chapter, I will try to correct five popular misconceptions about homeschooling.

Myth #1: I don't have the patience to homeschool.

Every homeschooler has heard this, and it is a legitimate concern for parents. And when you know the stress of helping a struggling learner in school, you might think that homeschooling him would be even harder. But if you are:

- helping the distracted child remember chores and find lost belongings, or
- practicing reading and writing with the child with learning disabilities, or
- training an autistic child to communicate and relate, and
- checking with the school on progress and assignments, and
- spending hours each night on homework, and
- teaching the social skills other children pick up on their own,

then you have been exercising a lot of patience. You may find homeschooling reduces your stress.

If you homeschool, there is no mad dash to catch the bus, no communication breakdowns between parent and teacher, and no tutoring after dinner when both of you are exhausted. Pat, who homeschools a hyperactive daughter in New York, told me, "Even though it was a struggle, [homeschooling was] the best thing we ever did for her, for her

1. National Center for Educational Statistics, Homeschooling in the United States: 2003. NCES 2006-042.

2. Ray, Brian, D., Ph.D. "Facts on Homeschooling." Salem, Oregon: National Home Education Research Institute, February 2003.

3. _____. Worldwide Guide to Homeschooling. Nashville: Broadman and Holman, 2005.

self-confidence and peace of mind. The stress level in our house dropped seven billion points." Many families I interviewed reported that homeschooling was less stressful than having a struggling learner in school.

Myth #2: Homeschooled children are isolated and do not learn how to socialize with others.

When I interviewed Sarita, a homeschooler in Georgia, she told me that was her initial impression. "You hear, 'homeschooling,' and you immediately think of anti-social weirdoes who sit in the house all day. You don't think of very social, very open, very bright children," she said. But Sarita's child had failed first grade in a small private school, so she tried homeschooling. She discovered homeschool does not mean isolation. She liked being able to teach to his needs, take many field trips, and enjoy activities with two homeschool groups.

Paul T. Hill, in the *Hoover Digest*, writes:

> *Home schoolers are not all recluses living in log cabins. Growing numbers of home-schooling families live in or near cities, are well educated, and hold down normal jobs. They are not all afraid of the modern world; many are inveterate users of the Internet, and large numbers of West Coast home-school parents work in the computer and software industries.*

> *Although large numbers of home schoolers are Christian fundamentalists and Mormons, many other religions are represented as well. There are active home-schooling organizations for Lutherans, Catholics, and Jews. In Washington, Oregon, and California, many of the new urban home schoolers are not active members of any church.*

> *Home schoolers' fierce independence rarely leads to isolationism. Increasingly, parents are bartering services—the mother who was a math major tutors children from several families in return for music or history lessons. Families come together to create basketball or soccer teams, hold social events, or put on plays and recitals.*[4]

4. Hill, Paul T. "How Home Schooling Will Change Public Education." Hoover Digest, No. 2, 2002. www.hoover. org/publications/ digest/3483911. html, accessed December 14, 2007.

Most of the homeschooling families I interviewed are very active outside the home and have opportunities to practice social skills. Homeschool parents have more natural opportunities to coach their children on social skills, and homeschooled children have more opportunities to relate to people of all ages, rather than being isolated with twenty-five people their age in a classroom. As homeschooling has grown, so have the opportunities for homeschoolers to socialize. One homeschooler I interviewed admitted social life was a problem: her family has too many social activities!

As one mother observed, for a child who needs social coaching, it is good not to have to try to master social skills while working on academics. Children on the autism spectrum, for example, may find a small homeschooled physical education class easier to adapt to than a public school class. A child with learning disabilities may do better in a homeschool math class with five children, than in a private school's class of fifteen.

Organizing social activities takes time and planning, and some families, particularly in some rural areas, do struggle to avoid isolation. But enrolling a student in public school does not guarantee good social skills, a good social life, or good friends. As one mother said of her autistic children's experiences in school, "They don't really get social skills at school and what they do get, I find to be negative."

In chapter 23, I will discuss activities outside the home.

Myth #3: I cannot homeschool because I am not trained as a teacher.

You can homeschool legally in the United States and Canada without being a teacher. Most states and provinces have laws authorizing homeschooling. In the rest, homeschoolers may operate legally as a small private school or provide what is called *equivalent instruction*. The laws vary, so you need to read the current law in your state or province. You may check with your local school district, but they may not keep up with the most current law. State and provincial homeschool organizations keep sharp eyes on legislative changes each year, and so their websites are excellent sources.

But even if you know you can homeschool legally, you may think you need teacher training courses to do a good job. While I earned a teaching certificate, enjoyed educational psychology classes, and had excellent professors, that did not qualify me to homeschool. Homeschooling successfully depends on information, preparation, and dedication. It does not require a teaching certificate.

Even the most dedicated public school teachers have limited resources, limited time, and many students. Every year, the school district, state, or nation expects the schools to do more: develop good citizens; build character; teach children about sex, drugs, hygiene, and exercise; and, especially, to pass the state standardized tests. As the government piles on the mandates, teachers have less time. That limits their ability to customize education for children with special needs.

Myth #4: A special needs child should have a special education teacher.

Again, there are legal and practical sides to this question. Let's discuss the legal side first. Two national homeschool organizations, the Home School Legal Defense Association (HSLDA) and the National Home Education Network (NHEN), discuss the legal issue well on their websites, but neither their websites nor this book should be considered legal advice. NHEN states:

> *[I]t is a crucial first step that you become educated about your specific state's requirements. This is especially important when deciding to home educate a child who has been in the public school system and who possesses an Individualized Educational Plan (IEP). The main concern is that frequently school officials will tell parents that it is not legal for them to homeschool their special needs child. Vulnerable parents, already anxious about their children's situations, will believe the school "experts" and not make the move to homeschooling. Schools also do not like for… children [with IEPs] to leave because these students bring in more money for the schools. Therefore, it is important to know your legal rights!* [5]

Practically, how can you homeschool a struggling learner when you are not a special education teacher?

First, I must say that I respect special education teachers. As a teen, I volunteered at a summer camp for special needs children. Working there

5. *National Home Education Network. "Legal Considerations." www.nhen.org/ specneed/default. asp?id=242, accessed November 27, 2007.*

under dedicated special education teachers is what drew me into teaching. Since then, as a parent and as a public school teacher, I have worked with wonderful special education teachers.

If you are not a special education teacher, you still can homeschool a struggling learner. There are two reasons why. First, the homeschooled child benefits greatly from getting individualized attention. Second, specialized help is available for you.

As I interviewed homeschooling parents for this book, I talked to three former special education teachers who are now homeschooling mothers. They urged homeschoolers to value their own work. One of those teachers, Jen, compared homeschooling to her classroom experience:

> *In a special education classroom, there may be up to twelve students in one classroom with different strengths and weaknesses. What works for two might not work for all twelve. In a homeschool setting, that student is receiving one-on-one attention from a parent who knows his strengths and weaknesses and can give that child exactly what he needs.*[6]

The research of psychologist Dr. Stephen Duvall supports the opinion of these parent educators. Education researchers know that the more time a student is engaged in *academic responses*—writing, answering orally, reading, or discussing academic material—the more the student will learn. Researchers call the amount of time a student spends on those activities *Academic Engaged Time* (AET). Duvall's research supports the notion that homeschooled special needs students spend more time engaged in academics than their public school peers. Duvall believes this is the key to understanding the high performance of homeschooled students.[7]

From our schooldays, most of us remember times in class when we hoped not to get called on. But homeschooled children have no crowds to hide in. They must engage more. When Mom or Dad is working with them, they cannot get away with fifteen minutes of daydreaming. As Duvall writes:

> *Specifically, if parents increase the amount of time that their children spend writing, making physical academic responses [e.g. typing*

6. E-mail to the author, July 6, 2007.

7. Duvall, Stephen F. "The Effectiveness of Homeschooling Students with Special Needs." Homeschooling in Full View: A Reader. Greenwich, Connecticut: Information Age, 2005, p. 157.

> *or using a calculator], reading aloud, reading silently, and engaging*
> *in academic talk about the curriculum or the instructor's lessons,*
> *then the pace of their children's learning will quicken.*[8]

It is not always easy for parents to find effective ways to teach their struggling learners, but they don't need to earn a special education certification. The disciplined, consistent effort of a parent who is actively engaging the child can work wonders.

The parents may need extra help and some training, especially for the child with more serious difficulties. Many families I interviewed used professional services such as psychologists, or occupational or speech therapists. Several parents hired special education consultants, meeting with them two or three times a year for advice. Several parents had taken special training, most often in teaching reading. In chapters 8, 10, and 18, I will discuss how parents can find an educational consultant and get the training they may need.

HSLDA recommends that you receive educational assistance, keep records documenting your child's progress, and obtain regular evaluations.[9] See chapters 7 and 8 on evaluations, testing, and assistance.

Myth #5: Homeschooling will solve all my struggling learner's problems.

As parents learn more about homeschooling, some think it will solve all their problems. Other parents assume this without realizing it. Removing distractions and customizing curriculum help. A flexible schedule and one-on-one training offers many advantages. But they do not make learning problems disappear. One parent advised, "Don't be delusional, seeking a magic bullet. Don't think everything will be cured if you homeschool and you'll reach normal."

Finding the right approach in homeschooling takes time Homeschooling is not something to decide on today and start tomorrow. Homeschooling a struggling learner is not easy, but it can provide your child a good education, reduce stress in your family, and help your child's self-esteem. It might be your best choice. The next chapter gives you advice on how to decide.

8. *Ibid., p. 160.*

9. *Home School Legal Defense Association. "Two Steps For Protecting Your Special Needs Homeschool." www.hslda.org/ strugglinglearner/ sn_TwoSteps. asp, accessed November 27, 2007.*

3

Deciding Whether
to Start Homeschooling

What questions should you ask when considering whether to homeschool? Even parents who were teachers may think long and hard before they begin. Here are some questions to ask yourself.

In this chapter:
- Can we do this?
- Can we afford to homeschool?
- What about relationships?
- What resources are available?
- Would homeschooling be good for my child?

Can We Do This?

Would homeschooling work for me and my family? To help you decide, ask yourself and your spouse these questions:

Do you enjoy learning? If you enjoy learning, you can pass on a love of learning. And as a new homeschooler, you have a lot to learn. Homeschoolers say that in the first year, the homeschooling mother learns more than the children. How much more when homeschooling a struggling learner! No doubt, you have begun to read about the special needs your child has. Perhaps you have read about possible treatments. You will need to shop and compare curricula, materials, methods, and possibly therapies—major research projects.

Can you admit mistakes? By not being flustered or impatient with your own mistakes, you can show your child how to be patient with herself. Homeschooling parents need to plan ahead and preview material, but we don't have to be perfect.

Do you like to teach? I don't mean in standing in front of a classroom. Do you like to share your knowledge and watch others understand? For instance, have you enjoyed teaching your child to cook, fish, or play checkers? Breaking a task into parts, doing it a different way, and noticing that a prerequisite skill needs to be learned or relearned—these are all parts of teaching.

Do you like to plan? Or have you learned that you have to plan to avoid disaster? If you are distractible or disorganized by nature, are you learning to compensate by using lists, timers, or other aids? Attention problems run in families, so the homeschooling parent may think, as I did, "I have a hard enough time organizing myself. Do I have to help my son organize his school work, too?" But your struggles can help you sympathize with your child, and your desire to help her can motivate you to organize yourself.

If you have trouble planning and are married, your spouse may be able to help. (If you are single, find a sympathetic homeschooling friend to help you plan, or hire a special education consultant as described in chapter 8.) Your spouse may not be at home most of the day, but can still help you set a schedule and goals. A second opinion can help anyone.

Are you wondering how you could stand being with the children all day? As you settle into a routine, you adjust. In later chapters, I'll discuss staying sane as you homeschool—tips for getting breaks and maintaining your own mental health. Here, I will simply observe that many parents report enjoying their time homeschooling their children. Anita's son has severe disabilities, but after homeschooling him for pre-kindergarten, she decided to homeschool his sisters, too, because "I got such great results with my son and we were having such a good time. I felt it was an opportunity to create a family environment that I wanted."

When you consider your ability to homeschool, don't worry about a few academic weaknesses. If you hate math, are terrified of chemistry, or can't stand dissection, that's no reason not to homeschool. As I will explain later, homeschooling parents don't have to teach every subject themselves.

Can We Afford To Homeschool?

Having looked at yourself, next count the cost. Chapters 11 through 15 will help you plan and purchase books and materials more efficiently.

Your first expense should not be buying curriculum, but preparing yourself. Buy or borrow books on your child's special needs and books on homeschooling. Some state homeschool groups offer seminars on how to begin homeschooling. Attend one. Go to a homeschool convention or conference. There, you can attend seminars inexpensively, look at curricula, and talk to homeschoolers. You will go from feeling you have no resources to realizing the problem will be choosing from among many. (Don't buy until you read chapter 13 on shopping.) Sign up for local homeschooling newsletters. Visit homeschooling websites. If you have not joined a patient advocacy association for your child's special need, start visiting your local chapters and the organization websites.

Next, let's look at the cost of books. You will buy or borrow books for your child: stories, novels, biographies, history, how-to books, and well-illustrated reference books. Get to know your library; mine saved me hundreds of dollars every year. Even a small library can help you, because with interlibrary loans, you can access the world. You will definitely need bookshelves.

You will want a computer, printer, and Internet access. You will probably buy more software because of homeschooling. Lots of websites offer information on disabilities and therapies. You need to be a skeptical reader and shopper, researching wisely. The Internet also is a great source of educational materials; again, some are junk and others are excellent. I'll discuss choosing materials in chapter 13.

Your goal is to create a home environment where learning is attractive. Home should be an interesting place to be. That can be done cheaply, but it should be done thoughtfully. You will want some art supplies, some manipulatives—plastic counters, pattern blocks, and other tools for hands-on learning. You may buy or make some educational games. You may need an inexpensive tape recorder and audio cassettes, so your child can dictate stories, or so you can make books on tape for her to listen to later. You can acquire these educational tools gradually.

You should budget a little for field trips. Many good trips are inexpensive or free, but remember admission fees, parking, and lunches. You may be travelling more as a homeschooler—if not to Europe, at least to the library! A car or a good public transit system helps. Even for field trips into fields or down to the creek, you may want a few simple supplies: water shoes for exploring creeks, for instance.

If your child is receiving speech therapy, occupational therapy, or other services through the public school, you might need to look at alternatives. Some school systems will not provide services to homeschooled families. Some homeschoolers find it prudent to discontinue receiving these services. Contact your national, state or provincial homeschool organizations for current advice and the latest news on the relations between your government services and homeschoolers. School systems are not always up-to-date on what services they are required to provide, so check with your state or provincial homeschool organization to see what current law requires your school district to do. Talk with your insurance company about what services they cover. Check with the local health department and universities, which provide some discounted services and may have research projects that would provide services for your child.

Homeschooling can be cheap, but it will cost you more than public school. In our case, it was much cheaper than private school.

Working mothers may think they cannot afford to homeschool. Some homeschoolers work from home for an employer or for their own small businesses. Others work shifts when their husbands can be home. Many homeschooling moms have put careers on hold. One mother brings her fifteen-year-old son to the family business. His reward for finishing his schoolwork is helping customers, which he enjoys. He also now sees reading, writing, and math are all needed to run a business. In another family, the father, a former high school teacher, homeschools his high-functioning autistic teen, while his wife works full-time.

These can be tough decisions when you are not sure homeschooling will work. But when you count costs, remember to include the savings from not working. You eliminate the costs of commuting, childcare, and a business wardrobe. Picking up carryout on the way home will be less of a temptation, and you will save on other incidental expenses related to work.

Single mothers can homeschool, but it takes dedication and organization to homeschool while working. Some state homeschooling organizations have special meetings and support for single homeschoolers. I know single mothers who homeschool, sandwiching work between their children's homeschool and outside activities. It's not easy, but one mother said she was glad that her struggling learners were not facing the strains of public school on top of their other struggles. She also figures that she is saving money by feeding her teens at home and is under less pressure to give in to clothing fads.

The biggest cost of homeschooling is time. Stay-at-home mothers who ponder pulling their children out of school may wonder how they will get their errands and housekeeping done. When I started homeschooling my son, I was frustrated that it was so much harder to keep up with housework, chores, and errands. Midway through the first year, my husband and I realized we needed to think of homeschooling as my job. He took on some more chores and we adjusted our expectations. Donna summed it up well, saying homeschooling "has to become one of your main purposes in life. You do have to give up a lot of things to do it." I'll discuss how to cope in chapter 26.

But also not homeschooling is costing you time, too. Having a struggling learner in school means long evenings helping your child with homework. It means trying to keep in touch with school staff and attending teacher conferences. There is your daily effort to figure out what is happening in the classroom: what the homework assignment really was, and who did what to whom on the playground.

What About Relationships?

After considering yourself and the cost, look at your relationship with your child. Do you enjoy spending time together? If the thought of spending day after day with your child worries you, there are many resources to help, as you will see.

In looking at your child who is struggling in school, it can be hard to judge how homeschooling will go. That's because if your student is unhappy in school now, you are living with the consequences at home. My son would come home from school emotionally spent, and explode when I asked him to put away his backpack. If you can't keep your daughter's attention as you try to help her through homework after supper, it may be that she's exhausted from trying to stay focused at school and has no more effort to give.

Apart from your relationship, look at your child. Is her choice of friends hurting her badly? Is she far from reaching her potential? If you are only afraid she won't get into a first-rate college, relax. But do you see her struggling with work that the average child can manage, though she seems reasonably intelligent? Is she miserable, starting to think of herself as stupid?

Is your child going to be lonely at homeschool? After public school, my son wanted someone to come over and play every day. But even very sociable children can thrive in a home school. It takes time to adjust, but they have more time and flexibility for extracurricular subjects and for activity with friends and family. For children who have difficulty with social skills, it's not clear to me nor parents I interviewed that being in school improved social skills; several parents who had put their children in public school for a time discussed undesirable social behaviors acquired there.

Chapter 23 describes homeschooling outside your home. Homeschooled students may take a class or two weekly with other home-school students, or at a growing number of private schools, which allow "a la carte" enrollment. Some public schools allow part-time enrollment, though this can cause problems, which I will also discuss. Homeschooled children have time to volunteer, learning to relate to people of all ages. Because parents are around to observe, they have more natural opportunities to teach manners and sensitivity.

What Resources Are Available?

Finally, look around you for resources. You probably know some people who homeschool. Get coffee with them. Visit homeschool support groups and some online ones, as well. Homeschool groups are multiplying and vary greatly. Some groups meet for dinner, some meet at playgrounds, and others run co-operatives with weekly classes.

Others work mainly by e-mail or message board, exchanging information, tips, and encouragement. While most of these online groups are national, a few are local, giving you a forum to ask questions such as, "Has anyone seen the new exhibit at the art museum? Is it worth the drive?" or "Anyone know a good dentist for a child who has trouble sitting still?"

While some groups provide support and information, other groups form for field trips and classes in everything imaginable. Special activities abound, such as Odyssey of the Mind, Math Olympiad, Jason Project, Junior Great Books, science fairs, and more. Those of us who homeschool for high school often join forces to keep our preparation manageable.

Don't be put off if the first groups you try do not suit you. We homeschoolers vary a lot, and we all have opinions about something. Even if you visit two groups with similar philosophies, activities and format, they will differ because people vary. So if you don't like the first groups you try, visit more.

There are homeschooling families all around, hundreds of curriculum vendors, a wide range of homeschool support groups—a wealth of resources. I'll say more about these later.

Would Homeschooling Be Good For My Child?

The biggest question most of us have as we consider homeschooling is, "Would this be good for my child?" If it is, and we can do it, we'll try nearly anything. Here are some reasons why homeschooling can be good for your child. I asked the homeschoolers I interviewed for this book what advantages they found in homeschooling. The most common answers:
- Customized curriculum,
- Flexible schedule,
- Learning at the child's pace,
- Better use of time,
- Limiting distractions and stress,
- Allowing more movement,

- Monitoring medical and psychological problems better,
- Avoiding bullying, ridicule, and other social problems.

Several parents told me their children's psychologists have told them that homeschooling is the best thing they could be doing for their struggling learners.

To decide about homeschooling, you need to look at yourself, the cost, your child, your relationship with your child, and the resources available to you. Homeschooling a struggling learner is a reasonable option for a growing number of families. It does take time and effort. From Alberta, Canada, Marjorie told me that her family made the big decision when her son was starting fifth grade, going into middle school, where:

> *They have lockers, and different teachers with different expectations—you know, the right book at the right time with the right classroom. We just knew that that was going to be a nightmare. We thought, well, we'll try this thing called homeschooling and try to save his sanity, even though I might lose mine! And it turned out to save everybody's sanity—for the most part. We just thought we would give it a shot because we knew he couldn't function in that setting, and it turned out to be the best thing we ever did.*

The next chapter is for parents who are already homeschooling, but are thinking of sending their child to public school. If that's not you, move on to chapter 5, and learn how your attitude and assumptions can make or break your homeschool.

4

Do You Need to Put
Your Homeschooled Child in School?

"I didn't really teach my older two. I just threw piles of books at them," Mary joked. Her third child is a different story.

For some parents, the problem is not deciding whether to homeschool. Homeschoolers know that different children may need different approaches to reading, math, and other subjects. But when we see one or more of our children struggling beyond what we ever imagined, we must decide whether and how to keep on. We may feel overwhelmed. We may long for professionals trained in special education to take over. We may fear we are failing our children.

Don't panic. What you need is knowledge, resources, and confidence. While I am not saying that every parent should homeschool every child, regardless of their special needs, you should realize that hardworking and well-trained as the best special education teachers are, you have many advantages as a homeschooler:

- You know the child better, while teachers face many new students every year.
- You have fewer students. You can be more flexible, limiting distractions and helping your child manage frustrations.
- You can modify your daily, weekly, and yearly schedule to suit the child.

- You can change curricula more easily.
- Finally, you are more determined to help your child succeed.

In this chapter:
- Figuring out what's wrong
- Dealing with professionals when you have been homeschooling
- Learning about your child's special needs
- Encouragement from special education teachers who now homeschool their own struggling learners

---

Figuring Out What's Wrong

If you have been homeschooling your child, you know better than anyone how he is doing. But you may not know what is abnormal. If your first child is bright, your second may look slow. When little brother passes big brother in math, it might alert you to big brother's learning problem. But it might just mean that little brother is brilliant in math. How to tell?

When problems persist, diagnostic testing by a special education teacher or psychologist can help you learn what's wrong and what to do about it. There is not one set answer for how soon to test. Some children's difficulties are so severe, they can be identified at birth. Sometimes parents can tell their children need to be tested by age two. Read a good book on child development. Your pediatrician can recommend one. (If your pediatrician is not helpful and knowledgeable, look for a better one.) Ask him or her what to expect in your child's mental development. As you read, study the developmental milestones of childhood and watch your child's progress. See chapter 7 for more on when to have a child evaluated.

While you know your child best, a good special education teacher, pediatrician, psychologist, or psychiatrist will have a better sense of what is in the normal range and more experience helping children with similar difficulties. In this book, I'll call these folks *professionals*. They can advise you on how to help your child. (Chapters 7 and 8 will discuss what they can do and help you decide which professionals you need.) You are still in charge, but by consulting with them, you may learn:

- the nature of your child's learning problem,
- how that will affect your teaching and his learning,
- teaching techniques, methods, and materials that can help you teach this child.

Some of us homeschool because we knew that our children would not succeed in public school. Some parents avoid public school because they do not want their child to be *labeled,* that is, diagnosed with special needs. They fear the school would see the child as a diagnosis rather than a person; as a set of weaknesses, rather than a person with strengths and weaknesses. They fear the child would see himself chiefly in terms of what he struggles to do. They worry that the child might let a label become an excuse for failure.

So why am I suggesting getting a psychological evaluation and a diagnosis? I'll discuss the pros and cons of labels in detail in chapter 7. Here, I'll simply say that the first step to solving a problem is to define it. You don't have to let a diagnosis define your child. Chapter 8 will explain in detail why and how to use medical and educational professionals to help you equip yourself to homeschool a struggling learner.

Dealing With Professionals When You Have Been Homeschooling

When you approach a professional to get help for your homeschool, you need to be prepared. You don't approach them only as a parent, but you also need to help them understand that you are the child's teacher.

Screen your potential professional by asking them about homeschooling. Do they have other patients or clients who homeschool? Do they believe it can be a viable option for education? If they don't know much about it, don't rule them out. Do they seem willing to learn about it? If one professional won't respect you as your child's teacher, look for another. One mother told me that every time she mentions homeschooling, her pediatrician rolls his eyes, while others said their doctors were the first to recommend homeschooling. If you have heard other people belittle your homeschooling, it is easy to mistake a professional's ignorance of homeschooling with rejection of it. Don't be touchy, but be observant.

When you visit professionals, you can do several things to convey your seriousness about your homeschooling. First, give them a picture of yourself as homeschool teacher. If you have been writing progress reports, bring the more recent ones. One or two completed lesson plans might be helpful. If your approach to homeschooling has been more relaxed, keep a brief diary of your activities. Keep it long enough to help others understand how your child is learning. These documents will show your typical week and, more importantly, show that you are serious about education.

Three years into homeschooling, we took our son in for his first private neuropsychological evaluation. After our pediatric neuropsychologist read my progress reports, my husband noticed a difference in the way he treated us. The neuropsychologist spoke to my husband as a parent, but to me as a fellow professional. He said homeschooling was the best possible thing we could have done for our son. He saw we were serious, not dabbling.

Second, along with progress reports and lessons, provide evidence of your child's struggle and achievement. Bring samples of his work: not the nicest work he's done, but work that shows his typical spelling, arithmetic, handwriting, or other struggles. Provide a brief list of books he has read for fun recently, as well as what he read for language arts. Your goal should not be to show off, but to give the professionals a good idea of what your child can do. If writing is a problem for your child, along with bringing writing samples, you might transcribe an oral report to show how writing is holding him back, or summarize other activities that show his ability. I would not bring in videos or displays, but perhaps a few labeled photos of projects and activities. Don't give the evaluator forty pages of material to read. Don't panic—remember the child is being evaluated, not you.

Third, keep a log recording samples of the worrisome behavior and difficulties. I find doctors take my written notes more seriously than anecdotes I tell them. For instance, just telling a professional that your son can't handle transitions from one subject to another isn't nearly as effective as sharing written dialogues recording a few examples of this behavior. You might use a recorder or make notes of your conversation, reminders, and actions. If hyperactivity is a concern, one day while your son is studying math, you might secretly keep track of how often he leaves his chair, drums his feet on the chair, or pokes his sister. Don't give the professionals a whole log to read, but a few pages of excerpts showing typical behaviors can help them understand.

Plans and progress reports, work samples, and logs convey to professionals that you are taking homeschooling seriously. That may help them to take you seriously. It also will help them understand your child better.

The cost of testing can be a bigger concern for homeschoolers than public schoolers, because many homeschoolers are one-paycheck families and some have larger families to support. Chapter 8 discusses ways to pay for testing.

Learning About Your Child's Special Needs

Although chapter 6 will cover learning about various special needs in more detail, here are a few remarks specifically to families already homeschooling.

Being creative and frugal, we homeschoolers are open to all kinds of ideas. Other homeschoolers may be sending information to help you, but as you read, consider the sources and their biases. Check the publication dates of books; note when Internet articles were last updated. Researching recently, two of the four online articles I found contained obsolete, inaccurate material. As you read about various treatments, read with a healthy skepticism. Every treatment I have read about has helped someone. But not every treatment will help your child. Investigate. Are there objective data to support their claims, published by someone who is not going to make the sale? Move cautiously before you spend money, time, or energy. More on this in chapter 9.

Learn from families who do not homeschool. Join patient advocacy organizations for your child's special needs, such as the Learning Disabilities Association of America, the Autism Society of America, the Autism Research Institute, and Children and Adults with Attention Deficit Disorder (CHADD), listed at the end of chapter 6. Several homeschoolers I interviewed who had children with ADD/ADHD recommended joining CHADD; one homeschooling mom is even starting a chapter. Visit such meetings and websites, look at their magazines, and see what helps you. I have found parents in these groups to be helpful and friendly.

When you visit, be patient. It may seem sad to homeschoolers how much effort other parents in these organizations spend communicating with their children's schools and negotiating for services. (Several families I interviewed for this book reported that one reason they began homeschooling was to avoid the stress of working with the schools.)

But these patient advocacy organizations provide an easy way to keep up with developments in research and treatment, alternative treatments, life skills training, and more. It can be very encouraging to meet adults in the group with the same disabilities as your child. I recently took my son, now a young adult, to a meeting for adults with ADD/ADHD. He was glad to hear and talk with interesting, articulate adults discussing their difficulties and their coping strategies.

Membership often provides useful magazine subscriptions, discounts on seminars, lending libraries, and support groups. It is also good for these groups to have homeschooling parents join, though the groups may not realize this at first. Homeschooling parents and public schooling parents know different resources and can help each other. As a homeschooling parent in such a group, your presence helps others learn that homeschooling is an option for them.

Last year I attended a good workshop on one particular learning disability. During the question time, one speaker asserted that homeschooling was not a good option because of the lack of opportunity to develop social skills. But several homeschoolers were present. An articulate mother graciously countered by explaining the many opportunities her homeschooled daughter had for socialization. The speaker backed down immediately, admitting she did not know much about homeschooling. By attending, that homeschooler helped the audience overcome a misconception about homeschooling.

Learn from a special education consultant. I'll discuss in detail how to find one in chapter 8, but as a parent already homeschooling, you want a consultant who is not opposed to homeschooling and who will respect what you have done so far.

Marcia, a homeschooling mother in Maryland and a former special education teacher, recommended having a consultant or mentor help you. Marcia's consultant runs an educational service. She provides annual

Homeschoolers Who Chose School—
But Returned to Homeschooling

Rose in New Hampshire adopted a son who was later diagnosed with ASD and other difficulties. I asked her if she homeschooled because she was already homeschooling his big sister. She replied, "No, in fact, that kept me from wanting to homeschool our special needs son," thinking school would serve him best. After one and a half years in public school and many difficult experiences, she brought him home two years ago. I asked her about the advantages and disadvantages of homeschooling a struggling learner:

Calm! He's more calm. We're more calm. He's soared ahead and I have no doubt he would have been trailing behind if left in public school. They were using occupational therapy techniques that were for the profoundly retarded and not for a very bright Asperger/ ASD child.

Disadvantages? Compared to dealing with professionals at the public school who did not get my son? There are no disadvantages.

In Florida, Denise homeschools three struggling learners. She wrote:

I planned to homeschool before I was even aware of my oldest child's learning challenges, based on the examples set by friends I admired. I tried to give up on that idea once the challenges became overwhelming, but that didn't work out well!

One and a half years in the public school system (third and fourth grade) got us on the path to diagnosis, but directed us back to homeschool. I was surprised to find that the teachers were no more patient than I was, and even more clueless on how to teach him! It wasn't just me! When it was evident public school would not work, we looked into private special education schools, but even the best school here used a self-paced workbook approach that would only have frustrated my dysgraphic child. In the end, it became evident that homeschooling was the only option—and I didn't want to try again! I had already failed at it once, and I didn't think it would work out, but now I am glad we ventured it. With the help of diet, medication, and less stressful methods, we are finally making progress!

He is dysgraphic with high comprehension, but very low processing scores. Getting him to output anything is virtually impossible—and why we gave up on public school for him. This year we finally got a diagnosis of bipolar, which has helped tremendously, but isn't the whole picture, just a part of who he is.

The main disadvantage of homeschooling is guilt over not being able to fix everything, thinking every shortcoming is somehow your fault—that you didn't teach it right or they would have learned! Especially when it's your oldest or only, you don't realize how little of it is you! It's a lot of pressure on mom.

Denise's advice for beginners:

Get professional help if you think there is problem. Don't wait. Everyone told me to just give my son time, so by the time I started looking into help he was in third grade, and immensely frustrated.

Second, don't push and don't try to keep up with public school, no matter how mild you may think the disability. Take cues from the kids on what they are ready to learn. Don't push, but be consistent on practice. Easy practice rather than frustrating challenges does amazing things, especially when it's covered in fun games and not drill.

evaluations and helps Marcia set goals. She also works with Marcia's son's reading tutor, speech therapist, occupational therapist, and others who help her child.

Encouragement From Special Education Teachers Who Homeschool Their Struggling Learners

Jen is a homeschooling mother in Virginia and a former special education teacher, whom I quoted in chapter 2 on the limitations she faced in a classroom with up to twelve special needs children at a time. She feels strongly that hard-working parents can give their children a good education:

> *In a homeschool setting, a student doesn't have to worry about answering a question wrong because someone might make fun of them. [In school] they learn that they are "stupid," "slow," and "special." They can experience much more success [being homeschooled] than if they were in a public school setting.*

I asked Hannah, a homeschooling mother in North Carolina, her advice for parents homeschooling a struggling learner:

> *I'm a special education teacher by training. I would say that you can do it. It's not just something the professionals know how to do. You know your child better than anyone else ever will.*

> *Don't be scared away by the jargon on the IEPs [Individualized Education Plans] and the jargon of those who are delivering the diagnoses. They might cause you to believe that you cannot possibly homeschool because you have not been specially trained in ADHD children. But your love and your logic, and going with what your heart tells you—like, "Hey, it's time to put this book down and take a jog"—those kinds of things will take you as far as you want to go with your child. You absolutely can do it.*

I think it's important for moms to know that they shouldn't feel guilty about becoming frustrated with their child, about feeling if they're not sure they want to do it, or if they're being loving enough in their homeschooling. We moms tend to beat ourselves up—and these are difficult children.

You can homeschool a struggling learner. It won't be easy. If you have been homeschooling other children and now must teach a struggling learner, the road ahead will be harder than for some other parents who homeschool. But for a conscientious parent, the rewards can be great. You can give your child an education customized to his strengths and weaknesses.

You need to learn more about how to help this child. But first read the next chapter to make sure your attitudes and assumptions are not derailing your homeschool.

It's not easy taking my problems one at a time
when they refuse to get in line.

Ashleigh Brilliant

Part II

Laying the Groundwork

5

Attitudes and Assumptions

When your son has lost his second soccer uniform or your daughter cannot read after three years of trying, you probably think you have more urgent concerns than your philosophy of education. Raising a struggling learner is demanding, so you want to focus on essentials. But thinking clearly about your views of education and human nature is essential to your success. Whether you are just launching your homeschool, or have been teaching at home for years, your attitudes and assumptions can help or hurt your homeschool.

In this chapter:
- Assumptions to avoid
- How do we view human nature?
- Attitudes to cultivate

Assumptions to Avoid

The School Mentality
Schools are designed for large classes of students. When you decide to homeschool, you can experiment with the structure of your homeschool to see what works best for your children. Ironically, when some people start to homeschool, they think they must duplicate the classroom at home to help

their children learn. Some parents copy school by buying old school desks. Furniture can help if it is the right size for the student and if it sets a tone for the parent and child that says, "We are serious about learning."

But school desks are not always necessary or even a good idea. The hyperactive child may find it too easy to move a school desk around and another child may just find it uncomfortable. One parent pointed out, "When you are trying to duplicate the school environment in a home, keep in mind that it didn't work in school; that's why he's at home. Duplicating that environment may bring negative emotions." (I will discuss setting up your homeschool in chapter 16.)

As a new homeschooler you may not only assume home has to look like school, you may think you have to lecture and rely on textbooks and workbooks. But when you teach at home, you have more options.

As I interviewed homeschoolers for this book, many said that their advice to new homeschoolers would be to overcome the school mentality—thinking homeschooling had to be just like school. (Some homeschoolers call this approach *school-at-home*.) As they adjusted to homeschooling, these parents enjoyed doing what schools could not. Many parents said they liked dividing lessons into short chunks. Many appreciated being able to deal with problems immediately. Others were un-school-like in different ways. For example, Lois in California discovered that if she was reading aloud, her son listened and recalled material much better if she let him play with LEGOS® as she read. In Alberta, Jody said her son likes to do his work while lying on the trampoline in the backyard. When he gets restless, he jumps a while and then settles back down to work. Homeschoolers also adjust their schedules for the physical needs of the child: letting a child with difficulty sleeping start school later, or a child with ADD/ADHD begin the day with lots of exercise. Others develop curriculum around their children's interests, engage in lots of hands-on activity, or travel extensively.

There is nothing wrong with borrowing ideas from school if they work or if you think they might help your child. But if they do not work, try something new.

Your Child's Learning Style and Your Own

Watch your child and think about how she learns best. That is her learning style. Would she rather read about something, listen to you explain it, or does she need to do it herself? Or, like many children (and adults), does she need a combination of these approaches to ensure she learns? Does she like to order material in a linear, logical sequence? Does she need to see the big picture first? Does she tend to perceive information concretely, or in abstractions? Learning styles can be defined many ways. (For example, study Howard Gardner's theory of multiple intelligences[1], Cynthia Ulrich Tobias' *The Way They Learn*,[2] or Carol Barnier's *The Big WHAT NOW Book of Learning Styles*.[3]) Whichever definitions you use, realize that different people learn, think, and recall differently. Experiment to find techniques that suit your child's learning styles.

If you are homeschooling more than one child, they may all learn differently. This is why parents may find they cannot use the same materials for all their children. You must observe each child.

Some parents assume their child's learning style is like their own. For example, a father who learns visually may wonder why his son, an auditory learner, is not helped by Dad's careful diagrams. A mother who learns best by doing can be frustrated by the child who prefers to read the book. Lisa, homeschooling in Pennsylvania, said, "Learn about learning styles, cater to their learning style, but also know your style. I am more free-flowing; I get excited, I go off on tangents. My son wants more structure. We butt heads sometimes. I have to keep thinking, 'No, this is what he needs. It's not about me, it's about him.'"

Life sometimes will require our children to learn in ways that are hard for them, so you should try to strengthen all means of learning. But if you know what comes easiest for your children, take advantage of it and teach them accordingly. For example, in *Take the Risk: Learning to Identify, Choose, and Live With Acceptable Risk*, neurosurgeon Dr. Ben Carson describes how after a terrible first semester in medical school, he considered his learning style. A very poor auditory learner, he couldn't absorb the seven hours of lectures he was supposed to attend daily. Knowing he learned best by reading and repetition, Carson skipped lectures and spent those hours

1. There are many sources on this theory, including Gardner's Multiple Intelligences: New Horizons in Theory and Practice. *New York: Basic Books, 2006.*

2 Tobias, Cynthia Ulrich. The Way They Learn: How to discover and teach to your child's strengths. *Colorado Springs, Colorado: Focus on the Family, 1994. www. AppleSt.com*

3. Barnier, Carol. The Big WHAT NOW Book of Learning Styles. *Lynnwood, Washington: Emerald, 2008.*

studying textbooks and detailed lecture notes, which he purchased from a note-taking service, among other study strategies.[4]

It can be hard to judge your child's learning style. But even if your child does not seem to fall squarely into one category or another, watching how she learns will help you improve your ability to teach and to choose and adapt curriculum.

Disabled or Defective?

Parents grieve when they think something is wrong with their child. They can feel guilty about their child's problem and blame themselves. Or they may think that by acknowledging a disability, they are condemning their child to a life of misery. How parents deal with these feelings about a struggling learner can make the child's way harder or easier.

Don't ignore your grief at the loss of a normal life when you have a child with special needs. You may experience the same stages of grief (denial, anger, bargaining, depression, and acceptance[5]) as you come to terms with your child's situation as you would in coping with bereavement.

Persistently imagining that the diagnosis is mistaken in the face of the evidence, or telling yourself that you can love the disability out of your child will not help her. Denying the fact that she has special needs wastes valuable time—time she needs getting help.

Parents need not be ashamed of children who are different. Shame or grief can make us unwilling to discuss our children's difficulties. But we need to inform teachers, camp counselors, and scoutmasters—any adults who supervise our children regularly—about our children's needs.

Your grief, denial, or anger won't help your child learn to cope calmly with their differences. Parents must not coddle their children. They do them harm if they permit them to use a disability as an excuse for being rude, lazy, self-pitying, or selfish. Deciding when their struggling learners are doing so is among the toughest judgment calls parents make. But letting your judgment be clouded by grief, guilt, or anger will not help you raise your children wisely.

Parents' denial of a problem can be selfish and harmful to the child. Some parents cling to dreams for their child that ignore the child's real limitations and gifts. Dreams are good, and parents want their children to aim

4. Carson, Ben, M.D. Take the Risk. Grand Rapids, Michigan: Zondervan. 2008, p. 95.

5. The five stages of grief were first described by Elisabeth Kübler-Ross in her 1969 book, On Death and Dying. New York: Scribner.

high. But for parents with children with milder learning problems, it may not become clear until later than some dreams are beyond their children's grasp.

Similarly, a parent's guilt about a child's learning problem only complicates the child's life. They may not accept a child's disability, because they imagine that the disability is their fault. Whether parents suspect better prenatal care, earlier diagnosis, or anything else would have lessened their children's difficulties—*whether right or wrong*—those who punish themselves with continuing guilt only cripple their effectiveness as parents.

Even when you want to accept your child's limitations, it is not something you achieve at once. Sometimes seeing our children struggle and fail with a new challenge can cause us to grieve or feel angry or guilty again. It is natural. For their sakes, we need to accept that they have struggles that others do not. Otherwise, we cannot look past their difficulties to enjoy their personalities and nurture their gifts. Emily Perl Kingsley's short essay, "Welcome to Holland," illustrates how accepting the situation you and your children are in enables you to enjoy what blessings you have.[6] But accepting the situation does not mean we resign ourselves to it, or pretend problems are a delight. It means we are ready to work to help our children grow.

Mindless Rushing

As you begin to homeschool, you need to stop and think about your long-term goals. Remembering them can help you avoid problems. And occasionally, you need to review your approach to teaching.

Modern living does not encourage us to stop to reflect, but we must, to help our children. It is good to step away and think how they are doing. Many homeschoolers spend a day or two each year at a homeschool convention, where speakers can challenge and encourage them about their priorities and goals and help them consider new techniques. Other homeschoolers arrange to go away for a night, or review and plan while their children are at camp or with grandparents.

Most parents share common goals for their children. We want them to grow up to be happy, useful, honest adults. Let's see how we are tempted to interfere with these goals:

6. Kingsley, Emily Perl. "Welcome to Holland," 1987. *www.creativeparents.com/Holland.html*

Sheltering or Coddling?

One mother in Michigan told me she was considering homeschooling because her son was struggling in school. But she did not want to make life too easy for him. She saw that struggle can be good for a child.

But if our children have become hopeless in school, and we have been unable to improve the situation, we do want to protect them. Several homeschoolers I interviewed had children who were very frustrated with school. Typical of those was Nancy, who said, "I had a third grader who couldn't read, had zero self-esteem, was so full of anger, just hated everything, and cried all the time." For those children who need to recover after prolonged pain in school, several parents recommended de-schooling, a relaxed period of transition to homeschooling, which I will discuss in chapter 16. But eventually, our children need to learn to cope with some stress.

Effective homeschooling is not about coddling or isolating a child. At home we can create a learning environment customized for our children, but our long-term goal must be to help them mature and become as independent as their difficulties allow. By nature, children want to grow up, and good parents want them to.

If we homeschool, how do we keep from overprotecting our children? We cannot let pity or sentimentality keep us from pushing them to develop. We have a responsibility to provide an education that will keep them challenged.

We must not isolate them. Despite the old misconception that homeschoolers live apart, nearly everyone I interviewed kept their children active outside the home. They all were concerned to help their children develop socially. They thoughtfully searched for and choose activities to help their children mature socially. (See chapter 23.)

As we plan we must think not only about academics, but also about life skills, social skills, and work skills. Like all parents, we have to help our children develop good habits—not depending on parents to organize life, or to fix every mistake. We must let them face the consequences of some bad choices while they are still home. With struggling learners, it can take years for lessons to sink in, even longer than the average teen, so we need to deliberately choose independence as a goal. It would be easier to do it all for them, but it would choke their self-esteem and independence.

As our children move toward independence, those who need special help must learn and choose to ask for it. This is called *self-advocacy*: the ability to go to the school, college, employer, or other authority and ask for reasonable help. We can train our children to think about what help is needed and coach them in how to get it.

The Entitlement Mentality

Popular culture encourages us to expect entertainment and instant gratification. Many of us have experienced peace and prosperity so often that we might feel we have a right to them. Because we are accustomed to quick fixes, we may expect to find a quick way to solve our child's difficulties.

While we all want simple solutions, they are often out of reach. As we homeschool, it is unlikely we will solve our children's problems with one book, technique, or seminar. Home education will not reward us with delightful, mature, adult children in one week or one year. We have to think and plan long term.

Despite adapting our homeschool to our children's needs, gifts, and interests, our children still may struggle. We have to remind ourselves that our work is a marathon, not a sprint. We must manage our expectations. Searching for years for a magic formula can keep us from using what we have. We can show our children they don't have to have all they want to enjoy what they do have. We can model for them the grace and humility of accepting and appreciating what we have. But we cannot teach them contentment if we are discontent.

Perfectionism

Not only can we feel entitled to find success in homeschooling, we may feel obliged to get everything just right. Are you a perfectionist, miserable unless everything is just so? Being responsible for our children's education is stressful. How do we run an excellent homeschool without becoming overanxious? Here are some tips:

Have you ever seen a child become furious over her inability to spell a word or solve a math problem? She erases a hole right through the paper, and is so mad or tearful that you cannot explain anything to her. Being a

perfectionist is contagious. Children need to see their parents deal construc-
tively with mistakes they have made. Our example shows them how to cope.

While some children learn how to recover from mistakes by watching
others, struggling learners can have trouble learning how to learn. We have
to deliberately and repeatedly talk about and demonstrate the right attitudes and responses. So not only do we need to observe how our children
think and learn, we must think about how we do, too.

Second, don't expect your children to have perfect attitudes as you
homeschool. Require a decent attitude toward work, but don't require
enthusiasm. You might want your child to be more excited about your
carefully-planned lessons, but don't insist on it.

Third, realize perfectionism is sometimes just a kind of pride and
grumpiness. It sounds very selfless to say, "I only want what's best for my
child." But are we making our families miserable by insisting on getting
everything just so for our homeschool?

My Child's Success Equals My Success

Another mistake parents can make is identifying too much with our
children. When we homeschool, the temptation to identify with our
children can be even stronger, because of the years of effort we put into
their education. We must be careful we are not requiring our children to
succeed in particular areas just so we can appear to be master teachers, or
parents of a prodigy—or even just parents of a normal child.

That may sound obvious when you teach a struggling learner, but it
can creep back into your thinking. My son gave me a good reminder one
day when he was a tenth-grader. We spent twenty-seven straight months on
Algebra I and Algebra II before I decided he—I first wrote "we"—would
not finish Algebra II. (It's hard to say who was the slower learner here: the
math student or the mother who dragged the agony out so long.) I was
tired of his learning disabilities. One day, after I chewed him out for forget-
ting something I had taught him many times before, my son excused himself a moment. He returned with a neatly printed motto, which he taped to
the chandelier over our school table.

His dangling sign read, "'Tis the way 'tis." In other words, "Mom, get
over it."

He was right. Don't let your pride make homeschooling harder for your child.

Resentment

When we work with a struggling learner, we may resent that life is so hard for our child, or that homeschooling can be hard for us. We read about homeschooled students who win spelling bees or are concert violinists. We know we are working hard and our kids are working hard, and we can be angry that we hear no applause for our children. It can be easy to resent people who seem to have life easier than we do.

We also can be resentful because we feel unappreciated. Rarely do children get up in the morning and thank their parents for homeschooling them. Occasionally a child will thank us for a book, a science experiment, or a field trip. We do need to teach our children to say thank you. But getting resentful does not teach good manners.

Resentment is easy to spot—in other people. In ourselves, it is insidious. We may need time with friends to blow off frustration, and times alone to examine ourselves and see if we are growing bitter. Whether you see your resentment or not, your child will notice it and be discouraged.

How Do We View Human Nature

As we read about different techniques, treatments, and learning difficulties, we encounter different views of human nature that shape how we treat our children. These views are not spelled out in the techniques, but are implied. They can affect our expectations for our children and how we treat them.

Behaviorism

Behaviorism is not behavior modification, which is an approach to training that reinforces good behavior with rewards, called *positive reinforcement*. Rewards are an important and natural part of life. For instance, the reward called a paycheck gets many adults up in the morning. Rewards help us train children. We all use behavior modification informally, starting when we reward an infant for looking at us by smiling and talking. Formal behavior modification can help us tackle tough discipline problems and teach vital safety and health rules. Behavior modification programs like Applied Behavior Analysis (ABA) do help some children.

But a behaviorist view of human nature is something else. From a strictly behaviorist view, people (or any organisms) are seen only in terms of how they respond to external forces, called *stimuli*. An extreme view of behaviorism can be dehumanizing, treating children coldly, only in terms of the behavior we want to see.

We need to see the whole child, not just the behavior. We miss something in our understanding of children if we don't try to understand why they behave certain ways. No one can raise a child, much less a teen, and ignore attitudes. If we only train children to avoid bad behaviors and do not develop their character, we fail them.

A Strictly Biochemical or Pharmacological Approach

Similarly, if we see our children's behavioral problems only as a result of chemical imbalances, we miss part of the picture. Chemical imbalances do cause problems. Medication can help some struggling learners. But medication is only part of the solution.

Parents I interviewed for this book varied in their use of psychiatric medication for children. Some homeschool to avoid it or to reduce the need for it. Others found medication a vital tool in helping their children learn, managing seizures, distractibility, severe mood disorders, and other conditions.

Psychiatrist Paul McHugh says that to understand mental disorders we have to understand their causes.[7] Depression in children, for example, can be chiefly the result of a chemical imbalance or can be caused by a difficult situation: death of a parent, divorce, or other crisis. Different causes require different solutions. McHugh says that knowing a cause of a disorder also can help us know which virtues we need to cultivate to become healthy.

While medication helps some struggling learners, it is rarely a complete solution. For example, most authorities on ADD/ADHD say that the best treatment is a *multi-modal* approach, combining medication with behavior training. Medication can work wonders. But there is no pill to make you want to do your work. Good attitudes, good habits, and effective study skills have to be taught, demonstrated, and rewarded.

7. McHugh, Paul, M.D. Interview by Ken Myers. Mars Hill Audio Journal, No. 83, Nov./Dec. 2006.

If a child has a learning problem, it is wrong to say that the child's problem is laziness or stubbornness. But it would be naive to assume that any child is incapable of being lazy or stubborn. We must train our children so they can develop the self-control they need to achieve independence.

A Psychoanalytical View

Some therapies for children are based on a psychoanalytical approach. Unlike behaviorism, this approach aims to understand why people behave a certain way. It recognizes that the child's thinking matters. According to this view, the child will tend to make good choices unless hampered by external causes. But this view can tempt us to blame inappropriate behavior only on external causes: genetics, an aloof mother, poor training, or neglect.

A psychoanalytical view leads to child-led approaches, such as play therapy,[8] which help some children. But like a strictly pharmacological approach, extreme versions of this view may lead us to overlook the possibility of the child making bad choices.

A Balanced View of Human Nature

Each of the views described above has some insight to help us. Behaviorists see that people respond to rewards and punishments. Biochemistry clearly affects behavior. A psychoanalytical view recognizes that environment and genetics can cause unhealthy behavior. We must also consider that our children make moral choices.

Are people basically good or bad? If we take either view, we are headed for trouble. If we think people are basically good, we will be surprised when our children are mean or selfish, and when they do not outgrow it. We have no way to account for our children's fundamental self-centeredness—or for our own. As Thomas Sowell wrote, "Each new generation born is in effect an invasion of civilization by little barbarians, who must be civilized before it is too late."[9] We need to understand that part of our mission as parents and educators is to civilize and to nurture a love of justice, truth, beauty, and wisdom.

But if we think people are basically selfish or self-centered, then we will concentrate on our children's moral failings and see our duty as parents largely as police work ("Who stole the cookies?") and jail-keeping ("You're

8. I'm indebted to Cathy Steere, who discusses the behaviorist, psychoanalytical, and pharmacological approaches to autism treatment on pages 145-147 of her account of raising her autistic son, Too Wise To Be Mistaken, Too Good To Be Unkind. *Sandy Spring, Oklahoma: Grace and Truth Books, 2005.*

9. Sowell, Thomas, A Conflict of Visions, *New York: Basic Books, 2007, p. 167.*

grounded.") We will miss the joy of watching our children's talents, generosity, and humor blossom; in fact, we can hinder their growth.

A balanced view of human nature sees that our children are capable of great good and, at the same time, are in great need of discipline, maturity, and grace.

Attitudes to Cultivate

What attitudes do we want to teach our children? Let me suggest five:

Respect

Insist that your child respect others, starting with you. You may have quit your job to homeschool, but you are not her personal cruise director, responsible to see that she has fun all day. Children need to respect parents. They must respect their parents' time and learn to balance family needs with their own. They need to respect their siblings and playmates. Life is not all about them.

We also need to respect our children. We are responsible for them, but we must help them learn to make wise choices for themselves. It is especially hard with struggling learners, because we know their immaturity and weakness. As they grow, we have to trust their judgment. For example, one homeschooler, Theresa, told me she has learned to respect her autistic daughter's ability to judge which situations were over-stimulating for her, such as a room full of noisy equipment they encountered on a field trip.

Because parents and children will disagree, a wise parent will teach their children how to raise objections politely and manage their feelings when things don't go their way. Developing a constructive means for disagreeing and the grace to accept the opinions of others will help our children develop into more resilient adults. When time permits, parents will listen to the objections and weigh them. When we overrule our children's objections, we must do it respectfully and without contempt.

Self Awareness

Theresa's story also illustrates that children need to become aware of their own strengths and weaknesses. Even though Theresa's daughter only began speaking at age nine and spoke her first sentence as a teen, she recognized that some situations were too much for her to bear. For our struggling learners, it is important to learn to work around their disabilities in social and work situations. We will need to spend time teaching these skills and encouraging our children to ask for accommodations politely. We also have to show our children how to respond maturely to people who choose not to help.

Passion for Learning

Several families I interviewed began homeschooling because their frustrated children were losing their love of learning. Many homeschooling parents told me they homeschool to nurture that passion. Some tailor their education to their child's interests.

Learning is not just vital to our children's ability to support themselves. It is an important part of being human: to be curious, exploring, inventive, and creative. Children are born wanting to learn. We must not let that urge be crushed by despair and failure.

Humility

A student who is humble does not become overwrought because of her own mistakes, but is calm enough to listen, learn, and admit she is confused. To teach humility, discuss it when you see it in action, whether it is your children or others who are showing it. Demonstrate it yourself.

Perseverance

My son astonished me once by saying he was glad he had studied algebra, because it taught him perseverance. Perseverance is a great word for struggling learners to know; it means not giving up. He learned it from a quotation from C. H. Spurgeon: "By perseverance, the snail reached the ark." Children who learn how to persevere will find it helps them the rest of their lives.

Conclusion

We have looked at common assumptions about schooling and human nature, and a few attitudes we want our children to develop. With that foundation, we are ready to look at our children's particular needs.

6

Common Learning Problems

Some readers might recently have removed their children from school, while others have homeschooled for years. Some of your children have taken a psycho-educational battery of tests in school or privately; a few a complete neuropsychological evaluation. Others have had no formal testing for learning problems. Some reader's children have medical help for their special needs; others have not.

For some children with less serious difficulties, just being home-schooled is enough to help a child succeed. Homeschooled children receive one-on-one instruction, spend more time engaged in academic tasks, receive a customized curriculum, benefit from a more flexible schedule, and face fewer distractions.

However, when learning issues are more challenging, many of us find that simply moving education home and buying curriculum does not help. As one mother wrote me recently, "I need help. For the first time, I am homeschooling my son. He struggled so much in school. I thought I could teach him with the attention he needs."

To help our children, first we need to know more about why our children are having trouble learning. If you are satisfied that you know what your child's learning problems are, skim this chapter.

In this chapter:
- First signs of learning problems
- A wide range of different conditions
- Gifts and talents
- Co-existing conditions
- Attention problems
- Learning disabilities
- Autism spectrum disorders or pervasive development disorders
- Becoming better informed

With this chapter's foundation, chapters 7 and 8 will discuss the why and how of getting a diagnosis and finding help from professionals.

First Signs of Learning Problems

No one ever wants to think anything is wrong with their children. When a child starts to falter physically, academically, or socially, parents notice. We may not worry at first, because we know that children vary. Some walk and talk late, others early. We may brush aside our doubts at first, or worry we are expecting too much, too soon. But when difficulties persist, wise parents start to ask questions.

Some children's difficulties become apparent very young, though they may puzzle parents. Parents may notice a child's unusual problems with coordination (large-motor or fine-motor) or with a child oddly seeking or avoiding certain sensations. For example, some signs of autism spectrum disorders (ASD, sometimes called pervasive development disorders, or PDD) may appear early, as in a six-month old who does not make eye contact or smile back at adults.[1] ASD usually become apparent before age three, though they may arise later or be diagnosed later. Similarly, some very hyperactive and impulsive children also are diagnosed in the preschool years. Some learning disabilities are apparent early, as well. As special education professor Dr. Joe Sutton says:

In the preschool years, failure to reach developmental milestones (e.g., crawling on all fours, saying one-word phrases, saying three-

1. ASD are a group of complex disorders characterized by difficulties with communication and social skills. They include Asperger Syndrome and High Functioning Autism (HFA), among others. See the U.S. Center for Disease Control's website, "Learn the Signs. Act Early." at cdc.gov/actearly.

*word phrases, following directions, toileting) in a timely manner
may be indicators of potential learning struggles to come. Language,
both receptive [understanding] and expressive [speaking], is a significant predictor of future learning success, too. Young children who
show weaknesses in communication are highly at risk for various
educational disabilities including learning disability.[2]*

But many problems don't emerge until school age. At home, we had
seen our son Pete's trouble with rhyming and learning the alphabet, but
when he started kindergarten, his teacher saw much more. He went to her
too often for help, was very easily distracted, and had trouble cutting out
simple shapes with scissors, among other difficulties.

If you are homeschooling already, you cannot compare your child to a
classroom-full of children the same age. But you may have begun to notice
differences from your other children at the same age: difficulty following
directions, recognizing letters, or drawing simple shapes, for example. And
you can check with your pediatrician, child development books, or the
Center for Disease Control's website for developmental milestones.[3]

Not every child is ready to sit down at a table and work at age five.
It has been popular among some homeschoolers to wait and see, argu-
ing that schools push children along too fast academically. It is true that
schools, obliged to serve crowds of children, must require more sitting still
and more workbooks than homeschoolers. But Dr. Sutton says if a child
at age six is not responding to traditional reading instruction, you should
consider having him evaluated.[4]

Around third to fifth grade, more learning difficulties can surface in
children. The pace of learning accelerates. Children move from "learning to
read" to "reading to learn." In other words, children are expected to learn
straight from a textbook. Some students are not ready to make that switch.
For them, as Donna said in chapter 1, "It's very hard to learn through your
weak areas."

Struggling learners can be bright students, and that may enable them
to cope with the workload of the upper elementary grades. They may put
in a huge amount of effort for a mediocre result. Unless their performance
is sufficiently poor and unless a parent raises concerns, schools may not give

*2. Field, Christine
with Dr. Joe
Sutton. "Strategies
for Struggling
Learners, Part
One." The Old
Schoolhouse,
2003. www.
theHomeschool-
Magazine.
com/How_To_
Homeschool/
articles/articles.
php?aid=83.*

*3. National
Center on Birth
Defects and
Developmental
Disabilities.
"Child
Development."
Accessed July 14,
2008. www.cdc.
gov/ncbddd/child/*

*4. Field with
Sutton, op. cit.*

the child much special help. Though U.S. law requires schools to provide a free and appropriate education, schools have limited resources and many children to serve with many different needs. Much as the school staff might wish for more time and resources, sometimes they settle for some children just getting by. That led some families I interviewed to decide to homeschool.

Homeschooling parents may first detect a problem when a younger sibling surpasses an older in math or reading. This is not a foolproof test, because that little brother or sister may be unusually gifted, but it is a sign for parents to consider whether the older child has some learning problems.

The beginnings of middle school, high school, and even the beginning of college are other times some learning problems are uncovered as the student begins to flounder with the increased pace of work. At those points, intelligence and determination may no longer be able to conceal learning difficulties. Schools and parents expect middle schoolers and high schoolers to be organized, not only managing more complex tasks, but keeping track of different assignments and tests. The social life and academic expectations are too much for some students, not to mention the emotional changes of puberty and the looming sense that soon they will be off to college or work.

So perhaps at one of these points—the beginning of schooling, the upper elementary grades, middle school, or high school—you notice your child is struggling to learn. How do you know if your child has a disability?

A Difficulty or a Disability?
The difference between a disability and a difficulty or difference is that anyone can see a difficulty or difference: a teacher, a parent, a friend. But to be called a disability, a condition has to be more severe and must be diagnosed by a trained professional. He or she should use both formal tests and the observations of people who know the person well. The symptoms should continue over six months and in different settings. I discuss advantages to getting a professional's opinion and how to find a good professional in chapter 8.

A Wide Range of Different Conditions

No one can describe all the conditions that cause a child to struggle with learning, and if I tried, this book would not fit in your lap. That is one reason you need to start with your pediatrician and talk with other professionals. Students can struggle because of physical, mental, and psychological problems—and from combinations of them.

To find parents to interview for this book, I appealed via e-mail and online forums for homeschoolers with struggling learners to contact me. If child was diagnosed with a learning disability, attention deficit disorder, or an autism spectrum disorder, I interviewed one or both parents, regardless of what other conditions the child or his homeschooled siblings had. Many of these children had more than one condition affecting learning. Here are the diagnoses of the children of the 64 parents I interviewed for this book:

- Allergies (severe enough to make a classroom intolerable)
- Anxiety Disorder
- Asthma
- Arthritis
- Attention Deficit Disorder (ADD) or Attention Deficit Hyperactive Disorder (ADHD)
- Autistic spectrum disorders, also called pervasive developmental disorders: Asperger Syndrome, High Functioning Autism, or Pervasive Developmental Delay-Not Otherwise Specified (PDD-NOS)
- Autonomic Nervous System Dysfunction
- Bipolar Disorder (formerly called manic-depressive)
- Central Auditory Processing Disorder
- Depression
- Down Syndrome
- Epilepsy
- Hearing problems
- Mental Retardation
- Fetal Alcohol Syndrome (FAS)
- Fibromyalgia

- Learning Disabilities (LD), including dyslexia, dysgraphia, dyscalculia (learning disability in math), fine motor disability or delay, language processing disorder, visual processing disorder, and others
- Migraines
- Nonverbal Learning Disorder[5]
- Obsessive Compulsive Disorder
- Oppositional Defiant Disorder
- Sensory Integration Dysfunction or Sensory Processing Disorder
- Post Traumatic Stress Disorder (PTSD)
- Syntactic Aphasia
- Temporomandibular Disorder
- Tourette's Syndrome
- Velocardiofacial Syndrome
- Vision problems

A few words about this list. Many of these children had co-existing conditions, that is, more than one of the problems listed. Several children were adopted after difficult infancies here or abroad. No doubt many other people I did not interview are homeschooling children with additional needs. I am not saying that I know about all of these conditions. Nor am I saying every child with these conditions should be homeschooled. But some parents are turning to homeschooling to help children with a wide range of needs, including disabilities.

To effectively homeschool your child, you should do what any good teacher should do: recognize that diagnoses can be complex. Because you, your family, and your child will live with the outcome, regardless of where your child is educated, you must learn what your child needs. It will take study on your part, and it may take expert help, whether or not you homeschool, to help your child reach his potential.

As you begin to meet others who are homeschooling children with special needs, it is not uncommon to meet someone whose child has a problem you have never heard of. What was striking as I interviewed parents was how many times parents of children with wildly different conditions had the same advice for new homeschoolers, as will be discussed later.

5. At this writing, Nonverbal Learning Disorder or Disability (NLD or NVLD) is not recognized by the American Psychiatric Association. Some parents and professionals use the term to describe a cluster of difficulties in nonverbal areas: motor, visual-spatial, and social learning. People with NLD are very verbal, and excel in vocabulary, reading, and rote memory, so this proposed diagnosis shares qualities with Asperger Syndrome. One homeschooler recommended Pamela Tanguay's book, Nonverbal Learning Disabilities at School: Educating Students With NLD, Asperger Syndrome and Related Conditions. *Philadelphia: Jessica Kingsley, 2002.*

It also was striking that these parents with such different children saw the same advantages to homeschooling, namely, being able to:

- customize curriculum to the child's interests, needs, and strengths,
- have a flexible schedule,
- teach at the child's pace,
- make better use of time,
- limit distractions and stress,
- allow more movement,
- monitor medical and psychological problems better,
- avoid bullying, ridicule, and other social problems.

If the list of diagnoses above were not long enough, the names of these disorders change, adding to the confusion as you try to educate yourself. Names also vary with location: in Britain, a learning disability is called a Developmental Disorder, while in the U.S. the very similar-sounding Developmental Delay means the child has an ongoing, serious delay in reaching various developmental milestones, but is not necessarily learning disabled. Some name changes are for the better: AD/HD was once called Minimal Brain Damage.

Gifts and Talents

Some struggling learners also are gifted, which can complicate their struggle. Gifted children who are bored may not do their work; bright students can become convinced they are stupid. Challenging and encouraging those children is as important as accommodating their needs. The better you understand their strengths and weaknesses, the better you can teach them.

Here is what I mean. One surprising result from my son's first neuro-psychological evaluation was that he scored in the top one percent in delayed recall—remembering details of a story half an hour after hearing it. That score shaped our homeschooling for years. His excellent memory for story detail became not just a strength I would notice and praise, it became a key to how to teach him. Is it any surprise that English and history are his favorite subjects?

Co-existing Conditions

Co-existing conditions are other conditions your child has in addition
to his main problem. They also are called co-occurring conditions, or
that dismal-sounding term, *co-morbidities*. Here is where things get really
complicated, both in diagnosing and helping the child. Many children have
co-existing conditions. For example, as many as two-thirds of students with
an attention deficit disorder have at least one other diagnosable condition.[6]
About fifty percent of people with learning disabilities also have one or
more related disorders, which might include: "other brain processing
disorders, attention-deficit/hyperactivity disorder, difficulties with
regulation of emotions, tic disorders, [and] bipolar disorders," according to
psychiatrist Larry Silver.[7]

    This is why getting a diagnosis will not solve all your child's problems,
though it is a beginning. Your child is a blend of personality, strengths,
and weaknesses. A diagnosis is helpful, but it will not lead you to the one
book you should read that will explain your child's mind to you, much less
inform you of the best curriculum for your child. Getting a diagnosis helps
you learn the strengths and weaknesses, which prepares you to search for
the best ways to help your children learn.

    And this is also why diagnosis should not be made by a parent who
has read some books. With untrained eyes, we may under- or over-estimate
our child's difficulties or misunderstand them completely. Once you start
reading about these disorders, there is a tendency to want to diagnose your
child yourself.

    You may be tempted to diagnosis yourself, too. You should not, for
the same reasons. But problems do run in families, so sometimes a child's
diagnosis leads his parent to be evaluated, diagnosed, and helped with a
related condition. So, your work to aid your child may help you to understand and manage your own life better.

    You know your child best, so it is worth paying attention to your
instincts. Many parents I interviewed urge new homeschoolers to do so.
But many also urged getting advice from professionals, who have seen
hundreds of children, and have studied and seen many different conditions,
individually and coexisting, so they have a better sense of what is in the
normal range, and can distinguish between similar problems.

6. MTA
Cooperative
Group. "A
14-month ran-
domized clinical
trial of treatment
strategies for
attention deficit
hyperactivity dis-
order." Archives
of General
Psychiatry 56
(1999): 12.

7. Silver,
Larry, M.D.
"Are Learning
Disabilities the
Only Problem?
You Should
Know About
Other Related
Disorders."
LDOnline.
2007. Accessed
June 10, 2008.
www.ldonline.
org/article/15815.

From the many conditions, combinations of conditions, and talents your child may have, let's look at a few common conditions. I also recommend you read Drs. Brock and Fernette Eide's book, *The Mislabeled Child*,[8] an excellent introduction to a variety of special needs.

Attention Problems

ADD/ADHD affects three percent to seven percent of adults[9] and nine percent of children in the United States.[10] Attention problems come in many flavors: distractible, hyperactive, impulsive, inattentive, or some combination. I think of some of my former students:

- Carla could not, even after seven months in eighth grade, remember to bring a pencil to math class.
- Charlie couldn't help rocking his desk and chair, and knocking them over in class. Once, when I didn't see him raising his hand, he stood on a table so his hand would be higher. Only when I told him to get down did he realize he was on the table.
- Brilliant Emily always blurted out things, then realized they sounded odd. She usually pretended she had been making a joke.

What is it like to have attention difficulties? Pat in New York describes her hyperactive daughter:

She can't help it. She's just a bundle of movement. It's not that she's not paying attention, it's that everything fascinates her. "Oh, look! Oh, look! Oh, look!" Everything I don't pay any attention to, she's absorbed by. It's not a plot to drive you out of your mind. [Laughs.] It feels that way, but it's not.

My son is not hyperactive, but distractible. He summarizes the difference between himself and the rest of us this way:

Pete: Look—up in the sky! It's a bird, it's a plane, it's …
Mom: Oh, get back to work!

We normal folks are so intent on completing our work that if Superman did fly by, we wouldn't notice.

8. Eide, Brock, M.D., and Fernette Eide, M.D. The Mislabeled Child. New York: Hyperion, 2006.

9. National Resource Center on AD/HD. Diagnosis of AD/HD in Adults. Landover, Maryland: NRC, 2003.

10. Centers for Disease Control and Prevention. "Diagnosed Attention Deficit Hyperactivity Disorder and Learning Disability: United States, 2004–2006." Vital and Health Statistics. July 2008. Accessed September 13, 2008. www.cdc.gov/nchs/data/series/sr_10/Sr10_237.pdf, p. 1.

How do you know if someone has ADD/ADHD? Everyone is distractible or inattentive sometimes. Some of us are always on the go. Does that make us hyperactive? The American Psychiatric Association publishes criteria for diagnoses in their *Diagnostic and Statistical Manual of Mental Disorder, Fourth Edition-Text Revision* (DSM-IV-TR). Doctors use these criteria to diagnose ADD and ADHD. The DSM-IV-TR divides the attention disorders into different types and lists symptoms for each.

The National Resource Center on ADHD website (help4adhd.org) has summarized these criteria. The patient needs to have at least six of the nine symptoms.

The symptoms for inattentiveness are:
- Fails to give close attention to details or makes careless mistakes.
- Has difficulty sustaining attention.
- Does not appear to listen.
- Struggles to follow through on instructions.
- Has difficulty with organization.
- Avoids or dislikes tasks requiring sustained mental effort.
- Loses things.
- Is easily distracted.
- Is forgetful in daily activities.

The symptoms for hyperactivity or impulsivity are:
- Fidgets with hands or feet or squirms in chair.
- Has difficulty remaining seated.
- Runs about or climbs excessively.
- Has difficulty engaging in activities quietly.
- Acts as if driven by a motor.
- Talks excessively.
- Blurts out answers before questions have been completed.
- Has difficulty waiting or taking turns.
- Interrupts or intrudes upon others.

If someone meets both sets of criteria, he is said to have AD/HD - Combined Type.[11]

The first time you read these lists, you might think many of these traits are true of many children. It is somewhat subjective, but to be

11. www.
help4adhd.org/en/
treatment/guides/
dsm

diagnosed, the child's symptoms must not be minor or temporary. Not only must one have at least six of the symptoms, the symptoms must be severe, affect the patient negatively, occur in multiple settings, and over a period of more than six months. (If someone says, "I have ADD only at work" or "only in math class," then it is not ADD.) At least some of the symptoms must be present from before age seven.

Learning Disabilities

About nine percent of children in the U.S. have a learning disability, according to the CDC.[12] It seems to me that saying "learning disability" is nearly as broad as saying "physical disability." Just as a physical disability could be many things—a vision or hearing problem, muscular dystrophy, cerebral palsy, or other difficulties—learning difficulties vary greatly. While it is still common to refer to dyslexia and its lesser known cousins, dysgraphia or dyscalculia, (trouble with reading, writing, or arithmetic, respectively), those are very broad categories. If your son has a reading problem (dyslexia), there could be many reasons. Is it because he cannot distinguish sounds or recognize letters? Can he follow the sequence of letters, sound out an unfamiliar word, or recognize a sight word? Can he remember the beginning of the sentence when he reaches the end, picture the scene, determine the main points?

It is helpful to distinguish learning disabilities by which parts of the learning process that are affected:

- Input
- Processing
- Memory
- Output or expression

Let's look at each of these in more detail. But realize that many combinations are possible, and the problems interweave. You will find a more detailed discussion of this in chapter 2 of Dr. Larry Silver's book, *The Misunderstood Child*,[13] which is my principal source for information on these four areas of disability, and which I recommend for parents with children with learning or attention problems. Here are a few examples from each area:

12. Centers for Disease Control and Prevention, op. cit., p. 1.

13. Silver, Larry B. The Misunderstood Child: Understanding and Coping with Your Child's Learning Disabilities. New York: Three Rivers Press, 2006.

Input. We receive information through our senses. But our brains turn those signals into perception and awareness. If someone has an input disability, that means that signals from the eyes, ears, skin, and nose are reaching his brain, but it is having trouble making sense of those messages. One visual perception problem is reversing or rotating letters or numbers as one reads, another is having trouble with depth perception. Or one might have difficulties perceiving the important figure against a background, which are called figure/ground problems. We use figure-ground discrimination to find a can opener in a drawer full of gadgets, or hear our names called out amid other sounds. Some people might take longer to make sense of what others say. Such a problem with receptive (receiving) language can make a bright person appear dull or inattentive.

We think of sight and hearing as being our main ways of learning, but other senses are equally important. Tactile perception is our brain's interpreting messages from our skin: not only what our fingertips touch, but anything our skin touches, or that presses on us, triggering signals from nerves below the skin. A child with a tactile perception disability might have very sensitive touch, and find the tag in his shirt drives him crazy, or think a kiss very unpleasant. Others with a tactile perception disability will be less aware of touch and may want stronger stimulation than most people; for example, they might hug others too hard and stand too close. (See also sensory processing disorder at the end of this chapter.) Proprioceptive perception helps us keep track of whether our joints are bent or straight, our muscles flexed or relaxed. (For example, you know without looking whether you are standing, and where your arms and legs are.) Vestibular perception enables us to balance, so we can walk, run, climb, and dance.

Processing or integrating. Once we take in what our senses tell us, we pull that information together in useful ways. We keep track of the sequence. (Did she say "63 divided by 7" or "7 divided by 63"? Was the headline "Man bites dog" or "Dog bites man"? Was that bus 604 or 406?) We interpret meaning, recognizing metaphors and idioms, tone of voice, context, jokes and purposes. ("Did you hear me?" can mean "Why aren't you answering or doing what I said?") We organize the information, relating parts to the whole.

Memory problems can vary, too. We may have problems with different kinds of memory: short-term or working memory, and long term. Working memory is the data you keep in your head to use for a short time, such as a phone number or license plate number you only remember long enough to write down or dial. Long-term memories are the ones that stick: your home address, how to get home, facts you remember from your own school days, the plots and details of stories you know. The Eides' book, *The Mislabeled Child*, has an excellent chapter on memory problems.

Output. You can have trouble expressing your thoughts in words for a number of reasons. You may have trouble constructing a sentence, speaking it, or writing it. Or you may have organizational trouble: you can say a sentence, but building a set of ideas to a conclusion may be hard, on paper or orally. Or you may have trouble coordinating large muscle movements, for instance skipping or dancing, a gross motor disability. A fine motor disability means you have trouble coordinating movements of the hand and eye, and would make handwriting and crafts more difficult.

Autism Spectrum Disorders or Pervasive Development Disorders

Asperger Syndrome (AS, also called Asperger's Disorder, AD) and High Functioning Autism (HFA) are two of a group of related brain development disorders generally called pervasive developmental disorders (PDD) or autism spectrum disorders (ASD). ASD are brain disorders that cause difficulties in nonverbal and verbal communication, relationships, and social skills.

The word "spectrum" in ASD emphasizes the variation among these conditions; parents sometimes refer to their children as being "on the spectrum." The more severe conditions often occur with mental retardation, but children on the spectrum may have normal to superior intelligence. They also may have superior spatial skills, mathematical skills, and superior powers of concentration and memory. Children with Asperger Syndrome may read early and speak more complex sentences than their peers.

The problems in communication and social skills generally appear before age three, although some are diagnosed later. (Two parents I interviewed reported receiving a diagnosis later in cases complicated by co-existing conditions.) Typically parents notice a child losing speech and other communication skills, avoiding eye contact, not responding to being called, not engaging in imaginative play, obsessively lining up toys, or other unusual behaviors.

Children with ASD also may:

- Not engage in conversation—by not speaking, by monologuing, or interrupting others, showing little sense of the give and take of social interaction.
- Not interpret facial expressions of others or respond to social cues.
- Engage in repetitive behaviors, such as flapping their arms, rocking their bodies, or repeatedly closing and opening doors.
- Have unusual, prolonged attachments to objects (say, a string or a spoon).
- Become very upset with changes in routine.
- Be hypersensitive—for example, be distressed by hugs, the feel of new clothing, or the texture of certain foods. Parents may have difficulty finding what few foods a child with ASD is willing to eat.
- Be hyposensitive—crave deep pressure, or not feel pants or shirts if they are too loose.
- Be prone to meltdowns when overwhelmed by new or uncomfortable events. Animal scientist Dr. Temple Grandin, probably the world's most famous autistic, says that the "fear is the main emotion in autism. I've got the nervous system of a prey species animal. … Before I started taking anti-depressant drugs, I was in a constant state of panic attacks…"[14]
- Seem unaware that other people have different knowledge and points of view. (The awareness of others' consciousness is called *theory of mind*.)

14. Grandin, Temple, Ph.D. Interview. "The Woman Who Thinks Like a Cow." Horizon. Dir. Emma Sutton. BBC, June 8, 2006.

Early diagnosis is important to training the child to develop social and communication skills. Homeschooling an autistic child allows you to devote more time to explicitly teaching communication, social and relational skills; to catch meltdowns early and help the child learn to manage them; and to create a peaceful atmosphere as you eliminate some of the over-stimulating parts of the school environment, among other advantages. For more about ASD, see the end of the chapter.

Becoming Better Informed

These sections above only give the briefest description of a few of many complicated conditions. Many books have been written on each of these conditions. I recommend several below, because your next step in helping your child is learning more about what help they need.

What next?

- Observe your child carefully. Make some notes about what is easy and hard for him.
- Begin to research conditions that seem to match your child's difficulties. Ask your child's doctor for ideas. Check your library and the resources below.
- Begin to seek out parents homeschooling struggling learners. See chapter 25 for ways to connect.
- Read the next chapter to find out why and how to get your child diagnosed.

Resources

Books on Special Needs
Attwood, Tony. *Asperger's Syndrome: A Guide for Parents and Professionals*. Philadelphia: Jessica Kingsley, 1998.

Bashe, Patricia Romanowski, Barbara L. Kirby, Simon Baron-Cohen, and Tony Attwood. *The OASIS Guide to Asperger Syndrome: Completely Revised and Updated: Advice, Support, Insight, and Inspiration*. New York: Random, 2005.

Bellis, Teri James, Ph.D. *When the Brain Can't Hear: Unraveling the Mystery of Auditory Processing Disorder*. New York: Pocket, 2002.

Eide, Brock, M.D., and Fernette Eide, M.D. *The Mislabeled Child: Looking Beyond Behavior to Find the True Sources—and Solutions—for Children's Learning Challenges.* New York: Hyperion, 2006.

Exkorn, Karen S. *The Autism Sourcebook.* New York: Harper Collins, 2006.

Ingersoll, Barbara D., Ph.D., and Sam Goldstein, Ph.D. *Attention Deficit Disorder and Learning Disabilities.* New York: Doubleday, 1993. Drs. Ingersoll and Goldstein have also written other helpful books in this field.

Gerber, Stephen W., Ph.D., Marianne Daniels Gerber, Ph.D., and Robyn Freedman Spizman. *Is Your Child Hyperactive? Inattentive? Impulsive? Distractible? Helping the ADD/Hyperactive Child.* New York: Random, 1990.

Grandin, Temple, Ph.D. *Thinking In Pictures: and Other Reports from My Life with Autism.* New York: Random, 1995.

Hallowell, Edward M., M.D., and John J. Ratey, M.D. *Delivered from Distraction: Getting the Most out of Life with Attention Deficit Disorder.* New York: Ballantine, 2005.

Kranowitz, Carol Stock, and Lucy Jane Miller. *The Out-of-Sync Child: Recognizing and Coping with Sensory Processing Disorder*, Revised Edition. New York, Penguin, 2006.

Levine, Mel, M.D. *Keeping A Head in School: A Student's Book About Learning Abilities and Learning Disorders.* Cambridge, Massachusetts: Educators Publishing Service, 1990.

Silver, Larry B., M.D. *The Misunderstood Child: Understanding and Coping with Your Child's Learning Disabilities.* New York: Three Rivers Press, 2006. Although only learning disabilities are mentioned in the title, Dr. Silver includes several chapters on attention deficit disorder, and material on related disorders.

Smith, Sally L. *No Easy Answers: The Learning Disabled Child at Home and School.* New York: Bantam, 1995.

Organizations and Websites on Special Needs
ADDitude Magazine: Living Well With ADD and Learning Disabilities.
www.additudemag.com/

A.D.D. Warehouse
300 Northwest 70th Avenue, Suite 102
Plantation, FL 33317
800-233-9273
www.addwarehouse.com
Book for parents, children and teachers on autism, learning problems, mood disorders, ADD/ADHD, and many other problems.

www.allkindsofminds.org
Dr. Mel Levine's website (see above, under Books)

Autism Society of America
7910 Woodmont Avenue, Suite 300
Bethesda, Maryland 20814-3067
www.autism-society.org
ASA has an annual national conference, state and local chapters, a magazine, and websites.

www.autismweb.com is "a free, informational web site run by parent-volunteers. It is not affiliated with any organization or service provider." It includes descriptions of teaching methods ABA, RDI, Floortime, and TEACCH, and information on diet and on research updates.

CHADD [Children and Adults with Attention Deficit Disorder]
8181 Professional Place - Suite 150
Landover, MD 20785
(301) 306-7070
CHADD.org
CHADD has local chapters, regional and national conferences, and
publishes *Attention!* Magazine.

Defeat Autism Now
www.defeatautismnow.com
"Dedicated to the exploration, evaluation, and dissemination of
scientifically documented biomedical interventions for individuals within
the autism spectrum, through the collaborative efforts of clinicians,
researchers, and parents."

Greatschools.net/content/specialneeds. This page offers articles on
AD/HD, learning disabilities, autism, and other learning differences.

International Dyslexia Association
40 York Rd., 4th Floor
Baltimore, MD 21204
(410) 296-0232
interdys.org
IDA has a helpful website, international and state conferences, workshops
and support groups, and a range of publications and fact sheets.

Jessica Kingsley Publishers
400 Market Street, Suite 400
Philadelphia, PA 19106
(866) 416-1078
www.jkp.com says, "We are well known for our long established lists on
the autism spectrum, on social work, and on the arts therapies."

LDOnline.org
Don't be misled by the name; it is not just about learning disabilities.
LDOnline is a wonderful, huge collection of articles on learning disabilities,
attention problems, and related issues.

Learning Disabilities Association
4156 Library Road
Pittsburgh, PA 15234-1349
(412) 341-1515
LDAAmerica.org
LDA has an annual national conference, and state and local chapters
and websites.

National Center for Learning Disabilities
381 Park Avenue South, Suite 1401
New York, NY 10016
(212) 545-7510
www.ncld.org
NCLD provides newsletters and other publications, a useful website
covering topics from "Early Learning" and "Parenting Strategies" to "At
College and Work," online discussions, and an online bookstore.

   National Resource Center on ADHD (help4adhd.org), an excellent
online resource, is a joint project of the Centers for Disease Control and
CHADD.

On Sensory Processing Disorder, see www.out-of-sync-child.com and
www.spdfoundation.net/

TEACCH

UNC School of Medicine

The University of North Carolina at Chapel Hill

www.teacch.com

The TEACCH method (Treatment and Education of Autistic and Related Communication Handicapped Children) was developed at UNC in the 1970s, and is used in some public schools. Part of the mission of TEACCH is "to enable individuals with autism to function as meaningfully and as independently as possible in the community." Though primarily serving North Carolinians, TEACCH's website and research are helpful to all. Some homeschoolers have received TEACCH training.

Woodbine House

6510 Bells Mill Road

Bethesda, MD 20817

800-843-7323

www.woodbinehouse.com

Woodbine House publishes many fine books for parents, teachers, and children on a wide range of disabilities.

7

Evaluation and Diagnosis

Our struggling learners differ. When some parents start homeschooling, problems disappear, the children revive, and their love of learning returns. But other parents struggle to homeschool effectively because their children's problems are more serious. This chapter will cover how to know whether and when you need a formal diagnosis of your child's learning problems or evaluation of her progress, and how to get them.

Like most homeschoolers, I am frugal. I do not think everyone needs to take their child to see a speech pathologist or occupational therapist for evaluation. Not everyone needs to have their children take a psycho-educational battery of tests, though probably most struggling learners do. Not every struggling learner needs a complete neuropsychological evaluation, though many do.

Almost every parent I interviewed said their doctors, their child's psychiatrists, their special education consultants, or therapists helped them homeschool. Understanding our children's needs enables us to customize our homeschool, and a good diagnosis also helps the professionals we work with help us and our children.

Some of you already have had a good, thorough evaluation by professionals you respect. You can skip much of this chapter, but read the sections on evaluation by occupational or speech therapists, and on understanding evaluations and benefiting from them, before you move on to chapter 8.

If you are homeschooling a child with mild learning problems who is making good progress, your child still can benefit from periodic evaluation by an special education consultant. If this is your situation, read the sections below on psycho-educational batteries, and on understanding evaluations and benefiting from them. In case other problems were missed, you should know the warning signs that you might need to have your child evaluated, so also read the sections on evaluations by occupational or speech therapists.

Some evaluations should be done before school age, long before you would have reason to read this book. Some of you will be all too familiar with them. For example, speech problems are best identified early, because from birth to age four is the critical time for language learning, and speech problems are more difficult to resolve if they are caught later. Autism is another problem usually diagnosed very early. Twelve-month-olds who do not point or notice adults, and two-year-olds who lose language skills should be screened by a pediatrician. Parents should learn the milestones of child development and talk with their health-care providers any time they are concerned about their children's progress.

But if difficulties worsen, if new symptoms emerge, if you are seeing a problem only now, or if your child seems to have been misdiagnosed, your child may need further testing. Some diagnoses are difficult and complex. One homeschooling mother in Virginia said her son was diagnosed with Tourette's Syndrome and ADHD at the age of five, but that his Asperger Syndrome was diagnosed at the age of twelve, at puberty, when his symptoms became much more pronounced. A homeschooler in Quebec said her eight-year-old son had been diagnosed last year with ADD and dyslexia, and is now waiting to be tested for autism. The important point is to keep looking for help if you suspect a problem.

The topics of how to find the right person to diagnose or evaluate your child and what to do if you cannot afford these services are covered in the next chapter, which also explains how different professionals can help you teach your child more effectively.

In this chapter:
- Objections to having a child diagnosed
- Why your child may need an evaluation or diagnosis
- Becoming informed
- A health assessment
- Different kinds of evaluations and diagnostic tools
- Does your child need an evaluation by occupational or speech therapists?
- Does your child need a psychoeducational battery or a neuropsychological evaluation?
- Other kinds of evaluations
- Preparing for an evaluation
- Understanding the results
- Your reactions to diagnosis
- Benefiting from an evaluation
- Talking to your child about the results

Objections to Having a Child Diagnosed

Some parents do not want their children diagnosed. Parents even may homeschool to avoid having their child *labeled*, that is, diagnosed with a special need. Why avoid diagnosis? Some parents do not want to admit the possibility something could be wrong with their child. Some fear what their friends and relatives will say. They may fear that their children will be stigmatized for having a condition or disorder. Others think that for the child, taking any tests with strangers will be too stressful. Some question whether the benefits outweigh the cost.

Others object to trends in modern mental health care. As more and more behaviors now are labeled disorders[1], the growing number of new disorders can make parents wonder which diagnoses are legitimate. To keep costs down, a few health professionals seem to give quick diagnoses and not take time to get the whole story. Some may seem quick to prescribe medication.

If getting your child diagnosed is expensive and uncomfortable, why do it? Why go to professionals if some diagnoses strike you as ridiculous?

1. See Allan V. Horwitz and Jerome C. Wakefield's book, The Loss of Sadness: How Psychiatry Transformed Normal Sorrow into Depressive Disorder, *(New York: Oxford U.P., 2007), or Christopher Lane's* Shyness: How Normal Behavior Became a Sickness. *(New Haven, Connecticut: Yale, 2007).*

Go because there are good therapists, consultants, psychologists, and psychiatrists who help many people. Don't go to a doctor who thinks a pill alone can fix a learning problem. A good health professional can help a child and her family tremendously. In chapter 8, I will discuss finding these good professionals. But if your friend had a bad experience at a car repair shop, that would not stop you from looking for a good mechanic for your car. How much more should you seek good care for your child!

Why Your Child May Need an Evaluation and Diagnosis

Dr. Barbara Ingersoll wrote in her book about ADD/ADHD, "The basis of a good treatment plan is a good diagnosis."[2] That is not just true for health professionals; it is true for homeschoolers, too. If you do not know clearly what the problems are, it becomes harder to help.

All the parents I interviewed had their children formally diagnosed. Why did they go to the expense and effort? An accurate diagnosis of their children's difficulties helps them help their children. I can summarize the parents' thinking in ten reasons:

- An evaluation helps you know your child's weaknesses and disabilities. Achievement tests compare your child's performance to her peers, and diagnostic inventories identify gaps in learning.
- Confirming the existence of a problem can be a relief to parents, because we sometimes worry that our bad parenting or poor teaching is the root of the trouble.
- A good diagnosis can help you set reasonable goals. (See chapter 11 on setting goals.)
- A good diagnosis or evaluation also reveals strengths, helping you teach more effectively. For example, as I wrote in the last chapter, we had no idea our son had exceptionally good delayed recall until he was tested for learning disabilities. Once we knew, we built on that ability in our homeschool.
- It is easier to find methods and materials to teach your child if you know what makes learning hard for them. It also helps you adapt curriculum.

2. Ingersoll, Barbara, Ph.D. Daredevils and Daydreamers: New Perspectives on Attention-Deficit/ Hyperactivity Disorder. New York: Doubleday, 1998, p. 47.

- An evaluation also reveals and records progress or regression, and provides useful details. Suppose you know you daughter is behind in reading. One form of evaluation, a reading achievement test, can help you measure the effectiveness of the reading methods you are using. (An experienced special education consultant can look at your child's diagnosis and determine a good rate of progress for the child. For some children, making six months progress in twelve months may be excellent.) A test also can confirm your suspicions of regression, making it clear you need to look for new teaching strategies. Or, you may see progress, but not realize how much progress your child has made until you see test results. I knew my son was working hard in math, but I did not appreciate his progress until he was re-evaluated at age sixteen. He had made so much progress he is no longer considered learning disabled in mathematics.

- In some states, you are required to demonstrate to the state the progress of children with special needs. The results of an evaluation are one way to do this. Even if the child is not making much progress, an evaluation can confirm the difficulties you and your child face.

- If you are involved in court litigation or custody disputes with family members who oppose homeschooling, diagnostic testing can demonstrate your child's special needs and progress.

- For an older, college-bound student, a disability can qualify her for accommodations on college entrance examinations and in college classes. (Accommodations are extra helps designed to give disabled students a fair chance to do their best work.) Documentation you receive through testing can show a legitimate need for these accommodations. Accommodations at college can include larger print tests, extra time, use of a word processor, or audio recordings of college textbooks. Other accommodations are available.

- A final reason to have your child's learning problems diagnosed professionally is because it is hard to diagnose learning problems. As explained in chapter 6, there are many kinds of struggling learners, and their problems can appear many different ways. It is even more complex if your child has co-existing conditions. Many children do. Most of the families I interviewed had children with more than one problem.

You know your child best. You should pay attention to your instincts. But experienced professionals, who have seen hundreds of children and who use standardized tests to compare your child's performance to thousands of other children, can notice qualities you may miss. There are too many disorders with overlapping symptoms for parents to diagnose serious problems at home. (Take problems in learning math, for instance. They can be caused by anxiety, frustration, poor instruction, a vision problem, or one of many different learning disabilities, among other things.) The right professionals can equip you to teach better.

Becoming Informed

To understand your child's learning problem, you need to learn about different kinds of learning problems. In the last chapter, I listed websites, patient advocacy organizations, and books to help you become informed. I found it helpful to read a few books and work through checklists of symptoms and descriptions of different kinds of problems. I also attended free lectures for parents and teachers given by local psychologists and patient advocacy groups.

Many homeschoolers I interviewed urged those beginning to homeschool a child with special needs to take time to become informed. One homeschooler, whose child has ADD/ADHD and is borderline bipolar, put it well:

> *Educate yourself. Don't just listen to the doctors or the therapists. Go online, read books. Ask questions. Get the answers. If you can't find them from the professionals, find them on your own. (In fact, my son's therapist now provides online resources to check out.) Learn what you can, so you can be better prepared.*

A Health Assessment

Why take the child to your medical doctor? There are several good reasons:

First, see a doctor to rule out physical conditions that mimic or cause learning problems. A sleep disorder can make your child seem depressed, anxious, inattentive, or learning disabled. An allergy can make your child inattentive or sleepy. Vitamin deficiencies can cause problems. So can many other factors.

Second, once we educate ourselves, we can ask our doctors good questions. If your child has many symptoms of a disorder, talk to your doctor about your suspicions. (When you make the appointment or phone call, ask for time to discuss these concerns.) If he or she won't listen, find a doctor who will, perhaps a specialist in the area of disability that your child seems to have.

Third, some problems are complex and must be diagnosed by a qualified specialist. Listen to your instincts, but don't think of them as infallible, any more than your general practitioner's or pediatrician's. Ask for a preliminary judgment and then to be referred to a specialist. As psychiatrist Larry Silver has said, if you suspected your child had strep throat, you would want the doctor to run a test before putting the child on antibiotics. Yet some parents told me their pediatricians simply listened to their stories, watched the child, and said, "Yes, that sounds like ADD. Let me write her a prescription." A doctor should first rule out anxiety, depression, or other problems that need different treatments, and which could be made worse by the wrong medication. Whatever the special need, you should work with a doctor experienced enough in treating children's learning or emotional problems to know that medication alone is not the most effective approach.

Different Kinds of Evaluations and Diagnostic Tools

There is no one test to determine what makes learning hard for a child. Diagnosis is made based on patient history, screenings, scales, and different tests. Some are based on how your child performs different tasks, while others ask the child and adults who know her to give their perspectives on her feelings, behavior, or performance.

Measuring ability and aptitude is not an exact science, so new tests are developed, and old ones are revised. As new treatments are developed and our understanding of these conditions improves, new tests will gain acceptance. Here are a few guidelines to help you as you learn about the tools used to diagnose various learning problems.

Patient History

Many evaluations begin with the tester asking the parents about the child's development. This developmental history should cover everything from the pregnancy to whether the child had trouble learning to ride a bike or tie her shoes. Testers often ask about family history as well, because learning problems can run in families, and family stresses can affect a child's ability to learn.

Screening, Scales, and Surveys

These tools include lists of questions for parents, the student, or the teacher to answer quickly. (Parents already homeschooling often have a coach, music teacher, or other adult who works with the child regularly complete these "teacher" questions.) Screening tests can rule out possible problems such as mood disorders, or show a need to investigate further.

When filling out a scale or screening, be honest, but do not agonize over the questions. Your choices may be "yes" or "no," and you may want to answer with a "sometimes." The individual answers may not matter. The testers look at how closely the overall pattern of your answers matches the typical results for a particular disorder.

If you are filling out a scale or survey for a child, record their answers objectively and without comment. This can be hard, and some of us know that our children are not very self-aware. But it is part of the data that can help form a picture of the child's needs.

Aptitude and Achievement Tests

Some educational tests measure aptitude in different areas, or inborn ability. Testers often use aptitude tests to measure intelligence, such as the Weschler Intelligence Scale for Children (WISC—there are also versions for preschoolers and for adults), the Stanford-Binet Intelligence Test, the

Kaufman Assessment Battery for Children, or the Woodcock-Johnson Cognitive Battery. Aptitude can be hard to measure, especially with a struggling learner, whose inattention or difficulties with communication may hurt her performance on the test.

On the other hand, achievement tests measure what level of work the student can do. The Woodcock-Johnson Tests of Achievement and the Weschler Individual Achievement Test are well-known examples. [These tests are more comprehensive than the achievement tests given in most school districts, such as the Stanford Achievement Tests (SAT-9 or SAT-10) or the Iowa Test of Basic Skills (ITBS). Some states require homeschooled children to take one of those achievement tests to give evidence of progress. See chapter 20 on taking such tests.]

Criterion-Referenced or Norm-Referenced?
Another way tests differ is in how the test scores are judged. A criterion-referenced test compares the test-taker's answers to a set of criteria or standards, but a norm-referenced test compares the test-taker's answers to her peers. For example, the written test for a driver's license is criterion-referenced; you have to get a certain score to pass. A norm-referenced test compares the test-taker's answers to a sample group of peers. Your child's achievement test score would be given in terms of her peers. "She is reading at a 3.2 grade level," means she is performing what is typical for someone in the second month of third grade. An intelligence quotient also is norm-referenced: on a scale of 0-200, a score of 100 is average intelligence.

Tests of Attention
Computerized tests can measure a person's ability to pay attention to a task over time. For these tests, the test taker completes an activity, sometimes a specially-designed, simple, and somewhat boring game on the computer, which measures how well the child pays attention to a task over time. The best known are the TOVA and Connor. These give clear numerical results, analyzing the child's performance. Those results are easy to compare to the norm for your child's sex and age. These kind of test results are attractively simple and clear, but by themselves, these tests

cannot diagnose ADD/ADHD, because inattention can have many causes. But they can be a useful part of a neuropsychological evaluation.

Does Your Child Need an Evaluation by
Occupational or Speech Therapists?

Many of us are not sure what occupational therapists and speech pathologists (also called speech therapists) do, so we don't know if our children need to see one. We know if the child has trouble dressing herself, she needs an occupational therapist, or if she stutters, she needs a speech pathologist. But there are many other difficulties these professionals can treat. Below is a brief look at some of the problems they can help our children with.

Generally, therapists will give two kinds of evaluations: a treatment evaluation or a written evaluation. A treatment evaluation enables the therapist to plan a good course of treatment for this child. A written evaluation may include more formal tests and evaluations, and will be more expensive because of the time required to write a formal report.

In the area of oral motor problems, either a speech or an occupational therapist can help. Your child may have oral motor problems if she has trouble swallowing or gags easily. To decide whether to see a speech or occupational therapist for oral motor problems, see if your child has any of the other needs described below.

Evaluation by an Occupational Therapist

Occupational therapists help people with skills they need for their occupations for daily living. Your child's main occupations are playing and learning. An occupational therapist can give different tests to look for difficulties in sensory processing (sensory integration), and in the development and coordination of gross motor skills (whole body), and fine motor skills (small muscle movements of the hands, like buttoning or typing), visual-motor skills, and other sensory motor skills.

Your child may need to see an occupational therapist for many reasons. Here are a few examples:

  ▪ Sensory processing or sensory integration problems: either over-sensitive or under-sensitive. For example, does she have a very high or very low tolerance for pain? Does she hate to be hugged unless she initiates, hug inappropriately, or stand too close to others? Is she bothered by textures? (Do shirt tags drive her crazy? Is she a very picky eater?) Is she unusually bothered by noise, smells, or lights?

- Sensory motor problems: difficulties with balance (vestibular system) or proprioception (awareness of where her body is in space),
- Low muscle tone,
- Problems with gross motor coordination, (such as skipping, balancing on one foot, riding a bike, throwing and catching a ball), or fine motor coordination (tying shoes, other tasks requiring dexterity),
- Visual motor problems, (hand-eye, such as difficulty with handwriting or awkward grasp of a pencil, or eye-foot, such as kicking a ball),
- Poor nonverbal communication,
- Difficulty managing anger,
- Difficulty mastering basic tasks of daily living.

These are just some of many signs an occupational therapist may be needed. To learn more, visit the websites listed at the end of the chapter.

Evaluation by a Speech and Language Pathologist

A speech therapist or speech and language pathologist can evaluate a child to identify articulation problems, hearing problems, or an auditory processing disorder. As with occupational therapists, they may give treatment evaluations or written evaluations.

Your child may need to see a speech pathologist if she has:

- Difficulty expressing herself—putting sounds together into words, vocabulary problems, putting thoughts into words, or putting words into sentences grammatically. This is called expressive language.
- Difficulty understanding the language of others. These are called receptive language problems, such as difficulty following directions, understanding who, what, or where questions, understanding sequences, idioms, or opposites.

- Difficulty pronouncing sounds, combinations of sounds, or words.
- Voice disorders (too breathy, nasal, or harsh; odd volume or pitch).
- Fluency disorders (stuttering, saying "um" too often, repeating or stretching sounds, repeating syllables, words or phrases).

For more information, talk to a certified speech pathologist in your area or visit the websites listed at the end of the chapter.

Does Your Child Need an Psycho-Educational Battery or a Neuropsychological Evaluation?

Let's look first at the difference between these two kinds of evaluations.

Psycho-Educational Battery

A psychologist can identify some cognitive and academic problems by giving a psycho-educational battery. It consists of a test of aptitude (often the WISC), a test of academic achievement, such as the Woodcock-Johnson, and a screening of social and emotional adjustment.

If the child's aptitude is much higher than her achievement scores, then she may have a learning disability. But other possible causes of a large gap between aptitude and achievement, such as ADD/ADHD, must be considered. If your child was identified as learning disabled at school, a school psychologist may have completed this kind of testing with your child.

Comprehensive Neuropsychological Evaluation

Pediatric neuropsychologists are "licensed psychologists with expertise in how learning and behavior are associated with the development of brain structures and systems."[4] A comprehensive neuropsychological evaluation includes all the elements of the psycho-educational battery, but also measures other brain functions to give a broader picture of the person's ability. It examines expressive and receptive language, phonological processing, visual motor ability, reasoning, executive skills (planning and organization), memory, attention, behavior, and emotional functions.

My son's neuropsychological evaluations were each completed over three visits, beginning with my providing a detailed patient history and a

4. American Psychological Association. "Pediatric Neuropsychology: A Guide For Parents." Public Interest Advisory Committee, Division 40 (Clinical Neuropsychology), 2001. Accessed May 10, 2008. www.div40.org/pdf/PedNeuropscyhBroch3.pdf.

review of earlier test results. A good neuropsychologist will observe results as the child is taking the various tests, and choose additional tests to sift out details of the child's difficulties. The history, the test results, and the tester's expert analysis provide a more detailed diagnosis of your child, giving you and anyone working with you better means for planning her education and treatment.

Does Your Child Need a Comprehensive Neuropsychological Evaluation?

Let's say you have started to suspect a problem, you have begun to learn about various learning problems, and you have checked with your child's physician to rule out physical problems. When should your child be evaluated? If your main concerns are with the child's trouble learning problems, how do you know if your child needs a neuropsychological evaluation? Watch for these signs:

- *Behavior problems:* Pediatric neuropsychologist Dr. Elliot Blumenstein said children need a neuropsychological evaluation

  when you see the child starting to become resistant. Behavioral problems are a signal. When parents have really put their all into teaching specific skills and the child isn't getting it, I think you need to look for a professional who can help you.

  Seven is not too young. We can tell at four years old if the child is going to have problems with the early reading process. We have tests that can look at phonological awareness.[5]

- *Discouragement.* Sometimes children are not resistant, but they are discouraged because they know they are falling further behind. Diagnosis and early intervention is important for preserving or restoring your child's self-esteem.

- *Falling behind on basic skills.* Dr. Joe Sutton, co-author of *Strategies for Struggling Learners: A Guide for the Teaching Parent*, said in an interview with Christine Field:

5. Blumenstein, Elliot, Psy.D. Telephone interview. November 16, 2007.

Researchers are now finding that children who do not respond to basic, traditional reading instruction at the age of six years and who show signs of not being ready to learn to read at that early age are highly at-risk. … Parents with young children who are struggling to read and acquire other basic academic skills, such as spelling and math, should seriously consider testing and evaluation for that child. … Parents can recover money spent on testing and assessment, … but they can never re-capture lost years of instruction.[6]

- *Other differences.* Though it can hard for any parent to identify learning delays, homeschooled parents have it harder in one sense: we cannot easily compare our children to a classroom full of peers. So if you are homeschooling already, be attuned to your child's progress, and learn about typical stages of children's academic, social, and emotional development. No one child follows them exactly, but major discrepancies are a sign to discuss with your health care professional.

One mother told me this story. When a group of children were asked to draw a tree, most of the children drew some variation of a brown trunk and green or colored leaves. But her son's drawing was drastically different. It led to the discovery that this bright boy has a number of disabilities. A discrepancy doesn't mean a child has a problem, but it could be a clue.

Several homeschoolers told me they wished they had had their children tested sooner. One woman's experience was common: "Lots of people told me just to give them time, and tried to make excuses. I wish I had followed my gut." Another recommended:

Don't wait like we did. It wasn't until I taught my younger son and I saw how he learned to read. Wow! What a difference! That's when I said to my husband, "We've waited long enough. We've got to have some testing for Joe. He's obviously bright, but he can't read. Something is not right here."

6. Christine Field interview with Dr. Joe Sutton. "Strategies for Struggling Learners, Part One." The Old Schoolhouse, 2003. www.TheHomeschool Magazine.com/How_ To_Homeschool/articles/ articles.php?aid=83

How extensive an evaluation to get for you your child is a personal decision. Parents I interviewed differed on this. Some choose a more comprehensive evaluation to get more detail, others choose a minimal amount of testing, often for financial reasons or difficulty in finding good services.

Remember your goal is to glean useful information, to gain insight into your child's strengths and weaknesses and how she learns best, so you can set realistic goals and plan her education. Some test givers are more accustomed to testing merely to see if a child qualifies for extra help or services in school.

You want information to help you teach effectively, not just a label. Pediatric occupational therapist and homeschooling mother Laurie Chuba advised, "Think need, not diagnosis. It's the deficit you are treating." You can spend a lot of money without getting that kind of help. In the next section, we will discuss questions to ask before testing begins to make sure you know what you are getting.

She recommended an occupational therapy (OT) evaluation as an ideal point of entry for special services, because it addresses so many areas of life. "There isn't any part of life that won't be touched in an OT evaluation,"[7] she concluded. An experienced occupational therapist can recognize other needs and refer you to other professionals.

Dr. Elliot Blumenstein, a pediatric neuropsychologist, makes the case for a comprehensive neuropsychological evaluation:

> *If you're struggling with getting your child to learn, what else are you supposed to do? If you don't get a broad-based look, there is so much you can miss.*
>
> *That's one of the reasons I became a neuropsychologist. When I was in graduate school performing very simple psycho-educational evaluations, I didn't have enough information to help parents figure out how to intervene. So I could see children who couldn't decode* [sound out words], *but why? Was it because their phonological awareness was weak? Because they had retrieval problems? Was it because they just couldn't focus on the text, because they were so*

7. Chuba, Laurie, OTR/L. Personal interview, February 29, 2008.

inattentive? Did they have visual processing problems? Could
they not track effectively? There are all sorts of things that go into
these problems.[8]

Other Kinds of Evaluations

This chapter has discussed a few kinds of evaluations given. What
is available in your area may be different. Many children's hospitals
give evaluations that include tests and screenings given by a team of
professionals, including psychologists, medical doctors, occupational and
speech therapists, and social workers. Some families I interviewed reported
seeing a developmental pediatrician or a developmental neurologist for
diagnosis. Some have gone to university clinics and had their children
tested by students who were training as psychologists. I discuss choosing an
evaluator and the cost of evaluations in the next chapter.

Children with learning problems often have emotional problems as
well. If you are concerned about your child suffering from symptoms of
depression or anxiety, having low self-esteem, engaging in obsessive behavior, or other serious behavior problems, don't wait. Several homeschoolers
reported their children had significant emotional problems, including bipolar disorder, anxiety disorder, and depression. These children were helped
by psychiatrists and therapists, and by being homeschooled by parents who
could work with them on these problems throughout the day as needed.
Learn about emotional problems in children, know the warning signs, and
get help. A psychiatric evaluation may be needed; see the resources included
at the end of the chapter for further assistance.

Preparing for an Evaluation

Diligent preparation for an evaluation will pay off, because you will be an
educated consumer. If you can study, find good evaluators, communicate,
and listen well, you can develop helpful working relationships.

One mother, Toni, a specialist in human resources, strategy, and organization, has put her expertise to work coordinating services for her child.

8. Blumenstein,
Elliot, Psy.D.
Op. cit.

She writes:

> *Some of the most important information you can give the testing team is letting them know that you are looking over your child's life span, not just the immediate educational problems. Write out your goals for your child, and let the lead examiner know about them. Your goals should not only depend on the potential problems you see, but also articulate how you want your child to function in life. For some, this may be as simple as:*

- *Someday, my child will need to have a job. I want my child to read and understand his assignments better.*
- *I want my child to have a full life, with friends, and a family if she wants one.*
- *I think my child can go to college someday, and I want to get him ready.*
- *She has a great imagination. I'd like her to be able to write her stories down and share them.*

> *This communicates your vision for your child, and it shows the context in which your child is living and working. It is important that the testing team understand this; it will help them in their recommendations.*

Make Sure You Know What You Are Getting

Accurate diagnoses depend on good data, so learn beforehand about the evaluation your child will have. Visit the websites listed at the end of the previous chapter. Look at the books mentioned, and review the sections on testing. Know the preparation required, the process, and the products of the testing. You may ask in advance for a written description of what work will be done. Find out:

- *Which tests will be given, at a minimum?* What are they supposed to measure? Dr. Blumenstein warned that some comprehensive neuropsychological evaluations are less than they should be:

    > *Some people will say they are doing a comprehensive assessment when they are not. There are people who derive all the*

*information that they put in their report from the WISC-IV. I
like to test my hypotheses out. So it's great to make hypotheses, but
please don't put them in the report unless you have information to
back it up, because it is a disservice to the family.*[9]

- *Will the test giver meet with you afterwards to discuss results?*
- *Will you receive a written report?* A written report should be
  included in psycho-educational or neuropsychological evaluations. A report less than three years old may qualify your
  child for extra time or other accommodations on standardized
  tests, such as the college entrance examinations, and in college
  classes. Older reports still are valuable as a baseline, revealing
  progress and continued struggles. For other evaluations, say
  from a speech pathologist or occupational therapist, ask for
  a written report, or it may not be included. Writing a report
  takes time, so it will cost more. But you can re-read and study
  a written evaluation later, and share it later with any other
  professionals helping your child.
- *Will you receive suggested reading and other resources to help you
  understand the results?* Will this professional refer you to materials or therapists who can train you and help you plan your
  homeschool?
- *How long will the tests take?* Ask about how many hours your
  child's evaluation will take, where it will be given, and who
  will be giving the test. A comprehensive neuropsychological
  evaluation may take seven hours or more, spread over two or
  three days. Some other evaluations can be done in one session.
- *How should you and your child prepare for the evaluation?*
  Obviously, you want the child rested, alert, and well-fed at
  testing time, but the test giver may have additional suggestions. If your child is taking medications, discuss whether she
  should take them on the testing days.
- *What will happen during the testing time?* Typically, the test
  giver will want to talk to the parents privately before testing

9. *Ibid.*

the child, so the parents can speak freely about their concerns
and give the child's history. The test giver may interview
and test the child without the parents in the room. You can
imagine that a parent's interruptions could give the child extra
help, which would skew the test results. Staying out of the
room makes some parents uncomfortable, but having parents
in the room can change the behavior of some children. If you
are very uncomfortable leaving a child alone with a test giver,
discuss that before the evaluation begins: perhaps you can
work out an agreement.

Does your child have other special needs the test giver needs to know
about in advance? If your child suffers from emotional difficulties, such as
post-traumatic stress syndrome, you should discuss this with each test giver
before the tests begin.

When you are interviewed to give your child's developmental history,
bring a few samples of your child's work, to help the test givers understand
your concerns, and show your child's strengths and weaknesses. A list of
books your child recently has read may interest them. If your child has been
in school, you might bring copies of a few of the most telling notes and
reports from her teachers. For parents who already homeschool, chapter 4
covers what to bring and ways you can help the professionals understand your
child's education to date. You also might bring in notes, describing examples
of some of your child's worrisome behaviors. I found that a few brief, typed
descriptions of specific behavior impressed doctors more than my spoken
comments. You should bring in copies of any previous evaluations, too.

Finally, take time to explain to your child what the evaluation is about
several days before you go. When my son was still in school, his reading
teacher explained why he needed testing: "We know he's smart. We know
he's trying. We need to figure what the problem is." I added, "We need to
find out why school is so hard, and what we can do to teach you better."
I chose that wording to help him see that it was not that he was broken, it
was that the adults needed to find different teaching approaches.

Understanding the Results

When you meet with the test givers to learn the results, ask them to:

- Explain any terms they use that you do not understand. Ask again if you still don't understand. In addition to grasping what the various tests measure, make sure you follow the wording of the results. For instance, which is more serious: being "low" or "at risk"?
- Recommend reading to help you understand the diagnosis.
- Recommend reading and other resources to help plan your child's education.
- Recommend materials and programs for the child—and advise you on what to look for in choosing curriculum. (They may need to think about that. You may need a special education consultant for those answers, but it is still worth asking.)

Your report may include paragraphs that seem irrelevant to home-schooling. These may be standard advice typically pasted into reports for children similar to yours. For example, I know homeschoolers who were amused to receive reports advising them to plan one-on-one or small group instruction. But that language still may be helpful to you later on, if you enroll the child in a public or private school someday.

Ask for how and who to call back or e-mail when you have digested the report and thought of follow-up questions. In the resource section at the end of this chapter, some materials are listed to help you understand these reports.

Your Reactions to Diagnosis

Parents often have one or more strong reactions to receiving a diagnosis: grief, relief, sense of being overwhelmed, guilt—or several of these at once.

Some of us feel grief as we receive confirmation that our child has a significant problem. Perhaps we were hoping it was something she would outgrow, or we could fix with a change of curriculum or setting. Some of us discover our child's problems were bigger than we imagined.

It is also common to feel a sense of relief that it is not our imaginations, it is not bad parenting, or a lazy child. This child really does struggle.

Parents can also feel relief for another reason. A mother in Texas said, "When my oldest son was diagnosed at Scottish Rite Hospital and they told us what it was, my husband started crying, because he realized it wasn't that he was lazy in school, it wasn't that he wasn't trying. He really did have an issue. It was reaffirming." Many adults are diagnosed with a learning or attention problem only after their children are diagnosed. It is common for these parents to feel relief. They finally understand the cause of their own struggles, too.

Some of us feel guilty for not figuring out what was wrong sooner. We may feel guilty for not getting the child tested sooner, or for not realizing how far behind this child was.

With a new diagnosis, some parents feel overwhelmed. They have much to learn about the diagnosis, treatment, and prognosis. They expect lots of work planning how to help this child succeed.

Benefiting From an Evaluation

Whether already homeschooling or trying to start, you need to understand the basics of the problem before you attempt to customize your homeschool to the child's needs. Don't think you can learn it all in a few weeks, and don't believe everything you read. Your learning about your child's problem will be an ongoing process. You'll want to explore the resources at the end of chapter 6, and refer back to them occasionally, updating them with new material from other reliable sources as it becomes available. The magazines and websites of the national patient advocacy organizations listed there can keep you posted about changes in understanding and treatment of different problems.

Don't put the evaluation results away and forget them. Commit to review them several times a year: before you make each year's goals and plans, midyear, and any time you are considering a new treatment or therapy. Those reviews will keep your child's strengths and needs fresh in your mind.

As you look at results, focus on your child's strengths. Not only can this help you be more positive as you work with your child, those strengths are the keys to your child's future success. Focusing on gifts and talents is vital to building self-esteem and perseverance.

Recognize that your child may have been making heroic efforts to achieve mediocre grades. Look for ways to recognize and encourage that hard-working, never-give-up attitude.

Talking to your Child about the Results

Once you have absorbed the information well enough to explain some of it simply, consider how to tell your child about the test results. Keep it simple and be sure to point out strengths: "The report says you are intelligent," "Your scores in ___ are very high," or "Now that I understand how difficult reading can be for you, I so am proud of how hard you keep trying." Children know they are struggling, and they need encouragement.

If a disability or other problem is identified, telling your child about it in a supportive way can be a big relief for the child, especially if you let her know you are looking for ways to change her education to help her. To help her understand her special needs, look for children's books on her disability. At the end of the chapter, I list some publishers to investigate. Read the books yourself first, before you read them or give them to your child. Even if you do not agree with their philosophy or conclusions, you may find helpful ideas to share with your child.

Explain the nature of her difficulties as she grows able to understand. Knowing about it can help her make good choices for herself as she gets older. Like other important news, you probably will discuss it in short conversations from time to time. If you dwell on it more than she wants, you will show her how much her problems bother you. Don't worry her.

It is important to let your child know when it is appropriate to share this privileged information and when doing so can make them more isolated, teased, or bullied. In one family I interviewed, two children have high functioning forms of ASD and receive psychological services. Because they are young (ages 8 and 11) and because reading social cues is not their strength, this family has designated some information as being "family information" which should only be shared with doctors, police officers, teachers, clergy, and other adults in charge The fact that they are seeing psychiatrists and psychologists is considered family information, not to be shared casually.

Don't let your child think that her problem is the most important thing about her. Don't let it become the main thing you talk about when you discuss her. Having a disability or difficulty does not make her better or worse than anyone. It does not excuse her from trying hard, being patient or kind, or doing chores to help the rest of the family.

Some disabilities seem to come hand-in-hand with gifts, but don't pretend her disability is an unmixed blessing. Praise and nurture her gifts, and tell your child, "I don't know why you were born with these difficulties, but I think it is making you kinder/stronger/tougher/more patient"—whatever virtues you see the struggle producing.

The elementary school my children attended had a motto: "Think you can. Work hard. Get smart." That slogan reflects the fact that intelligence and development are not fixed. Some people think test results are written in stone, but this is not always true. My son is no longer considered learning disabled in math, because after years of grueling work, he has closed the gap between his aptitude and achievement. Similarly, some individuals with autism improve their social and communication skills considerably with hard work and proactive therapeutic interventions. Some with other struggles use a combination of strategies to live successfully.

Conclusion

Getting a diagnosis can be a long, complex process. It can be expensive. But if your child has serious learning problems, it is a necessary investment that pays long-term dividends. Regardless of the news, knowing what the problems are is worth it. It can help you plan reasonable goals for your child, and help you find ways to teach her better.

Whether you are seeking a diagnosis for your child's difficulties, or seeking help for her areas of weakness, the next chapter discusses what help professionals can give you to equip you to better teach your child.

Resources

Occupational Therapy

American Occupational Therapy Association: www.aota.org
Canadian Association of Occupational Therapists' site for consumers:
www.otworks.ca.

Speech Therapy
kidshealth.org/parent/system/ill/speech_therapy.html

The Canadian Association of Speech and Language Pathologists and
Audiologists, www.caslpa.ca, has good consumer pages, including an
excellent article, "A Parents' Guide to Speech."

The American Speech and Hearing Association, asha.org, under their
public section, has "Speech Referral Guidelines for Pediatrics," and can
help you find a therapist, too.

Both of these last two sites include what milestones to expect your child to
achieve at various ages.

Information on Diagnosis and Treatment
of ADD/ADHD and Learning Disabilities
Barkley, Russell A., Ph.D. *Taking Charge of ADHD: The Complete,
Authoritative Guide for Parents.* New York: Guilford, 2000.

Eide, Brock, M.D., and Fernette Eide, M.D. *The Mislabeled Child: Looking
Beyond Behavior to Find the True Sources—and Solutions—for Children's
Learning Challenges.* New York: Hyperion, 2006.

Silver, Larry, M.D. *The Misunderstood Child*, Fourth Edition. New York:
Three Rivers, 2006.

Neuropsychological Evaluations

American Psychological Association. "Pediatric Neuropsychology: A Guide For Parents." Public Interest Advisory Committee, Division 40 (Clinical Neuropsychology), 2001. www.div40.org/pdf/PedNeuropsychBroch3.pdf

Psychiatric Evaluations

American Academy of Child and Adolescent Psychiatry www.aacap.org/ Click on "Facts for Families" to search or access their complete collection of brochures on many topics. Also see their "Resources for Families" section.

"Child and Adolescent Mental Health: Comprehensive Psychiatric Evaluation." www.healthsystem.virginia.edu/uvahealth/peds_mentalhealth/evaluat.cfm

Publishers Offering Books for Children with Special Needs, and Their Parents

A.D.D. Warehouse
300 Northwest 70th Avenue, Suite 102
Plantation, FL 33317
800-233-9273
www.addwarehouse.com
Book for parents, children and teachers on autism, learning problems, mood disorders, ADD/ADHD, and many other problems.

Autism Asperger Publishing Company
P.O. Box 23173
Shawnee Mission, KS 66283-0173
(877) 277-8254
www.asperger.net

Educators Publishing Service
PO Box 9031
Cambridge, MA 02139-9031
(800) 435-7728
epsbooks.com. See Dr. Mel Levine's books, including *Jarvis Clutch—Social Spy*, *All Kinds of Minds*, *Keeping A Head in School: A student's book about learning abilities and learning disorders*, and *The Concentration Cockpit*, explaining memory and attention deficits to children.

Woodbine House
6510 Bells Mill Road
Bethesda, MD 20817
800-843-7323
www.woodbinehouse.com
Woodbine House publishes many fine books for parents, teachers, and children on a wide range of disabilities.

8

Professionals Who Can
Help You Homeschool

If your child has serious learning problems, you can get assistance from professionals. What kind of help can you get? How do you get good help? This chapter will help you discover how the professionals can assist you.

In this chapter:
- Standard services professionals provide
- How to find a good professional
- What you need for a long-term working relationship
- Professionals helping you train
- How to pay for evaluations and services
- Traveling for help

Information in this chapter is based on my research and experience as a parent seeking services for a child with special needs. But it should not replace seeking advice from certified professionals; nor should any part of this book should be construed as medical or legal advice.

Standard Services Professionals Provide

As discussed in the last chapter, professionals can provide the critical help in your child's journey to become the best learner he can. Because diagnoses and the professional services are continually changing, this chapter provides a snapshot of services. I will discuss some newer treatments in chapter 9.

Services usually are available for children with special needs, but not in every community. In the communities with services, no two professionals are exactly alike. Not all struggling learners need every professional service, but it is important to be familiar with the range of services available. Homeschoolers I interviewed reported receiving help from:

- Medical doctors, including pediatricians, psychiatrists, and osteopaths,
- Psychologists and counselors,
- Speech pathologists and speech therapists,
- Occupational therapists,
- Special education consultants,
- Reading tutors and academic therapists.

We will look at each of these in turn below.

Medical doctors can diagnose attention deficit disorder (ADD/ADHD), autism spectrum disorders (ASD), and physical disorders. They can identify or rule out medical conditions that can create learning problems, such as sleep disorders or seizures, which can go unnoticed. They are qualified to prescribe medication when needed as part of a treatment plan.

Like other parents, homeschoolers I interviewed disagree on the use of medications to treat learning and psychological problems. Some parents homeschool to avoid pressure from schools to medicate their children. Some of these families have stopped medication. Others said homeschooling reduced their children's need for medication. And others consider medication an essential part of their child's treatment plan. One advantage of homeschooling, they said, was being able to monitor the use and effects of medications.

Not all doctors are knowledgeable about ADD/ADHD, ASD, and other disorders, so it may be important for you to ask your doctor for a referral to another doctor with expertise in your child's area of need, particularly if the diagnosis seems difficult or inconclusive. Developmental pediatricians (also known as pediatric developmentalists) are few, but their training and certification in developmental-behavioral pediatrics, makes them especially helpful in diagnosing some disorders such as autism spectrum disorders. For some conditions, your doctor may refer you to a psychologist, as ours did.

Psychologists are licensed by state and provincial licensing boards after completing graduate degrees, supervised experience, and an examination. Most psychologists have doctorates, but have no medical school training, so they cannot prescribe medication. However, they can provide many other kinds of help: testing, diagnosis, counseling for child and parent, family therapy, social skills classes, and other treatments.

Some families still feel there is a stigma with receiving mental health services, but many homeschooling parents like to know what the problems are and get help dealing with them. As far as your child is concerned, seeing a psychologist is only a big deal if you make it one, if your psychologist doesn't suit your child's personality (see the following section), or if you or the child discuss receiving mental health services with unkind or thoughtless people.

Counselors give advice and teach children, teens, and parents social skills, coping strategies, parenting strategies, and more. This teaching may be in classes or in private therapy sessions. Some counselors call themselves talk therapists, not to be confused with speech therapists. Counselors can help children understand their learning problems, which is an important part of coping with them. Counselors often are less expensive than professionals holding doctoral degrees. One note of caution: the term *therapist* is not equivalent to licensed professional counselor (LPC). In some states, therapists may not be licensed at all. Be sure to find an LPC.

Social workers help children and families by providing counseling and group and individual therapy, helping children develop social skills and improve relationships. They help children deal with academic and behavior problems and support parents and help them plan short- and long-term care. For families that choose to receive state-funded services, social workers can help parents navigate the often-confusing state system. Social workers usually have a master's degree and are certified as Licensed Clinical Social Workers (LCSW). I know homeschoolers with struggling learners who have benefited from group therapy or social skills classes offered by social workers who specialize in caring for children with learning problems.

Speech and language pathologists (SLPs), sometimes called speech therapists, help clients with speech disorders (trouble making sounds), language disorders (trouble understanding language or putting thoughts into words), and difficulty swallowing. According to kidshealth.org,[1] speech disorders include not only fluency disorders like stuttering, but also articulation disorders (difficulty making particular sounds), and voice or resonance disorders, in which the "pitch, volume, or quality of a child's voice that distract listeners from what's being said."[2] This can prevent a child from participating in group discussions, isolate them, or silence them for fear of ridicule.

Parents can miss speech problems, if they become so accustomed and attuned to a child's way of speaking, that they do not realize how different the child's speech is from normal speech. If friends or family comment on your child's speech or have difficulty understanding him, it may be your cue to have him evaluated. Don't wait—the younger a child is, the easier it is to treat speech problems.

Language disorders, as opposed to speech disorders, are diagnosed when a person has difficulty understanding language (a receptive language disorder) or expressing ideas or feelings (an expressive language disorder). Language therapy is intended to help increase a child's proficiency in language, often focusing on receptive, expressive, or pragmatic language.

SLPs give tests to determine their patients' needs and to prepare a plan of treatment. They give exercises to work on at home and provide individual and small group therapy.

Occupational therapists (OTs) help people with skills they need for work and daily life. Occupational therapy is much more than learning to button your shirt after a stroke or operate machinery after a serious injury. It helps children with many foundational skills including:

- fine motor skills like typing or handwriting problems (hand pain, pressing too hard, writing too lightly, poor spacing between words),
- balance or gross motor skills (trouble riding a bicycle, skipping, hand-eye coordination), and
- sensory integration difficulties, which might appear as inability to tolerate textures or sounds if the person is overly sensitive to them; or a lack of awareness that one is standing too close, talking too loud, hugging too much for the person who is insensitive to them.

1. Nemours Foundation. "Speech and Language Therapy." Accessed February 29, 2008. kidshealth. org/parent/system/ ill/speech_therapy. html.

2. Ibid.

OTs and SLPs both help children who:

- have language processing disorders, (e.g., difficulty following directions, needing tasks broken down into concrete steps),
- have working memory problems, and
- need to develop communication and social skills, (naïve or inappropriate interaction), non-verbal skills, trouble making friends.

Like SLPs, OTs give tests to assess the child's needs and to create a treatment plan. They also give exercises for home and may offer group as well as individual therapy.

Special education consultants are trained special education advocates or teachers who can assist with planning, offer strategies, and suggest materials. Some will give tests, such as the Woodcock-Johnson Psycho-Educational Battery. If you hire a special education teacher as a consultant, make sure they are not opposed to homeschooling, or better yet, have worked with other homeschoolers and know what resources are available to homeschoolers. These consultants need not be local; some help families long distance by telephone and the Internet.

A reading tutor might be the reading specialist at a local school, anyone trained in the teaching of reading, or even just anyone who can read and teach. Because tutors are not licensed, you should ask about their training and experience: what certifications they have and how much experience they have had tutoring, particularly in your child's area of need. For example, most of the reading tutors in my area specialized in teaching decoding (converting printed letters into words). Once my son mastered that, even though I spoke to many teachers certified to teach reading, we had trouble finding someone to help with training in comprehension and fluency.

This year we found an academic therapist, who is helping him make good progress, using Multisensory Structure Language (MSL). MSL is one of several methods using an approach based on the work of Samuel Orton and Anna Gillingham. Many of these methods have their own certification programs, and they vary in their thoroughness. Read more about various Orton-Gillingham programs in chapter 18. Because anyone can claim they are providing an Orton-Gillingham or multisensory approach, that chapter includes help finding certified reading instructors or becoming trained to give that instruction yourself.

How to Find a Good Professional

A good professional is one who is proficient in their field and suitable for your child. When you work with a professional, you are introducing them to your family and your life—you need to be sure they are going to support you as parents and homeschoolers. To identify good professionals:

- Make sure your professionals are certified. Learn the independent board or national professional organization that licenses or certifies practitioners.
- Ask other homeschoolers, as well as others with children who share your children's challenges, who they use. Check with support groups for parents of children with special needs and with local chapters of various patient advocacy organizations, such as Learning Disabilities Association of America, Children and Adults with Attention Deficit Disorder, or the Autism Society of America, to learn who other parents recommend. Ask state and local homeschool organizations and check their websites.
- Become familiar with the professional's services by reading over his or her materials and websites before your first meeting. Then you can more easily judge if the approach and manner are consistent with the advertising.
- Meet with the professionals you are considering. Listen to what they say and don't say. Consider their attitude and personality.
- Do they currently treat children with your child's particular needs? How frequently? What ages?
- Do they stay current in their field? How? Do they regularly read journals in their field and study research on treatments for your child's condition? Do they partner with a hospital or take credits for licensing?
- Will they track your child's progress and re-evaluate goals? How would you know their interventions are successful and complete, that is, how do you know when you are done?
- Will they support your working with your child between sessions when appropriate? Will they maximize your investment in their

services by suggesting a home-based program for parents to apply between professional visits?

- Are they open to homeschooling or at least not opposed to it? One mother reported that every time she mentions homeschooling her pediatrician rolls his eyes, while another said her pediatrician was the first to suggest homeschooling. A third has a supportive doctor who helps her cope with her son's ADHD. She advised new home-schoolers to "have a good heart to heart with a physician. That was the biggest help for me to stay at it and not give it up."

- Are they well connected in the community? Do they belong to CHADD, ASA, LDA, or other patient advocacy groups, or interact with other professionals? Your goal is to have a professional who is well connected in the community, who knows and can refer you to other helpful professionals should you need them. For example, a neuropsychologist should be able to refer you to good local reading experts and occupational therapists, an occupational therapist should be able to recommend a good speech pathologist, and so on.

- Do they communicate well? Do they take time to explain things to you? Are they willing to provide you with titles, articles, and websites to help you be better informed? Do they follow through on providing promised titles and articles?

- Do they respect you? Do they listen to what you say, and respond, or are they more interested in talking, like a walkie-talkie that can only transmit, not receive?

Finding Professionals Who Listen

Kim's experience illustrates the importance of doctors who listen. Her two-year-old son Calvin began showing symptoms of autism, losing verbal skills, and not making eye contact:

> *At three, he could not learn his colors, he couldn't focus, he couldn't learn his letters, he couldn't sit still for a story. It was very obvious that there was a problem.*

I took him from doctor to doctor, and they said, "Oh, he's just a boy, you need to let him play." I took him to a specialist who specializes in ADHD and autism. And he said, "He's definitely ADHD, but he's not autistic, he's just delayed. He'll catch up in time." In my gut I knew he was wrong, because I had been reading and he had all the signs. He's on the spectrum, but there are things about him that are not autistic.

I kept going along with the doctors. At four, he was still not counting "one" or knowing even one color. We kept going back to the doctor, who kept saying, "Oh, he's just a boy. He's just delayed. He's fine. Relax. Take him outside for walks."

"I do!," I answered. "But he should be learning some things."

Later a friend said, "I have this wonderful pediatrician who listens."

I said, "Give me his name!" I went last autumn when Calvin was five. At our first appointment, the doctor was listening to me, but all the time he was observing Calvin. The doctor said, sighing, "I know you don't know me and I hate to start off with parents that don't know me with something serious like this. Has anybody mentioned the word 'autism' to you?"

I said, "Thank God!"

He looked at me funny, because it wasn't the response he was expecting.

"For two years, I have been trying to get somebody to listen to me," I answered.

Kim's advice for beginners:

Read a lot.
Immerse yourself in information.
Find a doctor who is supportive.
Be in tune with your child's learning style.
Join Home School Legal Defense Association (HSLDA).

What You Need for a Long-Term Working Relationship

It's one thing to meet with a professional once or twice for an evaluation, but when you expect to be working together over months and years, you need to ask more questions.

Ask medical doctors what their approach is to medication and managing side effects. It is especially important that doctors keep up with current research because this is a rapidly changing field.

Ask all providers how they usually teach children and teens about their condition and involve them in their own treatment.

Ask how they see parents involved in a child's treatment. As you interview professionals and learn about proposed treatments, you need to explore with them how active you want or need to be in your child's therapy. Many treatments require or benefit enormously from follow-up exercises at home, reinforcing what your child is learning. (Some treatments should not be done at home. See Anita's comments below, for example.) Your professional may be cautious at first, wanting to see if you are careful to follow their guidance. Poorly implemented therapy can harm your child, so if you are giving a home-based program, learn from the expert.

You should not expect to be treated as if you were a licensed expert; however, as one parent tells her child's professionals, "I may not be an expert in your field, but I'm an expert in my child!" You can offer valuable insights. You must be willing to listen and learn new ideas yourself, though.

Speech pathologist-turned-homeschooler Anita writes about other speech pathologists, but her idea applies to some other therapies, as well:

It's also very important that they have the mindset that it's the parent who must ultimately be trained. I've seen many who literally shut parents out of the therapy session and it makes no sense at all. I really like home-based therapy for younger children and particularly those that are homeschooled. It is most helpful for the therapist to see how the child communicates in their environment, and set up a program for parents based on factors such as daily routine and communicative opportunities.

[However,] *if the child is older and needs specific equipment for remediation, such as stuttering, then home-based is not recommended. …*

I have not seen enough therapists give parents the confidence and training to take on a much more active role in remediation of speech and language issues. The homeschool parent is in the best possible position to administer therapy effectively and consistently. I've seen too many therapists guard their role and make it inaccessible to parents.

Ask all providers if they will be comfortable working with other professionals who are serving your child. Are they willing to confer with them and coordinate care? Several parents I interviewed work with multiple therapists and professionals, including counselors, speech therapists, and occupational therapists. Several homeschooling parents receive multiple services from special educational services or mental health centers. For example, one family with a child on the autism spectrum receives help at one center from a psychiatrist, a nutritionist, an applied behavior analysis[3] (ABA) therapist, and a special education consultant, who evaluates the child's progress, and assists with coordination and planning.

What if you need a team, but don't have such a clinic or practice in your area that offers all the services you need? If you cannot work with a clinic long distance, perhaps because your child needs regular therapy sessions, you might try to build your own team. Toni, a human resources professional quoted in the last chapter, is not a homeschooler, but offers good advice from her experience coordinating the team that helps her

3. ABA therapists train children (and adults) with pervasive developmental and other special needs. ABA is a form of behavior modification, in which specific skills are slowly and explicitly taught and consistently rewarded.

autistic children. Her team includes a speech therapist, a physical therapist, and an occupational therapist. She chooses professionals who are willing to work together, recognizing that therapies are more effective if they are given consistently through the day. She arranges team meetings to discuss and agree on strategies to use while introducing new approaches to her children. (Those who cannot attend in person attend by phone.) She looks for professionals with some knowledge of each other's fields, who can look for teachable moments, and support each other's training.

It's not just children who need to "play well with others." Your professionals do, too.

Ask all providers about their philosophical approach and therapeutic model. Do they strongly favor an approach based exclusively on behavior modification, medication, psychoanalysis, or neurodevelopmental exercises[4]? Does the approach they use seem reasonable to you? Are they open to combining approaches if that is something you want to consider, that is, a multi-modal approach, such as using medication and training to treat ADD/ADHD, or Applied Behavior Analysis (ABA) along with diet changes for a child with ASD.

Finally, don't ask, but watch how they treat your child. Do they respect him? Is their manner too loud, cheery, or dull for him? Does their approach fit your child? Be prepared for your child to surprise you by getting along well with someone whose manner you do not expect to suit him. Observe. How does your child work with them?

Partnering with Professionals

In Virginia, speech pathologist turned-homeschooler Anita homeschools her three children: girls age seven and ten, and a son, age eleven, who has Down Syndrome, sensory integration disorder, and a mood disorder (which are more severe difficulties than faced by most families interviewed for this book). Anita brought her son home five years ago after a very difficult time in public school. She said:

4. Neuro-developmentalists develop programs of exercises for children to do with them and with their parents daily at home. Their theory is that because the brain is remarkably adaptable, a program of intense daily exercises to stimulate different areas of the brain can help "rewire" the brain. Several parents I spoke with found help from this approach. More at icando.org and nacd.org, groups that certify these trainers, but at this writing, cite no research in refereed journals to support their therapy. See chapter 9 on evaluating newer treatments.

He has multiple disabilities. I don't believe the school system is equipped to handle that. …

I got such great results homeschooling my son and we were having such a good time, that I decided to try it with the girls. By that time it had become something that I believed in, that I felt was best for kids with special needs or typical kids. I felt it was an opportunity to create a family environment that I wanted.

Anita also looked at the big picture for families with children with more severe needs:

The bottom line is, the therapy recommendations have to make sense. For children with multiple disabilities, for whom therapy is an on-going endeavor, it is often unreasonable for parents to be expected to keep up a weekly schedule of therapies for twenty-plus years. In this case, the therapist must really partner with the parent and consider intensive therapy during "windows" of progress, and back off at other times and consult periodically. For these parents therapy can be exhausting and both parent and child need breaks. And let's not forget the tremendous drain on finances.

Given her son's severe needs, Anita has assembled a team of professional helpers.

An occupational therapist comes weekly and a physical therapist comes every other week. Anita provides speech therapy through the day. They see a neurologist and a behavioral psychologist regularly.

I wondered how she managed it all. A college student comes twenty hours a week to assist with the homeschool or to babysit, so Anita can give the children individual attention. Anita's mother comes and helps one morning a week, and she has lots of family close by.

Anita connects with the community in many ways. Her son competes in Special Olympics and Challenger baseball, and he takes private swim lessons. She is in local and online homeschool support groups and active in her local chapter of the Down Syndrome Association. She is just starting a support group for homeschoolers with children with Down Syndrome. Their activities don't all revolve around her special needs child. Her daughters both take piano lessons and go to tennis clinics. The older girl takes art classes at a local art academy, while her younger daughter takes classes at a local science center and plays softball.

Anita's advice to beginners:

I would encourage them to get support. When I started, I thought I could do it all. As my son got older, I realized if I'm in for long haul, I have got to set up a lot of support. Second, parents should give themselves room to fumble around, let themselves off the hook a bit. There will be good and bad days. It takes a while for the teacher-parent and the child to get in the groove. I put a lot of pressure on myself the first couple years. Realize that you are not going to get it all done. You have to remind yourself the school isn't getting it all done, either.

Professionals Helping You Train

When you homeschool, you are becoming a teacher. Working with a struggling learner, you may need to attend workshops and take courses to become better equipped to help your child. Good professionals may know of opportunities for you to learn: workshops, classes, and books. You also might ask your professional's advice on various training and treatment programs your child can do at home with you or online, such as the speech therapy program *Straight Talk* by speech pathologist Marisa Lapish, available at www.nathhan.com, or *TeachTown*, an online teaching program for children with ASD. While most professionals, except some special education teachers, won't be familiar with different curricula, you can get advice on what features would be helpful.

In chapter 10, I will discuss other ways to improve your teaching.

How to Pay for Evaluation and Services

First, check with your health insurance or health maintenance organization (HMO) and make sure you understand what they will cover. One homeschooling mother wrote, "I called my insurance company (the mental health division) and asked if there are any participating providers that do ADD testing and there were! We only have to pay a twenty dollar co-pay for the cognitive and personality testing."

However, there are two disadvantages to having insurance or managed care pay for testing. First, you may have to wait many months for service.

Second, insurance companies limit where you can go for testing and limit the hours that professionals can spend giving tests and evaluating scores. For children with more serious needs, more comprehensive testing is important. Pediatric neuropsychologist Dr. Elliot Blumenstein is dismayed by the effect of insurance on testing:

> *You will rarely see a good assessment from someone who works for insurance companies. When I'm trying to get reimbursed from insurance companies, they will offer me seven hours. That includes working with the kids, meeting with the parents, and writing the report. I test for seven hours. The insurance company's response is, "Those are school issues, not psychological issues." My response is, "School issues are their life issues and related to their psychology. School is their job. We have to figure out what's going on here."* [5]

5. Blumenstein, Elliot, Psy.D. Telephone interview, November 16, 2007.

6. Ibid.

Though not required, many psychologists give back to community by providing pro bono or reduced fee evaluations, Blumenstein said.[6] Talk with professionals in your area and see what you can afford.

Since not every child needs a comprehensive neuropsychological evaluation, you may consider other options. Some psychologists will give simply a few tests, though others feel that gives a dangerously incomplete picture.

U.S. public schools will provide limited testing and may provide services to homeschooled families. Canadian homeschooling law varies by province. But current U.S. federal law, the Individuals with Disabilities Educational Act (IDEA 2004), does not require public schools to provide services to students who are in private schools or homeschools. According to Pamela Wright and Pete Wright, Esq.:

> *The Individuals with Disabilities Education Act includes the Child Find mandate. Child Find requires all school districts to identify, locate and evaluate all children with disabilities, regardless of the severity of their disabilities. This obligation to identify all children who may need special education services exists even if the school is not providing special education services to the child.[7]*

The Wrights also explain that parents of infants and preschoolers also should know that:

> *Another purpose of the law is to help each State implement a statewide, comprehensive, coordinated multi-disciplinary system of Early Intervention Services for infants and toddlers with disabilities. Young children with disabilities must receive appropriate early intervention services to "prepare them for further education, employment, and independent living."*
>
> *Congress encourages states to provide Early Intervention Services so children with developmental delays and other disabilities will receive treatment early. Congress enacted the Early Intervention Program for Infants and Toddlers to provide interagency coordination of services to children from birth to two years of age. Under IDEA, states must ensure that children with disabilities are eligible for special education services by age three.[8]*

7. Wright, Pamela, Esq., and Pete Wright, Esq. "The Child Find Mandate: What Does It Mean to You?" Accessed March 8, 2008. www.wrightslaw.com/info/child.find.mandate.htm. The Wrightslaw website is a valuable resource on special education law, education law, testing, and advocacy for children with disabilities.

8. Ibid.

If your child was in public school, received an Individualized Education Plan (IEP) or 504 Plan, and has been receiving special services (such as speech therapy) from the public schools, consider whether you want to try to continue to receive those services from the schools. Although not required, some public schools will continue to provide the services. Check with your state or provincial homeschool organization for advice on your school district's policy and practice with homeschooling families.

Also check with HSLDA, an excellent resource on federal and state law. Generally, this association is very wary of homeschoolers' involvement with public schools, based on their experience defending homeschooling families whose right to homeschool is threatened by local authorities.

HSLDA reports that:

many families have found themselves mired in legal difficulties as a result of their involvement in public school services. … We understand that as a matter of economics and ease of access, free public school services are very attractive. We also understand, however, that regulatory strings may come attached to these programs. Generally, we find that the longer a family uses these programs, the tighter the strings of control become.[9]

Experiences vary. Some homeschoolers have received some testing services from public school with no trouble. Others have experienced difficulty afterwards, with schools pressing them to enroll and insisting that their homeschooling is inadequate. Other parents have been unable to receive services they wanted. It varies with location, personalities, and laws. So ask other homeschoolers in your area. In summary, public school testing:

- Is free,
- Is less comprehensive than good private testing,
- May come with strings attached, including increasing pressure from the school to enroll your child.

Other sources of less expensive testing are medical research centers and universities with graduate program in psychology. Some of these facilities have research projects and need participants, who may receive free evaluations and treatment. Some universities run clinics where graduate

9. Home School Legal Defense Association. "Two Steps For Protecting Your Special Needs Homeschool." Accessed November 27, 2007. www. hslda.org/strugglinglearner/ sn_TwoSteps.asp

students in psychology give tests under the supervision of licensed psychologists. In our family's experience, the supervision meant that the graduate student tape-recorded her testing for her advisor to review. The advisor also reviewed her results and written report before we saw it, but we never met the advisor, a licensed psychologist. One parent observed that a problem with receiving an evaluation at a university clinic is that there is no way to know who will evaluate or what they are like.

Such testing by graduate students is cheaper than private testing, but good testing is an art, involving the use of a variety of tests. A good evaluator will notice details and subtleties in some test results, and may choose different tests to understand the nature of the child's learning problems. An inexperienced tester may miss those clues.

Traveling for Help

Some parents I interviewed traveled great distances to find good testing and training. They thought it worth the trouble and expense. If you live far away from experts and you cannot otherwise find out how to help your child, this may be a necessary route. If you choose this option, prepare ahead of time by conducting your own research, completing all paperwork, and seeking an opportunity to talk directly (by phone or e-mail exchange) with the facility, so you have everything you need to ensure your trip will provide you with accurate answers. If you are required to send paperwork in before your visit, I recommend you make two extra copies of your completed forms, leaving one at home, and bringing a copy with you, just in case they are lost at the facility. By being prepared, you can get the most benefit out of your trip.

Conclusion

The stereotype of homeschoolers as recluses is particularly mistaken when it comes to parents homeschooling struggling learners. Finding the right people to assist you as you homeschool is important. You need qualified experts you respect, who respect and work with you. The greater your child's needs, the greater your need of good help.

Resources

Speech and Language Pathologists
American Speech-Language-Hearing Association (ASHA) is the
professional association for audiologists, speech-language pathologists,
and speech, language, and hearing scientists. asha.org

Occupational Therapy
American Occupational Therapy Association: www.aota.org
Canadian Association of Occupational Therapists' site for consumers:
www.otworks.ca

Help for learning disabilities, see OT or SLP above and also:
Academic Language Therapy Association
To find an academic therapist, see www.altaread.org/ and click on
"Find a therapist."

Wilson Reading System
To find a teacher or to be trained to teach the Wilson Reading System:
www.wilsonlanguage.com/ Use the "Contact us" page, and include
your zip or postal code.

9

Newer Therapies and Treatments

What will you try to help your child? "Anything!" many parents reply. But when it comes to choosing treatments and therapies, how do we know which are effective? Some are standard practice in the health care community. Some newer treatments and therapies may become standard one day. Other so-called treatments are useless or, worse yet, dangerous. How do we know what is going to help or hurt our children?

In this chapter:
- The gold standard
- Buyer beware
- Why try anything else?
- How to decide

Like other parents with struggling learners, homeschoolers have limited money and time to invest in treatments. Yet safe treatments can improve our children's ability to learn. Learning about different approaches helps us decide what is best for our children.

Seeking and evaluating new treatments can be an all-consuming job. Such treatments offer to ease our children's problems, but families with struggling learners know that choosing effective treatments can be a gamble.

The Gold Standard

When considering treatments, one homeschooler advised, "Beware junk science." To be sure treatments are worth the time, energy, and money they take, and because researchers' wishes can affect their results, scientists have developed rigorous standards for trials of new treatments. Known as the *gold standard*, these criteria enable researchers to test their assumptions rigorously, to help remove bias and prove a given treatment is effective. To meet the criteria for gold standard, the trials should be *placebo-controlled, double blind, randomized, replicated*, and *published in a recognized, refereed professional journal*. That is no simple feat. Let me explain those terms to show the scrutiny given to meet the gold standard.

A well-designed experiment must include two groups: the *experimental group*, who receive the new treatment, and the *control group* of similar people who do not. Only well-designed testing and experiments can prove or disprove the effectiveness of a treatment.

Psychologists have long known about the placebo effect: if we think something we are getting will do us good, some of us will feel better. In a *placebo-controlled trial*, the control group receives a placebo, a fake treatment that does no harm. To test a medication, for instance, the placebo might be a sugar pill that looks like real medication. To evaluate the effectiveness of training, the placebo treatment could be similar training with key ingredients missing. Participants don't know which group they are in.

Parents need to ask hard questions when something is claimed as proven. Advertisements for one treatment claimed that their therapy was proven effective. But their research only compared students receiving frequent therapy sessions to those receiving no special treatment at all. Any one-on-one work with an adult often helps students because it increases their Academic Engaged Time (AET), so the test only showed that the advertised therapy was better than nothing. A more useful comparison would have been to have children in the experimental group receive the therapy and those in the control group receive conventional tutoring.

In a *double-blind* experiment, not only do the participants not know if they are receiving the experimental treatment, neither do the researchers.

This insures that the researchers and the participants are not influenced by the researchers' hopes or doubts about the new treatment.

Randomized means that the participants are randomly assigned either to the experimental group or the control group. A well-designed experiment will measure the participants first with several assessments to make sure the groups are evenly matched. Ideally, the only difference between the two groups is that one is receiving the experimental treatments and the other is not.

If research is *published in refereed, professional scientific journals*, that provides another layer of protection to consumers. Anyone can publish a study privately or even make up a professional-sounding journal name to publish it in. But for research to appear in respected professional journals, the work must be refereed by peers, that is, reviewed by qualified professionals with no personal interest in the project.

Replicated means the experiment was repeated at other independent reputable research facilities. One experiment does not prove anything. Independent verification helps prevent error and ensures impartiality.

This combination of requirements is the *gold standard* in research: a randomized, double-blind, placebo-controlled study, published in a peer-reviewed scientific journal, and replicated independently. These safeguards of the scientific method are not flawless, but they help prevent fraud and mistakes.

Buyer Beware

Fraud is rampant. As Rita, a homeschooling mother in Pennsylvania noted, "Learning disabilities are big business," and she advised caution. Of course, other special needs are big business, also, so be wary.

Even an alternative treatment that does not harm your child physically can harm your family in other ways. Many treatments are very expensive, and the prices are not well-advertised. Even if a family decides a treatment is affordable, it often requires an investment of many hours in therapy at a clinic or at home, and sometimes hours of commuting. It is not only time, but also energy. A family can only do so much; a struggling child may feel worn out or exhausted by months or years of treatments.

Why Try Anything Else?

So why don't all parents wait for every theory to be tested so rigorously? In *Attention Deficit Disorder and Learning Disabilities*,[1] Psychologists Dr. Barbara Ingersoll and Dr. Sam Goldstein point out several reasons that apply to alternative treatments for other conditions, as well. Some parents are too easily swayed by dramatic success stories. However unlikely a treatment sounds—and there are some bizarre treatments available—any sign of improvement naturally captures our attention. Seeking sensational successes, the news media are likely to showcase treatments that are dramatic, new, and different. The success of a few others may seem to point the way for you. Reading testimonials on a website or brochure gives you no idea how many people were not helped by the treatment, or whether anyone was harmed by it. Unscrupulous providers can write fake testimonials, misquote respected authorities, manufacture so-called studies, or place great weight on a study based on the experience of one or a few patients.

So beware. Almost anyone selling any treatment can probably find a few people who have been helped by it and want to share that hope.

Another, more understandable reason that all parents don't wait for treatments to be rigorously tested is that they realize that such independent verification takes time, staff, and lots of money. Because a few of today's alternative treatments may become tomorrow's accepted practices, some parents do not think they should wait for the gold standard to be completely met.

How to Decide

We want to help our children and protect them at the same time, so what can we do? Parents I interviewed had differing opinions, but many stressed the need to become informed and keep current on their children's disabilities.

For example, because I am a member of Learning Disabilities of America, in 2007 I learned about a workshop by Dr. Ingersoll, on CogMed, a five-week program of daily home computer exercises to improve working

1. Ingersoll, Barbara, Ph.D., and Sam Goldstein, Ph.D. Attention Deficit Disorder and Learning Disabilities: Realities, Myths, and Controversial Treatments. *New York: Doubleday Publishing Group, 1993.*

2. Ibid.

3. Arnold, L. Eugene, M.D., Robert A. DiSilvestro, Ph.D., et. al. *"Serum Zinc Correlates with Parent- and Teacher-Rated Inattention in Children with Attention-Deficit/ Hyperactivity Disorder."* Journal of Child and Adolescent Psychopharmacology, 15:4, 2005, pp. 628-638.

memory. (Working memory is the ability to hold information in one's mind for a few seconds and is closely linked to paying attention, to problem solving, and to academic tasks such as studying or writing a paragraph.) I knew Dr. Ingersoll was one of the authors of *Attention Deficit Disorder and Learning Disabilities*,[2] and had debunked many alternative treatments. My son was skeptical, but we investigated. We learned CogMed had been the subject of randomized, double-blind placebo controlled studies, published in refereed journals, which were being replicated. My skeptical son was convinced and decided to train with her. Since he completed the training, we saw improvement, which helped his reading, math, and daily living. But we never would have heard of this treatment if we had not kept informed.

Keeping informed can make you aware of other kinds of treatments, too. Because I attended Children and Adults with Attention Deficit (CHADD)'s international conference in 2007, I learned about research by Drs. Eugene Arnold and Robert DiSilvestro at Ohio State University on the effect of serum zinc on children with ADD/ADHD[3], and about Dr. Alexandra Richardson's study at Oxford, which linked a relative lack of omega-3 and -6 fatty acids to dyslexia and ADD/ADHD[4].

While parents do not have time to keep up with every research paper, joining patient advocacy organizations and talking with knowledgeable professionals wherever we meet them can point us to important news and new practices, as they become recommended. For example, I met Dr. John Umhau, one of the authors of the chapter on omega-3 fatty acids in the National Institutes of Health's book, *Low-Cost Approaches to Promote Physical and Mental Health*, which says:

> *Our message is that omega-3 fats can contribute to a longer and healthier life and that seafood is a healthy food. For those who do not care to eat fish, omega-3 rich fish oils are a safe and inexpensive alternative to the pharmaceuticals used to treat diseases that fish oil might prevent.*[5]

As homeschooling mother Corazon told me, in explaining why they tried a biomedical treatment for her autistic son, "I'm not going to wait for something to be one hundred percent scientifically proved." Corazon found

4. Richardson, Alexandra J., Dphil, and Paul Montgomery, DPhil. "The Oxford-Durham Study: A Randomized, Controlled Trial of Dietary Supplementation With Fatty Acids in Children With Developmental Coordination Disorder." Pediatrics. *Vol. 115: 5 May 2005, pp. 1360-1366.*

5. Umhau, JC, and KM Dauphinais. "Omega 3 - Polyunsaturated Fatty Acids and Health." Low-Cost Approaches to Promote Physical and Mental Health: Theory, Research, and Practice. *Luciano L'Abate , editor. Springer, 2007.*

some scientific research supporting biomedical treatment, as advocated by some medical doctors and parents affiliated with *Defeat Autism Now*. She read and evaluated possible side effects, and decided to try the treatment, involving dietary changes, supplements, and prescription dietary enzymes, under the supervision of a physician. She saw improvement almost immediately. More than six years later, she continues to see good results.

Several parents I interviewed reported discovering their children responded well to changes in diet, such as eliminating red dye or going on a gluten-free, casein-free (GFCF) diet. Since gluten is found in wheat and casein is in dairy products, this diet is a major and expensive effort to undertake, but several families I interviewed found it helpful, and there is some research to support a benefit for some children with autism spectrum disorders.[6] These parents did not wait for that research to be replicated and published in peer-reviewed research in refereed journals.

Drs. Edward Hallowell and John Ratey take a similar approach in *Delivered From Distraction*, recommending readers learn about alternative treatments for attention deficit disorder. They suggested that some treatments, such as taking fish oil, are worth trying, since these treatments help some people, are not expensive or difficult, and are safe if you follow dosage guidelines and buy from manufacturers with high standards of purity.[7] Of course, always consult with your doctor first.

Homeschooling parents differ on their views of new treatments. But the parents I interviewed agreed on approaching them skeptically, doing your homework, and evaluating all the costs (money, time, and energy), before you decide to give something a try.

Conclusion

If you are planning to try an alternative treatment, check with your own health-care professionals. But from my reading of Ingersoll and Goldstein, Hallowell and Ratey, and from my interviews of homeschooling parents, I summarize their advice on alternative treatments by asking the following questions:

- If you are considering a supplement, what is in it? Is it safe? Who is supervising the quality? Herbal remedies and other non-regulated

6. For one survey of studies, see A. M. Knivberg, K.L. Reichelt, et al. "Reports on dietary intervention in autistic disorders." Nutritional Neuroscience. 4(1):25-37, 2001.

7. Hallowell, Edward, M.D., and John Ratey, M.D. Delivered From Distraction. *New York: Ballantine, 2005.*

treatments can become contaminated. Even substances that are good for you can be very dangerous if taken excessively—including vitamins. If you are going to try a dietary supplement, even a vitamin, a mineral, like zinc, or omega fatty acid supplements, and especially if you think of deviating from the recommended dosage, talk with your primary-care doctor.

- Has this therapy been tested? Could it harm my child? What are the risks (short- and long-term) associated with this therapy?
- Is this treatment expensive? Few websites I have seen for alternative treatments display the price. Ask for details about the duration and dosage and do the math: what will this cost you per year?
- If you are looking at treatments or exercises, how many hours a week are recommended? How many hours a week can you and your family devote to maintaining it? How many months or years?
- Is the treatment supervised by licensed or certified professionals?
- What sort of research backs up the claims of success? What do skeptics say about this treatment?

Alternative treatments may help your child; however, they should not be undertaken lightly. Medical advice on possible treatments is crucial to making informed family decisions. Doing your homework will help you know whether your child may benefit from a treatment, or whether it is potentially time-consuming, expensive, or harmful.

Resources

General

Eide, Brock, M.D., and Fernette Eide, M.D. *The Mislabeled Child: Looking Beyond Behavior to Find the True Sources—and Solutions—for Children's Learning Challenges.* New York: Hyperion, 2006.

Ingersoll, Barbara, Ph.D, and Sam Goldstein, Ph.D. *Attention Deficit Disorder and Learning Disabilities: Realities, Myths, and Controversial Treatments.* New York: Doubleday, 1993.

Assistive Technology

Green, Joan L., M.A., CCC-SLP. *Technology for Communication and Cognitive Treatment: The Clinician's Guide.* Potomac, Maryland: Innovative Speech Therapy, 2007. Not just for clinicians, this book or (a consultation with the author) is a good source of information on many different manufacturer's software to improve verbal and written expression, auditory comprehension, reading comprehension, and memory, as well as tools, from special keyboards to speaking software. innovativespeech.com and especially theymaynotknow.com.
1-800-IST-2550.

ADD/ADHD

CHADD's website on complementary treatments for ADD/ADHD: www.help4adhd.org/en/treatment/complementary

Hallowell, Edward, M.D., and John Ratey, M.D. *Delivered From Distraction: Getting the Most Out of Life With Attention Deficit Disorder.* New York: Ballantine, 2005.

Autism

www.autism-society.org

Organization for Autism Research www.researchautism.org/ has a "Parents' Guide to Research" at www.researchautism.org/resources/parents%20guide.pdf

Autism Research Institute, affiliated with Defeat Autism Now, a coalition of doctors and parents favoring a biomedical approach. See www.autism.com

Sicile-Kira, Chantal. *Autism Spectrum Disorders.* New York: Perigee, 2004.

Learning Disabilities

At www.LDonline.org you can find articles on diet, fish oil, and other newer treatments.

10

Teacher Preparation
and Training

Starting homeschooling is exciting: launching a new work, a new school, a new lifestyle. We aim high, wanting to find a better education for our children, save their love of learning, and nurture their self-esteem. But it is also hard work and many of us feel ill-prepared.

At home, we have no teacher work days, when the children stay away and we are paid to plan, and no in-service days, as teachers have, when the students stay home from school and the teachers attend workshops to help them teach better.

Homeschooling parents have to make time to become and remain effective teachers. We can get help with our planning and we can find support. While I have included this chapter in the second part of this book, training is not a one-time event, but rather as an occasional, ongoing part of your homeschooling.

In this chapter:
- Becoming a teacher
- Help with planning
- Read to improve your teaching
- Lectures, workshops, and seminars

Becoming a teacher

How do you make the transition from parent to teacher? If you begin homeschooling on a whim, without preparation, materials, or forethought, you will probably not last long. Once a woman told me she homeschooled for a few weeks, out of disappointment with her son's school, on a sudden impulse. She had no plan; she just bought a few workbooks. Quickly she became discouraged and re-enrolled him. Another mother said her son was skeptical whether she could teach him, until he saw her planning and preparing. Preparation and knowledge give you confidence, and give your children confidence in you. In the classroom or in the home, if you fumble about, expecting a child to wait quietly while you figure out what to do, you are in trouble. In this chapter we will look at acquiring knowledge about teaching. In the following chapters, I will discuss how to prepare: setting and revising goals, reviewing progress, finding materials and approaches.

Homeschooling can be tough some days, like parenting. Sarita in Georgia admitted, "Your children don't see you necessarily as the teacher. They see you as Mom, as more easily manipulated. They feel, 'If I whine hard enough, she'll change her mind.'"

Just like any other parent or teacher, if you reward whining by giving in, children will whine again. How do you make them do the schoolwork when they don't want to? It is not much different from making them do their homework when they don't want to. You have the same discipline tools: encouragement, punishments, and rewards. Good discipline will save your child's life. To continue to discipline firmly and patiently, read wise books on child-rearing. You also must make time for yourself, to have the energy you need to keep on. In the final chapters of this book, I will turn to keeping you and your child encouraged.

Help With Planning

Support for the parent homeschooling a special needs child can come from many sources. According to several families I interviewed, hiring a special education consultant can make homeschooling easier. The consultant, either a former homeschooling parent or a special education teacher knowledgeable about homeschooling, can assist you in finding resources, with planning and strategies, and testing and evaluating. You will see more about setting goals and planning in chapters 11 and 15. See more about finding the right professionals in chapter 8.

With or without additional help, regular planning time is important. Much as I enjoyed teaching eighth graders in public school, one of my favorite days was the day between semesters, when the students stayed home and I could organize and prepare for the coming months. Homeschooling parents also set aside time for planning and organizing. For example, one summer, while her three boys were at camp, Donna in Maryland planned an entire year of homeschool, including her eldest son's first year of high school.

For those who don't have the luxury of a quiet week or two, you may need help getting time to plan. Perhaps you can swap afternoons with a homeschooling friend, so one can stay home alone and plan, while the other takes the children for a half-day at a park or field trip. If you operate your homeschool on a September to May schedule, you may want that planning time in the spring and summer, to prepare for the coming year. But it is also helpful to take a few hours every couple months to assess progress. Stepping back and reviewing not only showed me how we were doing, it also refreshed me. I'll discuss ways to do this in chapter 16.

Another form of support for parents is umbrella schools, also called cover schools or independent study programs (ISPs). An umbrella school functions as a liaison between homeschooling families and the government, maintaining school records with information it gathers from the parents, and assisting parents with planning. Umbrella schools prepare transcripts, so that, on paper, your child looks like a private school student. Some umbrella schools assist families across the country, working by mail and telephone, such as Almaden Valley Christian School in California. Other umbrella schools work locally. Cedarbrook Academy in Clarksburg, Maryland, for instance, assigns each family a consultant to review and assist them, has a special education consultant, and offers optional activities: weekly classes for kindergarten through twelfth grades, field trips, social activities, and workshops for parents.

Read to Improve Your Teaching

You do not need a teaching certificate or a special education degree to homeschool, but training can help. You can learn at home from good books and websites, from online self-paced courses, and virtual lectures and workshops. You can go to daylong workshops designed for teachers.

But reading is the easiest way to become a better teacher. Homeschooler Angela said, "When in doubt, I always do *bibliotherapy*. Whatever the problem is, there's always one more book." Reading is easier to fit into your schedule than a class, and books are always cheaper and more portable than coursework.

There are a few good books on homeschooling struggling learners by homeschooling parents, with a different focus from this book. I give details on these books at the end of the chapter. I also recommend authors who did not homeschool, but have extensive training and experience in special education and in working with homeschooling families with children with special needs.

In addition to those books on homeschooling children with special needs, look for books on teaching children with your child's particular problem. But examine them before you buy. Some materials for teachers are written in Educationalese rather than English, and unnecessarily obtuse. You should skim the book's suggestions to see if they are practical or necessary for homeschooling. For instance, books full of activities that require one to two dozen children are generally impractical for homeschoolers (that is why co-ops and group classes thrive; see chapter 23 for more information), and homeschoolers don't need books telling them that the distractible child should sit near the teacher.

Lectures, Workshops, and Seminars

Beyond books, you can become a better teacher by reading websites, taking online self-paced courses or lectures you can download, and interactive workshops, sometimes called webinars. You often can attend workshops and conferences designed for teachers. How do you find them?

- Patient advocacy organizations, such Learning Disabilities Association (ldaamerica.org), Children and Adults with Attention Deficit Disorder (chadd.org), and the Autism Society of America (www.autism-society.org), can help you find out about training for parents and teachers. (You may need to remind them that you fall in both groups.) Sign up for their local chapter e-lists and newsletters for information about workshops.

- These national association websites are good sources of information: some have on-line introductory courses, and online libraries of articles, notably CHADD's www.help4adhd.org. These associations also have regional and national conferences that may educate you and help you to teach more effectively.

- LDonline.org not only provides excellent articles on learning disabilities but on other special needs, such as autism and attention deficit disorder, as well as webcasts.

- Many state and provincial homeschool organizations have annual conventions. As the homeschooling of struggling learners increases, these organizations are increasing the number of workshops they have on special needs topics. Join your area's homeschool organization, check their workshops, and tell them what you would like to learn more about.

- GIFTSNC (Giving and Getting Information to Teach Our Special Needs Children, www.giftsnc.com) has held conferences specifically on homeschooling children with special needs. Begun as a support group in the Raleigh, North Carolina, area, GIFTSNC has grown through its Yahoo group, and launched several sister groups in other states. Hundreds of attendees have found the GIFTSNC conferences encouraging and informative, and even more people exchange information and encouragement through their Yahoo group.

- Can't get to a convention? Some of the authors mentioned in this book speak at conventions and have lectures available to download as MP3s or to order as recordings. If you know of a conference where they have spoken, visit the organizer's website, or try www.rhino-technologies.com, www.best-christian-conferences.com, or www.aven.com, which carry recordings from multiple conferences.

- If there are private schools in your area for struggling learners, check to see if they offer parent seminars or workshops for local teachers, and whether you may attend. Phone around and get on their mailing lists. For example, I have attended excellent teacher workshops at the Lab School of Washington, D.C., and was welcomed warmly by the other participants, although I was the only homeschooler.
- Hospitals, clinics, state and local educational agencies, and psychological, educational, and tutoring services sometimes offer training for teachers and parents. If they do, ask to join their mailing lists.
- Ask your professionals—psychologist, speech pathologist, pediatrician, special education consultant, occupational therapist—where you can learn more.
- Private firms offer various parent workshops and teacher training in therapies, assistive technologies, reading methods, and more. Some of these are hoping to sell you a product or approach, but may still be worth your time. Some offer free or inexpensive introductory workshops, in person or online.

Before you sign up for courses, ask about the course content and about how relevant the material is for homeschoolers.

Specific training on teaching reading is covered in chapter 18.

Conclusion

Most of us begin homeschooling without special education training, and it can feel intimidating at times. But there are a wealth of resources to help you become a more effective teacher at home. With love for your child, practice, and the many resources available, you can help your child succeed.

Resources

Books by homeschoolers with children with special needs

Baker, Janice, Kathleen Julicher, and Maggie Hogan. *Gifted Children at Home: A Practical Guide for Homeschooling Families.* Cheswold, Delaware: Gifted Group, 2001. This book discusses how to know if your child is gifted, why you should homeschool gifted children, how to parent the intellectually gifted learner, curriculum, teaching techniques, acceleration and grade skipping, activities, computers, and what to do about high school and college.

Barnier, Carol. *How to Get Your Child Off the Refrigerator and Onto Learning.* Lynnwood, Washington: Emerald, 2000. Not just for the hyperactive, this book helps with distractible or fidgety children, too. It is geared to the elementary grades. Wise and humorous, Barnier believes in enjoying what she calls your "spirited child," and gives great tips on making educational games and other hands-on activities.

Boring, Melinda L. *Heads Up Helping! Teaching Tips and Techniques for Working with ADD, ADHD, and Other Children with Challenges.* Victoria, British Columbia: Trafford, 2002. A speech pathologist and homeschooling mother of three (two with ADD/ADHD), she focuses on dealing with daydreamers, fidgety, distractible, or hyperactive children, and children with sensory integration problems. Practical tips on adapting your homeschool and curriculum for these behaviors.

Hensley, Sharon C., M.A. *Home Schooling Children with Special Needs,* Vancouver, Washington: Noble, 2001. www.noblepublishing.com Founder and director of Almaden Valley Christian School, Sharon homeschools her three children, one of whom is autistic. Her book includes sections on disabilities beyond the scope of this book, expectations, behavior, planning, and teaching techniques.

Other helpful books for homeschooling special needs children
Gerber, Stephen W., Ph.D., Marianne Daniels Gerber, Ph.D., and Robyn Freedman Spizman. I*s Your Child Hyperactive? Inattentive? Impulsive? Distractible? Helping the ADD/Hyperactive Child.* New York: Random, 1990.

Green, Joan L., M.A., CCC-SLP. *Technology for Communication and Cognitive Treatment: The Clinician's Guide.* Potomac, Maryland: Innovative Speech Therapy, 2007. Not just for clinicians, this book (or a consultation with the author) provides information on many different manufacturers' software to improve verbal and written expression, auditory comprehension, reading comprehension, and memory, and tools from special keyboards to speaking software. *Cf.* innovativespeech.com, theymaynotknow.com, or 1-800-IST-2550.

Herzog, Joyce, *Learning in Spite of Labels.* Lebanon, Tennessee: Greenleaf, 1994.

_____. *Choosing and Using Curriculum: Your Guide to Home Education.* JoyceHerzog.com Inc., 2004.

Levine, Mel, M.D. *Educational Care.* Cambridge, Massachusetts: Educators Publishing Service, 1994.

Munday, Judith. *Teaching Your Special Needs Student: Strategies and Tools that Really Work.* Chesapeake, Virginia: H.I.S. Place, 2007. Available from www.heav.org.

Naglieri, Jack, Ph.D., and Eric B. Pickering, Ph.D. *Helping Children Learn: Intervention Handouts for Use in School and at Home.* Baltimore: Brookes, 2003. This is a collection of very short articles explaining practical strategies. It's clear, concise, and based on interesting research.

Rief, Sandra F. *How To Reach And Teach Children with ADD/ADHD: Practical Techniques, Strategies, and Interventions.* San Francisco: Jossey-Bass, 2005.

_____. *The ADD/ADHD Checklist.* San Francisco: Jossey-Bass, 1998.

Sutton, Joe, Ph.D., and Connie Sutton. *Strategies for Struggling Learners: A Guide for the Teaching Parent.* Simpsonsville, South Carolina: Exceptional Diagnostics, 1997. Available from www.heav.org.

[Alice asked,] "Would you tell me, please, which way I ought to go from here?" "That depends a good deal on where you want to get to," said the Cat.

Lewis Carroll, Alice's Adventures in Wonderland

Part III

Planning

11

Setting Goals

While "Ready, Fire! Oops! Aim," is a way of life for some struggling learners, don't let it summarize how you homeschool. Here we'll look at how to choose your goals for your homeschool. In the following chapters, we'll consider your teaching approach, finding and adapting teaching materials, and turning these goals into plans.

In this chapter:
- Keep it manageable
- List your observations and ideas
- Reading difficulties
- Other basic needs
- What to expect of your child
- Other sources of possible goals
- Goals and accommodations across academic subjects
- Beyond academics
- Revise your lists

Keep It Manageable

First, a warning. Here I include many different suggestions because you readers have children at different stages with different needs, abilities, and talents. No one can do everything listed here. As you read this chapter, observe your child, brainstorm, write, and then focus on a few goals. As you read these suggested goals, you may say "Not this year" or "Not for us." Or you may say, "I can't believe she left out foreign languages and _____ [insert your favorite goal here]."

Everyone has different goals for their children. Some parents have children who are college-bound, and others just aim to help their struggling learners live and work independently. One mother, whose daughters have epilepsy and significant learning disabilities, said, "My personal goal is to raise godly women. Academics are just one part of life. Life skills are very important." Whatever your long-term goals for your children, setting goals for your homeschool will improve your teaching. It is a great guilt reliever, too.

List Your Observations and Ideas

To develop your goals as you work through the following section, make three lists. On the first, jot down your observations about what your child can do. On the second, write down rough ideas for goals for your child for the coming year, and on the third, longer term goals. (You may find it easier to initially combine the two goals lists, and later sort out which goals to focus on for this year.) These observations and ideas may not be very precise at first, but they will cover the most striking weaknesses in schoolwork, practical skills, and behavior.

Your observation list may have:
- Sam loves to be read to.
- Sarah likes to recite the dialogue from her favorite movies.
- Nathan can summarize a story well.
- Katie knows her times tables.

Your goals list for this year might include:
- Read third grade level books by next May,[1]
- Make change from a five dollar bill,
- Leave a message on an answering machine, clearly stating the caller's name and phone number,

1. See end of chapter 18 on using readability formulas to determine the reading level of a book.

- Write a letter to the editor about a local problem and propose a solution.

Your long-term goals might be:
- Live independently,
- Write a ten-page research paper,
- Attend college,
- Know how to behave at a job interview.

Just watch your child as you learn, think, and brainstorm. Later you will need to choose among the goals to focus on this year. But your long-term goal list can help you plan next year, and help you set intermediate goals to reach the long-term goals.

Reading Difficulties

How do you assess your child's ability in reading? Just knowing she is behind is not enough to help you plan. Reading is a complex task. You look at a word and either recognize it on sight or else recognize the letters, associate them with sounds, assemble the sounds, check to see if that makes a known word, check to see if that makes sense in context, move to the next word, and repeat. Then you keep all those words in your working memory to see if that makes a reasonable sentence, recalling the context.

One way to find out at what level your child is reading is to hire a reading tutor or special education teacher to give the child a standardized reading test. Your state or provincial homeschool organization may provide a list of specialists who can help. The International Dyslexia Association also provides lists of individuals who tutor and test. Some private or public schools will have a list of reading or special education teachers available to tutor; these also may give reading tests. See the end of this chapter and chapter 18 for more on reading.

Interview potential tutors by phone. Ask about their training and experience with children with disabilities like your child's. Sound them out on homeschooling. You don't want to pay for an hour of someone telling you to stop homeschooling. I have paid reading and special education teachers to administer standardized reading tests, such as the *Woodcock*

Reading Mastery Test, Revised, and the *Gray Oral Reading Test*. These tests produced helpful reports. I also asked for and received advice from the tutors when they gave me the test results.

Reading is not easy. But there are many ways you can help your child at home with reading without special training in reading, if you are willing to learn and work steadily at it. There are also ways to get training to help your child with more severe problems. See chapters 10 and 18.

Other Basic Needs

After reading, look at all the other language arts—literature, spelling, writing, and speaking—and mathematics. Feeling discouraged by all your child's areas of weakness? As you write your lists of observations and ideas for goals, don't be too negative. Remember to note the areas where your child is successful. If she is in second grade and able to do a second grade math book, add it to the list. It may not sound like much, but if she is two years behind in reading, don't neglect her success in math. And if the child cannot multiply, but can add, don't neglect the success in addition. Also note other areas of strength, whether your child is a gifted young artist, athlete, or expert on frogs. Noting areas of strength and success on your observation list can keep you from being discouraged. If you are discouraged, you will convey that to your child. These areas of success can also be the keys to the child's future. There may be ways to build on those strengths to work around the child's weakness. And praise for your child's successes (be it expertise in horses, rocks, or building intricate LEGO® creations) can encourage her if she has heard about her failures too often.

Your list of observations should give an informal overview of the child's present level of performance (which schools abbreviate as PLP, PLEP, or my favorite, PLOP). However you abbreviate it, it summarizes strengths and weaknesses. In public school, the staff writes a PLP as a first step to their planning an Individualized Educational Plan (IEP). The PLP considers the academic areas affected by the student's disability, chiefly reading and math, though a trend in public school is also to report on skills related to independent living and working.

What to Expect of Your Child

What if you aren't sure what to expect of your child academically at a particular age? It can be tricky. If she was in school before, how did she do by their standards? Look at her classmates' work and behavior. (This is one of the benefits of volunteering in the classroom.) Ask her teachers. If the school uses criterion-referenced tests, the test results may indicate what skills she has mastered. But you may not get a thorough picture.

If you have taught other children, you may have an idea, provided you know if those other children were above or below average. If your child's text or workbook is not marked by grade level, how do you find out at which level she is performing? And what if you don't use workbooks or textbooks?

The *Brigance Diagnostic Inventories* are excellent tools. These tests determine what skills a child has mastered. They can be given by teachers at school or parents at home. These inventories test individual skills defined very specifically (e.g., "reads lower case letters," "prints first name," "addresses envelope"), so they make it easy to write detailed, specific goals. See the end of this chapter for ways to buy or rent this test. I have used the Brigance Comprehensive Inventory of Basic Skills-Revised (CIBS-R), nicknamed the *Brigance Green*, which is for pre-kindergarten through grade nine, but there are other Brigance Inventories for different age ranges, including:

- Inventory of Early Development-II (IED-II) (yellow cover)—birth through developmental age 7,
- Life Skills Inventory (LSI —designed for "Secondary Special Ed., Vocational, ESL [English for Speakers of Other Languages] Programs, assesses listening, speaking, reading, writing, comprehending, and computing skills."[2]
- Employability Skills Inventory (ESI). Also designed for Secondary Special Ed, Vocational, ESL Programs, this "assesses basic skills and employability skills in the context of job-seeking or employment situations."[3]

If your child was evaluated by a psychologist, special education teacher, reading teacher, or classroom teacher, you should review those

2. "Assessment - Brigance Inventories." Accessed June 21, 2008. www.curriculumassociates.com

3. Ibid.

reports to help you identify areas of need or strength. If your child was in school, look at the teacher's notes on old report cards, and standardized test scores. The reports indicate areas of progress to add to your list of observations and may help you add to your lists of goals. If your child was in public school and had an Individualized Education Plan (IEP), certainly you'll want to consider the goals and objectives listed in there.

Other Sources of Possible Goals

When you consider your goals, you might look at what other people think should be required. But remember, you are the boss when you homeschool.

State Standards. Some states publish requirements or suggested standards for their public schools. Whether they are called Standards of Learning (Virginia), Content Standards (California), or Content and Performance Standards (Hawaii), you might want to read one or two and see what you think. They are posted on the Internet and also available in print. You may find an idea you wish to incorporate, such as requiring your fourth grader to demonstrate that she can use "word processing software and standard touch-typing keyboarding skills to create documents,"[4] or you might decide sixth grade (or third) is the time for that. (For children with handwriting problems, learning to type early may help them with their other subjects.) Or you might decide that you place a higher priority on other skills. It's your call.

State standards are controversial even in public schools. I am not suggesting you follow them, unless you are planning to move your child into public school soon. In that case, you might consider following them. But even then, realize that many public schools receive students from out of state who have not been trained according to your states' guidelines. If you put your child in school later, she will not be the first transfer student who has been taught toward different goals.

Privately published guidelines can be another source of ideas for your goals. The best known is E.D. Hirsch's *Core Knowledge series,* including titles such as *What Your Third Grader Needs to Know.* Another is Barron's Making the Grade series, with titles like *Making the Grade: Everything Your Third Grader Needs to Know.*

4. Hawaii State Department of Education. Hawaii Content and Performance Standards Database. *Accessed February 21, 2007. standardstoolkit. k12.hi.us/sdb/ database/display_pis.jsp*

The dangers in looking at any of these published standards, whether published by a state or private company, are that you may feel obliged to follow them or to try to do too much. Jot down ideas that sound excellent to you, but don't get carried away.

Depending on the severity of your child's needs, you may not find many goals reasonable for your child, or you may find that your child can go beyond grade level in some subjects and below grade level in others. With homeschooling, you have that flexibility. When asking any home-schooled child, "What grade are you in?" folks may be surprised by the long answers, such as, "I'm in fourth grade science and math, but I study sixth grade history with my big brother, and fifth grade spelling." Homeschooled children don't have to fit neatly into one grade.

Goals and Accommodations Across Academic Subjects

Whether you've looked at other sources of goals or brainstormed alone, along with language arts and mathematics, consider other academic areas. The following is a short list to get you thinking. Review these subjects and list a few goals. Brainstorm. What would your child enjoy? What does she need?

Remember to devote time to developing her gifts. When I was in school, I was required to go to physical education daily, and it was good for me. But no one said that I couldn't take advanced English until I learned to play basketball well. They let me go on with my strengths. Is your child a compulsive sketcher? Does she adore music or create unusual designs? Nurture those talents.

And as you look in areas where your child is doing satisfactory work, make note of what sort of special help she might require. For example, if she loves stories but doesn't read well, don't rule out novels. She may just need a large print text or a recorded book. These helps are called *accommodations*. As I suggest other goals, I have included some accommodations for struggling learners, not because they are goals, but to help you see that more goals are in reach than you may realize.

Language arts

For literature, your child can memorize and recite poetry, and enjoy the sounds of language. If reading is hard, use recorded books and read aloud to the child or buy software that can read text aloud. If writing is a problem, discuss the reading, give oral quizzes, and let the child make posters, collages, or dioramas in shoeboxes to illustrate key scenes.

For drama, you can read scenes and plays aloud together, watch and discuss videos of excellent productions, take her to local productions of plays, or sign her up for drama classes.

For speech, students can give oral reports and presentations to family, friends, clubs, and homeschool groups. You coach them to be better speakers. They can join homeschool speech and debate teams and classes, and compete in local, regional, and national tournaments. Don't let a speech problem rule these activities out. Actor James Earl Jones overcame years of speaking problems when Donald Crouch, his high school teacher, encouraged him to write and recite poetry.[5]

For writing, don't wait for your child to spell or capitalize correctly before beginning to teach organization of a paragraph or an essay. Don't let her miss the pleasure of making up a good story. If handwriting is a problem, keep her practicing daily, but also let her develop these other writing skills by dictating into tape recorder or learning to type. Don't let dysgraphia hold her education hostage. Eventually, she might shift to having the computer type by using a microphone and dictation software such as *Dragon Naturally Speaking*.

For spelling, I recommend first choosing a program based on your child's needs (see chapter 19), then using that program to determine your child's grade level, and setting a goal of improving one or one-half grade level per year, depending on how severe her spelling difficulties are. Remember that you don't have to check spelling on every assignment. It may go against your nature (it does mine), but you won't be graded on how well you correct her! A page covered in corrections can discourage a student. She knows she has trouble spelling without your marking every misspelled word wrong. Just add some of the regular misspellings to her spelling list.

For grammar and usage, I suggest you use Brigance Green as a guide to setting goals.

5. Academy of Achievement. "James Earl Jones Interview." June 29, 1996. Accessed July 15, 2008. www. achievement.org/ autodoc/page/ jon2int-2

Mathematics

Just as you can work on writing essays before your child masters spelling and punctuation, your child can advance in mathematics despite prolonged trouble learning arithmetic facts. Look for areas of math that are appropriate to the age and see what the child can do. Hands-on work with measurement, fractions, and probability can help your child. See chapter 17 for more on teaching math.

Science

Science has so many fascinating topics; don't leave it out of your homeschool. You can study dinosaurs, volcanoes, insects, horses, frogs, trees, a nearby creek, jungles, predators, electricity, magnets, waves, or even potato cannons. Look for hands-on projects, which help the child with learning or attention differences. You can use science to support language arts by requiring the child to write journal entries or to give short talks about the science they are studying. You can incorporate art into science by having them draw specimens, create leaf rubbings, or make a poster about life in an anthill. Local science fairs give children opportunities to follow the steps to organize, complete, and present a long-term project.

Social Studies

Social studies also can make your schooling more fun. You can study places, cultures, mountains, beaches, climates, and the important life skill of map reading. Your student can begin by drawing a rough map (floor plan) of your house, and then move on mapping to your street and neighborhood. History can be tied to literature by studying biographies and historical fiction. You can cook foods and sew clothes from the place or time you study, visit historic sites, and try crafts of the period.

Beyond Academics

Along with academic subjects, include other areas in your goals. As a homeschooler, you have the freedom to include what you think is important. Here are some ideas to get you started; a few resources are listed at the end of the chapter. Pick out a few areas to work on each year.

Health and Hygiene

Some school-age children need help to master the basics of using the toilet, hand washing, covering their noses when they sneeze, and bathing themselves well. You may want to work on other health topics: nutrition, healthy meal planning, germ theory, anatomy, drug and alcohol education, and sex education. You can train them in keeping a room clean, changing sheets, washing dishes, and washing clothes. These last are sometimes grouped with *Life Skills*.

Physical Education

Children need to move. Exercise helps children with attention problems focus and is good for everyone's mental health, including the parents'. Even coordination-challenged people like me can find exercise they enjoy if they keep looking, even if it's just a walk in the stillness of early morning.

What sports or skills do you want to work on? Your goals can be as simple as taking fifteen minute breaks every morning for kicking a soccer ball around, shooting hoops, jumping jacks and push-ups. Your child can try biking, in-line skating, or dancing. She can jump rope or bounce on a mini-trampoline while reciting math facts. Your exercise goals can be as ambitious as a weeklong canoe or backpacking trip, a monthly family hike, participation in a swim team or a league sport, or a career as a professional athlete. Remember that team sports can be difficult for a child with attention or communication problems. They may prefer an activity where they primarily compete against themselves, such as martial arts.

The Fine Arts

Too many public schools are pressed to get everyone to pass standardized tests at the expense of music, art, drama, and other activities that enrich life. Don't make that mistake. The rhythms of music can help a child focus. Trying an instrument and attending a variety of performances can lead to lifelong interests. I am amazed by the artistic and dramatic skills of some struggling learners. As a homeschooler, you have the freedom to explore these, trying different activities and developing your child's strengths. Your opportunities will vary with your area. It may take some looking to find what you want. You'll see some arts resources at the end of chapter 13.

Study and Organization Skills

Struggling learners need to be taught study skills carefully, even though some of their peers seem to learn them effortlessly. As your child matures, you need to teach them to keep track of assignments, use a planner and calendar, and break long-term projects into manageable chunks. You want them to understand what sort of environment they need to work effectively, what distracts them, and how they learn best. This can take years of teaching and re-teaching. You child needs to learn how to learn from books, to take notes, and to summarize. She needs to learn how to take tests. From lost mittens and math assignments, to lost W-2 forms and car keys, some people struggle to be organized all their lives. There are books with helpful techniques you can teach and learn. I discuss these skills in chapter 20.

Life Skills

In addition to those listed under health and hygiene, think about the skills your child will need when she moves out: answering the telephone, leaving a message on an answering machine, balancing a checkbook, planning meals, buying groceries, and paying bills on time. You want her to be able to sew on a button, cook, do her laundry, and clean a bathroom. As she grows, you want her to read want ads, fill out a job application, present herself well in an interview, and be punctual. As you choose life skills for each year, think of the big picture and what's appropriate for your child now. Most second graders can learn to answer the phone. They do not yet need to know how to fill out a job application, but you needn't wait until age sixteen for this.

Interpersonal Skills

Even with the best intentions, a child isn't born knowing how to behave politely. Manners must be taught. A polite tone of voice must be taught. Some struggling learners have to work hard to grasp that other people don't know what they know or see what they see. Learning to read faces takes time for some struggling learners. Teens' brains are still developing those skills.[6] For children and teens on the autistic spectrum, developing these skills and the life skills above are major concerns, so I'll discuss this further in the chapter 20.

6. In an August 1, 1999, article "Inside the Teen Brain," US News cited research by Deborah Yurgelun-Todd, a neuropsychologist at McLean Hospital in Belmont, Massachusetts. Yurgelun-Todd and graduate student Abigail Baird showed adults and teens photographs of faces expressing fear. All the adults read the expressions correctly, but many teens could not. This may explain some parent-teen communication problems.

Character

Wise friends told me once their main goals for their children's elementary school years are manners and chores. Chores require discipline and teach responsibility.

Children must be taught to be honest and appreciate honest friends. I don't know anyone who needed to be taught how to lie. There is no standardized test to see if your child is more honest than last year, but if you have added "developing honesty" and other virtues to your list, and review it occasionally, you will think about it more.

To help a child develop character, read and discuss stories stressing the value of different virtues, or point out the virtues of important people in history. Teach character as circumstances arise, as you ride in the car, at the breakfast table, through the course of each day.

Don't forget to praise the child for being virtuous when it would have been easier not to. When honesty gets her into trouble, make sure that she knows there would have been worse trouble had she been dishonest. When she is punctual or kind, praise her.

Love of Learning

Does your child enjoy learning? When you homeschool, you can nurture a passion for knowledge. Several families I interviewed homeschool to build or restore a passion for learning, by pursuing their children's interests, encouraging their curiosity, and enjoying learning together.

Good Habits

Think a moment about which of your child's habits bothers you most. Does she leave lights on when she leaves a room? Interrupt you when you are on the telephone? Forget to flush? Whine? Pick one or two good habits to develop for this school year. Be encouraging, firm, and patient. Praise progress. I was delighted one day when one of my offspring complained about a loudly whining child at the grocery store. I asked, "Remember all those times I said, 'I can't hear you when you use that whiney voice'?" Surprised, my child replied, "Thank you!"

Revise Your Lists

Now take your list of observations and ideas for goals. Write a paragraph summarizing the child's needs and strengths. Tentatively choose top goals for this year, and save the rest as a starting point for planning next year. You'll revise this list as you see what materials and opportunities are available.

Keep it simple. A page might be plenty. My first years, I had a page or two, handwritten. Your amount will vary from mine, depending on how specific you are, how much time you have, and how great your child's needs are. We did not meet all my goals, but they helped me focus my work.

Remember that these goals are only guidelines for you. In three months you may realize some are already met and others were overly ambitious. That is okay. The point is to develop goals to help you plan, not to make you feel guilty or inept. Writing goals gets easier with practice. Don't spend more time on this exercise than you can afford.

You have brought this child home to provide individualized help and let them progress at a pace they can manage. Do not let your goals turn you into a nag or a tyrant. If the child is discouraged from school failures, you will need to build her morale. That should be one of *your* major goals.

Discuss this year's goals with your spouse. (If you have no spouse, perhaps a wise friend who knows your child well can spare an hour or two to help you prioritize.) The parent who does most of the homeschooling may be too close to the situation. Your spouse or other friend may find it easier to prioritize, or see something you have overlooked.

When you have a sense of what is more important to you, you may find it helpful to group your goals (remedial, artistic, life skills, or whatever groupings makes sense to you). In the next chapters, we'll consider your teaching style and how to find, adapt, or write curriculum, so you will be ready to write your plans: a Student Education Plan (SEP) and your other plans.

Resources

Reading Test Resources
International Dyslexia Association, 40 York Rd., 4th Floor, Baltimore, MD 21204-5202. Online store, conferences, web pages for parents, college students, and educators. www.interdys.org/. IDA provides lists of tutors and testers.

Other teacher training programs in reading have lists of trained people in your area. I suggest you read up on any approach that interests you and then look for certified trainees in your area. I am not a reading teacher, but tutors I respect have referred me to Academic Therapy (altaread. org), Phono-Graphix (readamerica.net), Orton-Gillingham (www.orton-gillingham.com), Wilson Language Training (www.wilsonlanguage.com/), and Lindamood-Bell Learning Process (www.lblp.com/).

Curriculum Associates sells Reading Grade-Placement Tests for Grades 1-8 on their homeschool web pages. The tests look easy to use. See Curriculum Associates, P.O. Box 2001, North Billerica, MA 01862-9914, www. curriculumassociates.com/ USA & Canada: (800) 225-0248.

Setting Goals
Brigance Diagnostic Inventories can be purchased from the publisher, Curriculum Associates. See the previous listing. It can be rented from Home School Legal Defense Association, if you are a member. See www.hslda.org.

Hirsch, Jr., E.D. Core Knowledge series [*What Your First Grader Needs to Know, What your Second Grader Needs to Know*, etc.]. New York: Delta, 2001.

Barron's Making the Grade series [*Making the Grade: Everything Your First Grader Needs to Know*, etc.] by various authors, for grades kindergarten through six. Hauppauge, New York: Barron's Educational Series, 2003.

Field, Christine. *Life Skills for Kids: Equipping Your Child for the Real World.* Colorado Springs: Shaw, 2000.

Munday, Judith B., "Present Level of Performance," www.hishelpinschool.com/plans/plop.html.

Other Resources Mentioned In This Chapter
Kurzweil 3000 software reads text aloud. www.kurzweiledu.com.

Bookshare.org and RFBD.org provide recorded books for those with disabilities.

Dictation software does the typing for your student, who speaks into a headset. We have used *Dragon Naturally Speaking 9*, by Nuance Communications. www.nuance.com.

12

Teaching Styles

"So, if I want to homeschool, I'll just stop in at the teacher supply store, get textbooks and workbooks for each subject, write a schedule, and get going, right? Or wait! I'll call up Brand X homeschool curriculum and order a third grade package."

An approach like this make both experienced homeschoolers and special education teachers cringe for many reasons. It neglects the development, strengths, weaknesses, and interests of the student. It overlooks the opportunities and importance of our environment. It ignores the rich variety of ways we can teach and learn.

Thoughts about educational philosophy, child psychology, and learning methods are reflected in the many different teaching styles that are popular among homeschoolers. As David Guterson wrote in *Family Matters: Why Homeschooling Makes Sense*, "If you're going to keep your children out of schools, you had better decide what an education means because no one is going to do it for you."[1]

Homeschoolers I spoke with use many different approaches, described below. As you read, you may decide that some of these styles will not work for you or your family. At the end of the chapter are resources for learning more about each approach. Explore what appeals to you.

1. Guterson, David. Family Matters: Why Homeschooling Makes Sense. New York: Harvest, 1993, p. 117.

In this chapter:
- Unit studies
- Charlotte Mason
- Classical education
- Unschooling or relaxed homeschooling
- Eclectic style
- Resources for various teaching styles

Unit Studies

A unit study is a way to organize much or all of your school around one theme for a few weeks. Usually, all the children in one family complete a unit study together. That doesn't mean they work together all day, but most or all their work is geared to the theme of the unit, with harder assignments for the older children.

For instance, if you decide to study ancient Egypt,
- For geography, you could draw maps, build clay or paper-maché maps, and study the importance of the Nile and its floods.
- For math, you might learn how to figure the volume of the pyramids, the perimeter of their bases, and create word problems, such as, "If Moses' father makes twenty bricks an hour and the overseer demands two hundred bricks a day, how many hours must Moses' father work?" To get a thorough grounding in math, you might work through a math curriculum without trying to integrate it into your unit study.
- For art, your child could make models of the Egyptian gods or other artifacts.
- For writing, you might have him write a story, imagining he was a slave or a prince in ancient Egypt.
- For literature, read, discuss, and write about a novel set in ancient Egypt.

Unit studies take more planning and preparation time than working through a textbook. But as one mother, who has homeschooled her son with ADHD for three years, told me, "Unit studies spark their interest.

When he loses interest, we move on to a different unit or to a different activity in the unit study." Like some of the other approaches described below, unit studies lend themselves to active learning. Marcia in Maryland reported that her struggling learners wore frontier clothes and spent most of several days outside while studying the United States westward expansion.

While some parents prefer to design their own unit studies, you may purchase unit studies from Design-A-Study or Konos. Denise, homeschooling her three children in Florida, told me she uses Konos, and enjoys their online co-op. Konos sends weekly lesson plans and videos on how to teach them. Parents discuss them online through a Yahoo group. Denise said, "On my own, I would have avoided the activities that didn't seem worth my effort to set up, but my kids have re-discovered a love of learning that I would not have helped them find without the online co-op."

Whether you seek outside help or not, unit studies take time to plan, but they can be fun, stimulating, and motivating for your child.

Charlotte Mason

Several parents I interviewed were enthusiastic about the Charlotte Mason method. A British educator, Charlotte Mason (1842-1923) developed a philosophy of education that has influenced schools, homes, and homeschoolers. She was a lecturer at a teacher training college, a popular public lecturer and author, and founder of a school for governesses, which became Charlotte Mason College[2]. She founded the Parents National Educational Union, which formed a group of parent-directed schools in England. Her ideas became less popular around World War II, but have grown in popularity in recent years, with the publication of Susan Schaeffer Macaulay's 1984 book, *For The Children's Sake: Foundations of Education for Home and School*.[3]

Charlotte Mason believed that "education is an Atmosphere, a Discipline, a Life," not chiefly the means to getting a diploma or job. She thought children learned best from good books, nature, art and music, and ought to encounter great ideas and literature directly, not watered down though textbooks. The Charlotte Mason method emphasizes:

2. Hocraffer, Lynn B. "The A-B-Cs of Charlotte Mason." Accessed March 11, 2008. homepage.bushnell.net/~peanuts/faq1.html

3. Macauley, Susan Schaeffer. For the Children's Sake: Foundations of Education for Home and School. Wheaton, Illinois: Crossway, 1984.

- Copywork, beginning with learning to neatly copy the alphabet, then increasingly longer passages of good literature, and learning elements of good composition from these texts,
- Narration, in which the child tells the story he has heard, and eventually writes his own version,
- Short lessons,
- Time outdoors: "Never be within doors when you can rightly be without."[4]
- Nature study: developing skills of observation, curiosity, an appreciation of creation, and an awareness of its Creator. Weekly nature walks include sketching, painting, and recording observations, and bringing samples home for study.
- Living books, by which she meant well-written, interesting books written by people who loved their subjects,
- A study of music appreciation, art appreciation, and handicrafts,
- Habit training: such as obedience, honesty, neatness, respect, kindness. These are taught explicitly, focusing on one at a time for several weeks.
- Grammar is not introduced until age nine.
- Poetry and the Bible are read, memorized, and recited. Memory work is intended to stock and stimulate the child's mind, not to be done mindlessly.

Classical Education

In 1948, British author Dorothy L. Sayers wrote an essay, "The Lost Tools of Learning."[5] In it, she imagined a return to the medieval approach to education. For the primary grades, the *trivium* were the three basic elements: grammar, dialectic, and rhetoric. Rather than learning subjects, children were first taught the tools to learn. Grammar meant language skills, taught in the teaching of Latin, which taught the clear expression of thought and how languages work. Memory work was emphasized because, according to this approach, memorizing the grammar of a subject is always the first step in learning new material. Dialectic was "how to use language: how to define his terms and make accurate statements; how to construct

4. Mason, Charlotte. "Out-Of-Door Life For The Children," Home Education, *Vol. 1, p. 43. Accessed March 11, 2008. www.amblesideonline.org/CM/1_2_01to08.html.*

5. Sayers, Dorothy L. "The Lost Tools of Learning," a pamphlet republished in A Matter of Eternity, *Grand Rapids, Michigan: Eerdmans, 1973.*

an argument and how to detect fallacies in argument."[6] Rhetoric taught students how to speak compellingly and elegantly. A classical approach takes advantage of the developmental stages of children: Little children often like to memorize, repeat, and recite, older children like to debate and argue, and teens like to be expressive and communicate with style. Secondary education covered the *quadrivium*: astronomy, arithmetic, music, and geometry.

Though Sayers wrote that "it is in the highest degree improbable that the reforms I propose will ever be carried into effect,"[7] her essay inspired Doug Wilson's 1991 book, *Recovering the Lost Tools of Learning* [8], which sparked the movement of classical schools and classical homeschooling. Jessie Wise and Susan Wise Bauer's 1991 *The Well-Trained Mind: A Guide to Classical Education at Home* [9] is the best-known work on classical education at home.

But how can you expect a struggling learner to learn anything involving Latin? It may surprise you that families modify classical approaches successfully. The multi-sensory and historical approaches appeal to some children. Pam, homeschooling in Virginia, told me,

> *I hated memorizing in school and decided my children wouldn't do that. I wanted them to understand the material—not memorize it. Then one summer we tried memorizing states and state capitals. I was stunned to discover that they thoroughly enjoyed the process. Reviewing our memory work became the most enjoyable time of our day. There is something intrinsically rewarding in mastering the material that keeps them motivated.*

She enrolled them in Classical Conversations Foundations Program, a classical program for homeschoolers that meets three hours, once a week, requiring memory work and oral presentations. The program includes weekly art and science activities. The multi-sensory approach of using timeline cards works well for her children. Pam helps them memorize their weekly history sentences by having them or helping them create simple symbols, such as an Eiffel Tower for France. She noted that Classical Conversations also has Challenge level classes for older students, which

6. *Ibid.*

7. *Ibid.*

8. *Wilson, Doug.* Recovering the Lost Tools of Learning. *Wheaton, Illinois: Crossway, 1991.*

9. *Bauer, Susan Wise, and Jessie Wise.* The Well-Trained Mind: A Guide to Classical Education at Home, Revised and Updated Edition. *New York: Norton, 2004. See also www. welltrainedmind. com*

focus on the skills developed during the dialectic and rhetoric stages. The Challenge level classes meet for a full day once a week. Pam also noted that Classical Conversation teachers were not trained in special education, and she was working to explain her child's needs to them and to suggest simple accommodations.

Her family is not alone. One of the www.welltrainedmind.com's online forums discusses classical homeschooling for special needs children, more evidence that a classical approach can be modified to suit a struggling learner.

Unschooling or Relaxed Homeschooling

The term *unschooling* was coined by John Holt (1923-1985). Holt was a private school teacher for many years, and became a controversial proponent, first of school reform, and then of children's rights, homeschooling, and unschooling. In 1964, he wrote his first book, *How Children Fail*, blaming schools for the failures of children and launching reforms. His later book, *How Children Learn*, suggested new strategies, and concluded:

> *Birds fly, fish swim, man thinks and learns. … What we need to do, and all we need to do, is bring as much of the world as we can into the school and classroom; give children as much help and guidance as they ask for; listen respectfully when they feel like talking; and then get out of the way. We can trust them to do the rest.*[10]

In 1976, Holt wrote *Instead of Education; Ways to Help People Do Things Better*, which suggested illegally keeping children out of school. When homeschoolers contacted him and described their teaching at home, he corresponded with them and began a newsletter, *Growing Without Schooling*, which became a magazine. He later wrote a book on home-schooling, *Teach Your Own*.

John Taylor Gatto's books also influenced the unschooling movement. Three-time winner of New York City's Teacher of the Year, Gatto developed unorthodox ways to motivate his failing students, getting them out into

10. Holt, John. How Children Learn. New York: Perseus, 1983, page 293.

the community to survey their neighbors, producing reports and recommendations about issues they cared about,[11] the sort of projects unschoolers and other homeschooling families sometimes undertake. Disillusioned
with schools, Gatto quit in 1991 and became a lecture and author. His
books include *Dumbing Us Down: The Hidden Curriculum of Compulsory
Schooling.*

People disagree on whether unschooling is the same as relaxed homeschooling. Some relaxed homeschoolers argue that their homes have more
underlying structure (both in educational goals and in relationships) than
unschoolers, but others say the terms are interchangeable. Several parents I
interviewed identified themselves as relaxed homeschoolers or unschoolers.
When I asked them about the difference, a parent in Kentucky replied:

> *I don't honestly have an answer other than that saying we are
> relaxed homeschoolers makes me think that I will be less frowned
> on than if I said we unschool. I don't know if the experts would say
> there's a difference or not. Either way, my kids are not doing school.
> They are just living their everyday lives, reading about and research-
> ing whatever interests them, and they are happy. And smart!*

Unschooling is not as lax as you may imagine. Parents do not merely
watch their children wander in the fields and find more books about their
passion (say, botany), but actively propose pursuits in line with the children's interests, such as trips to meet forest rangers and botanists, volunteer
work on horticultural centers, or studies and surveys of plant species—
which will involve wandering in the fields! Unschooling parents look to
the interests, abilities, and needs of their children. They help them set their
long-term goals, such as getting into college, and help them acquire the
skills and education they need to achieve them. Unschooled students may
choose to enroll in some classes, take online courses, or use textbooks.

But letting the student plot the course may sound risky. Does it sound
like a waste of time if the child spends two years focused on a subject, such
as insects or Japanese animated films, but then decides not to be an ento-
mologist or animator? Unschoolers would say not, because their children
learned how to learn, organize, write, and relate to adults. Unschoolers and

11. Gatto,
John Taylor.
Homeschool
Appreciation
Day. Six Flags
America, Bowie,
Maryland, May
22, 2003.

relaxed homeschoolers see homeschooling as being a way to develop a life-style of learning as a family. They see themselves as a family, not a school.[12]

Like any approach to homeschooling, unschooling requires conscientious parents. Unschooling makes some parents nervous. But some families I interviewed loved the flexibility and freedom it provides and the love of learning it encourages. Kate in Alberta said that unschooling has been great for her two very different students:

> *My older one is above grade level in many subject areas and my other son is below grade level in many subject areas and has attention difficulties. The best thing for us, for both my children, has been unschooling. We don't follow a curriculum, we just follow the children's own interests.*
>
> *…*
>
> *[On unschooling,] the books that I enjoyed most were anything by John Holt. He turned my thinking around.*

Eclectic Style

Many parents I interviewed for this book did not identify themselves with any single teaching style. They use a combination of curricula and approaches, called an eclectic approach. One mother calls it a buffet curriculum. Such families may use textbooks for some subjects, but combine historical fiction, biography, and other resources for their history and literature. They often include some subjects reflecting their child's interests, such as Japanese, film studies, debate, or drama. Occasionally, even families who have enrolled in classes for homeschooled students will pull their child from class, to travel, perform in a concert, or attend a weeklong educational seminar. Another parent said she is "as non-textbook-ish as possible," incorporating field trips and projects like hatching chicks, and once devoting a whole semester to the War of 1812, using videos, movies, and field trips to supplement the unit. For math, she uses *Math-U-See* [13], because it is "manipulative-based, the videos provide him a good introduction, and the workbook gives good reinforcement."

12. Hood, Mary, Ph.D. "The Relaxed Homeschool Mindset," Home Educator's Family Times. July/August 2003. Accessed July 25, 2008. www. homeeducator. com/FamilyTimes/ articles/11-4arti-cle8.htm.

13. Math-U-See is a K-12 math curriculum used by several families I interviewed. mathusee.com.

Conclusion

Philosophically, homeschoolers vary widely, but share a concern to help their children love learning and learn to contribute to society. They emphasize their children's interests, family time, and conversation.

This chapter has given you a taste of a number of homeschooling styles. You probably have been interested in some and put off by others. Your homework assignment is to look into those that interest you using the resources below. Ask homeschoolers you know what they do, and if they know anyone using the styles you are interested in. Check on the Internet; there are websites discussing these methods. Of course, some of these sites are vendors who want to make a sale, and so consider your sources.

One style does not suit everyone or cure all learning problems, whatever anyone says. Look for the philosophical underpinnings of the websites and styles. All children are born wanting to learn, but most of us are born with a lazy streak, too, so you need to teach in a style that nurtures learning, encourages, and prods, without overwhelming the student. You know your child best. As the child grows, the challenge of parenthood is to find a changing balance.

You also may find it helpful to read online group discussions among homeschoolers already using these approaches. Homeschoolers love to give advice, which you may or may not find helpful. Mull it over as you move on to the next chapter. As you shop for curriculum, you'll gain more sense of which styles appeal to you. As you begin to homeschool, invest a little of your time and money into a style you like, communicate with others using it, and give it a try.

Resources for Various Teaching Styles

Unit studies
Kathryn Stout, author of the Design-a-Study educational materials, www.designastudy.com

Wade and Jessica Hulcy, authors of the KONOS unit study curriculum, www.konos.com and www.homeschoolmentor.com

Charlotte Mason

Charlotte Mason's original six volumes of lectures and articles are available online from www.amblesideonline.org/CM/

They also may be purchased, along with other materials, from Dean and Karen Andreola's website, www.charlottemason.com

Macaulay, Susan Schaeffer. *For the Children's Sake: Foundations of Education for Home and School.* Wheaton, Illinois: Crossway, 1984.

simplycharlottemason.com

Anne White's online article, "An Introduction to CM," is an excellent summary of the Charlotte Mason method. www.amblesideonline.org/WhatIsCM.shtml

One homeschooler I interviewed recommended Charlotte Mason for Special Kids, a Yahoo group "for those using Charlotte Mason homeschooling methods for special needs children. A wide range of special children are represented on our list, from learning differences to developmental delays, audio and visual processing disorders to deafness and blindness."[14] Go to groups.yahoo.com and enter "CMspecialkids" in the search box.

Classical

Bauer, Susan Wise, and Jessie Wise. *The Well Trained Mind: A Guide to Classical Education at Home,* Revised and Updated Edition. New York: Norton, 2004.

Also see their websites, www.welltrainedmind.com, and their curriculum publishing company, Peace Hill Press, www.peacehillpress.com. Bluedorn, Harvey and Laurie. Teaching the Trivium: *Christian Homeschooling in a Classical Style.* Muscatine, Iowa: Trivium Pursuit, 2001.

14. groups.
yahoo.com/group/
CMspecialkids/
?v=1
&t=search
&ch=web
&pub=groups
&sec=group
&slk=1

Classical Conversations, www.classicalconversations.com, provides training, books, local classes, and other resources for homeschoolers.

Wilson, Doug. *Recovering the Lost Tools of Learning*. Wheaton, Illinois: Crossway, 1991.

Veritas Press, a publisher of classical homeschooling materials, also offers parent training seminars. www.veritaspress.com

Unschooling

Holt, John. *How Children Fail*. New York: Pittman, 1964, revised 1982.

_____. *How Children Learn*. New York: Pittman, 1964, revised 1983.

Holt, John, and Pat Farenga. *Teach Your Own: The John Holt Book of Homeschooling*. Cambridge, Massachusetts: Perseus, 2003.

John Holt and Growing Without Schooling website www.holtgws.com

Gatto, John Taylor. *Dumbing Us Down: The Hidden Curriculum of Compulsory Schooling*. Gabriola Island, British Columbia: New Society, 2002.

www.johntaylorgatto.com

13

Shopping For Curriculum

In this chapter:
- Textbooks and workbooks
- Where to find good textbooks and workbooks
- Audio books
- Books, not textbooks
- Video and computer courses
- Other computer resources
- Special education tools, games, kits, and other fun stuff
- How to choose

In the last chapters, you have set goals and considered teaching styles, so you have some idea which approaches appeal to you and are likely to work with your child. Now you need materials to help you reach those goals.

Your options are to buy or borrow, to adapt, or to write your own curriculum. *Curriculum* is simply the course of study; the plural is curricula. Curriculum can mean your whole educational program, or the course of study for one subject, as in, "I'm going to the homeschool convention to shop for a better math curriculum."

We all know how to shop. Some of us love to hunt for good selection and prices. Sometimes we browse and find great things we need but weren't even looking for. It is wise to have a budget and a shopping list. The same things are true when we shop for curricula.

Now I will discuss how to find and choose teaching materials. In the next chapter, I will give advice on adapting or writing your own curriculum.

Textbooks and Workbooks

I will begin with textbooks and workbooks, not because they are best, but because they come to mind when most new homeschoolers think about curricula. Textbooks and workbooks are convenient, enabling good readers to teach themselves. Workbooks are easier and quicker to grade than longer written assignments. Even in adulthood, if you need to pass an examination to advance your career or earn a license or certificate, you turn to good textbooks and workbooks, because they put all the information you need in one place.

However, textbooks and workbooks may not be a good fit for your struggling learner. The books may advance too quickly, may not have enough examples or practice problems, or may inadequately review the background material. Or a book may go too slowly. If so, you can skip sections or exercises, of course, but even then, a student can become bored. Textbooks and workbooks are orderly, and for some students just out of school, textbooks feel like real school, which is comforting, familiar, and for some, easy. But for the child who thinks differently, and loves creativity and spontaneity, such books can be dreary.

Another concern for homeschoolers considering textbooks is their cost. However, because a good textbook can provide a solid basis for a course, you may decide that you want textbooks for one, two, or more subjects, perhaps subjects with which you are less confident.

What Makes a Good Textbook or Workbook?

When shopping for a textbook or workbook for your struggling learner, you need to see the book and examine it. You can begin with a catalog or website, but getting the book in your hands is best. If you must buy a book unseen, ask about the return policy.

When you examine a book, check the table of contents, and then browse through the book. Does it cover what your child needs to learn?

Does it seem clear? Does the order in which the material is presented make sense?

Next consider the book's appearance. How big is the font? Is it hard to read? (Does your child think so? Ask her.) How are the pages laid out? Is there good use of white space? In a large textbook, two columns are better than one, because a seven-inch wide single column is harder to read than double columns. (Readers can lose their place when their eyes return to the left margin.) Are the headings and subheadings easy to find? Is the page hard on the eyes, crammed with material?

Your child may work better with materials with good illustrations and colorful borders. Or she may be distracted by those features, and prefer plainer materials. If you must buy material with the small print crammed together, find a photocopier and enlarge pages, if the copyright permits. (Some copyright notices allow limited copying for classroom use. If not, contact the publisher. If you are making a single enlargement for one student, they may grant you permission.)

The following textbook features are helpful:

- Chapters and sections begin with a list of topics covered.
- Sections include preview and review questions.
- Chapters end with a good summary and review section.
- Illustrations are apt and have good, clear captions.
- Charts and diagrams are well-designed and clear.
- Pages are not cluttered.
- Unfamiliar words are highlighted in bold face.

Check that your student can find out the meanings of unfamiliar words. Some books define words in the text or the margin. Others give definitions in a glossary at the back, which is less convenient. Consider the level of difficulty of the words defined. Does the book interrupt itself with definitions of many words your student already knows? My son found that annoying and distracting.

Check the back of the book for resources. Are the maps and charts easy to read and well-suited to the subject and your student? Look up a few items in the index. Is it hard to use? One of the study skills you will have to teach is how to use an index, and it is tough to work with a bad one.

Some publishers offer placement tests to help you judge where to begin. Other may want you to start from the beginning, knowing you might be able to rush through early levels, reviewing and solidifying knowledge. Do not let that added expense rule out a new program, though. You may be able to buy secondhand, or re-sell that first unit once you finish it.

A good textbook for your child may be a grade level or two below her official grade level. Often the difference between a fifth and sixth grade book is minimal: slightly smaller font and a little more detail in the sixth grade book. For a slow reader, the lower level book with its larger font can be easier on the eyes. Textbook publishers have caught on to this need for flexibility, and so many now conceal the grade level or do not mark it at all.

Specific Tips for Choosing Workbooks
If you are shopping for a workbook, here are some additional features to check. Are the blanks long and the spaces between the lines wide enough for your child to write in? You want pages with lots of blank space, like the *Keys to…* math series (see the end of this chapter). How about the paper? If the book is printed on cheap newsprint, it may tear if she erases vigorously. Some workbook pages include a puzzle or some other activity designed to make the page more fun. If that motivates your child, that is great. However, for some children, a puzzle is another struggle and not a reward at all.

Some workbook pages have *word banks*, lists with all the possible answers for the page. This can help poor spellers. Matching problems can, too. With word banks or matching problems, the students only have to recognize correct answers, not recall them on their own. But word banks and matching lists that only give all the correct answers make it too easy to guess the last problems.

Where to Find Good Textbooks and Workbooks

When you begin to shop for your homeschool, the best places to begin are catalogs from educational publishers and retailers. Businesses serving the homeschool market have boomed in the last decades. Most of these educational vendors will now send you a catalog on request by phone or via their websites. Ask homeschoolers you know to lend you their catalogs, or tell you which they use, and start your own catalog collection.

I had about thirty catalogs on a shelf when I started homeschooling. I did not use them all, but they helped. It sounds silly, but they gave me a sense of security, reminding me there were many resources and a large homeschooling community, even though at first, I did not know anyone homeschooling within forty miles of my new home. The catalogs saved me time: some I could look through in five minutes and discard, faster than clicking through a website. Other catalogs I circled, dog-eared, and carried around as I brainstormed. Some catalogs review curricula or materials, and include stories of homeschooling families, or tips about starting out. Some catalogs inspired me to buy materials (or at least get them from the library to try), to plan field trips, and science projects.

Several families I interviewed recommended particular workbook-based programs. Two families recommended ACE Curriculum/School of Tomorrow, which divides each subject into twelve workbooks called PACEs, which include lessons, vocabulary, quizzes, and tests. Another parent reports that her son likes Alpha Omega's LIFEPAC, in which each subject comes in a set of small workbook/textbooks. "He doesn't think, 'I'll never get it done,'" she said. Some children appreciate the structure and completeness of workbooks. There are many publishers of workbooks that cater to the homeschool market, and any homeschool convention will have their representatives. See the curriculum guides and catalogs at the end of the chapter.

Mainstream Textbook Publishers

If you are homeschooling, it's easy to overlook the major textbook publishers such as Houghton Mifflin, Harcourt Brace Jovanovich, and Pearson Educational (which includes Addison Wesley, Scott Foresman, and Prentice Hall). Some textbook publishers deal only with school systems, but others now sell individual copies. These books will not be cheap, but some are excellent: well laid out, easy to read, well-illustrated, and comprehensive. Online sources of used books, such as www.abebooks.com, may help you find a bookstore with a better price, but used books may not be returnable, so check with the bookseller first. The publishers I have bought new textbooks directly from had a thirty-day return policy, and accepted payment by credit card.

The publishers' websites often are good, with sample pages to read from the student and teacher editions of books. I sometimes ordered one teacher's copy and one student copy. But when the teachers' books mainly included features to help in a large class, I ordered two student copies, one for me and one for my son. We liked to have two copies of the book so I don't have to read over my son's shoulder; other families get by with one copy. Teacher's editions are often larger and more expensive. For two years, my father taught my son social studies using Glencoe McGraw Hill text-books, and found the teacher's editions unnecessary.

Many publishers' websites also offer supplemental materials for teach-ers and learning activities for the students. Some of these materials will be helpful for homeschooling; others require purchase of expensive DVDs or other materials beyond a homeschooler's budget.

If you are on good terms with your local school staff, you might ask to meet with a teacher (ideally someone you already know), and have a look at what they are using first. A middle school teacher let me borrow a civics book to examine. I also have e-mailed with a government teacher at an area magnet high school and with an astronomy professor at a nearby university, describing my son's interests and special needs, and received good advice on books. One homeschooler I interviewed borrows materials from a local school occasionally.

As you work with textbook publishers directly, remember that it is expensive for publishers to sell single copies, when they usually sell books by the dozens, hundreds, and thousands. It is as if car manufacturers started selling single cars by catalog from the factory, instead of through dealers: to serve homeschoolers the publishers have to manage all the minor details of setting up small accounts, verifying your credit card, packing, shipping, and returns. The major publishers are not going to make much money from homeschoolers ordering one or two copies at a time, so bear with them as they serve us.

Another problem textbook publishers face is that a few unscrupulous students with credit cards have tried to buy teachers' editions and answer keys to avoid work. That is why some publishers ask you for proof of your homeschooling. It wasn't difficult in my case: I faxed the publishers the letter of acknowledgement that my county had sent me, as proof that I had registered as a homeschooler. The publishers I have purchased from have shipped me textbooks quickly.

High-low Books

Some publishers, or branches of publishing houses, sell books designed for special education. They may sell stories written at low reading levels, but designed to be more interesting to teens than the average easy readers. These are sometimes call high-low books (high interest, low readability). Some sell textbooks with high school content, but with larger print, less complex sentences, and with the harder words defined in the margin. My father, chairman of our homeschool social studies department, and my son were satisfied with one, a Globe world history textbook.

Audio Books

Whether you use textbooks or other books, consider an audio format if your child has reading or vision problems. You probably have seen recorded books on cassette or CD at your public library, but there are other options. Here are three:

- Recordings for the Blind and Dyslexic (RFB&D, www.rfbd.org) has a library of over 500,000 titles, including textbooks, read aloud by volunteers, which can be played only on specially-adapted DVD players and software they sell. Begun as a service of the New York Public Library to help veterans blinded in World War II attend college, now most of their members, who range from kindergarten through adult professionals, have learning disabilities.[1]
- Bookshare.org "provides print disabled people in the United States with legal access to over 40,000 books and 150 periodicals that are converted to Braille, large print or digital formats for text to speech audio."[2] Through Bookshare, people using scanners to digitize printed text can share these scans. The scans then can be used in different ways, such as having them read aloud by the synthetic voice of text-to-speech software.

   Any visitor to the Bookshare.org website can download public domain books. Copyrighted books are only available for

1. Recordings for the Blind and Dyslexic. "The RFB&D Story." Accessed August 26, 2008. www.rfbd.org/about.htm

2. Bookshare. "Welcome to Bookshare." Accessed August 26, 2008. www.bookshare.org/web/Welcome.html.

download in the specialized formats of digital Braille and the digital talking book format, and are only available to people with disabilities who have provided certification of disability.[3] Participation in Bookshare is cheaper than RFB&D (see above), but their library is less extensive.

- Kurzweil 3000 software (www.kurzweiledu.com) helps struggling learners. It can read aloud text in printed or electronic form, help students to read actively with study skills features, including adding notes and electronic highlighting. It also helps students write, because using Kurzweil, "As students type, the software speaks each letter or word, so they can quickly recognize and correct spelling mistakes. The Check Spelling As You Type feature underlines misspelled words in red."[4]

Books, Not Textbooks

You do not have to teach from textbooks and workbooks. Working from a book that is not a textbook—with no questions, no chapter reviews, no suggested projects, and no tests—may sound like too much work and time for the new parent educator. But for others, textbooks and workbooks represent what is wrong with public education: a one-size fits all approach that ignores the needs and gifts of each student. A mother in New Hampshire said they use "anything and everything that isn't workbook!"

Why use books that are not textbooks? First, there are more books than textbooks, covering more topics, at more levels of detail, from more perspectives. If your child loves to learn about reptiles, rocks, asteroids, or the French and Indian War, you'll have a hard time finding many textbooks on those topics, and if you do, they may not be written at the right level for your struggling learner. Second, a child who is bored with textbooks may tolerate the technicalities of a book about a topic she loves. One homeschooler said her son does not enjoy reading, especially textbooks, but is willing to read "real books." Using "real books" may motivate your child to push herself into higher level reading, too.

3. Bookshare. "About Bookshare. org," Accessed August 26, 2008. www.bookshare.org/web/BookshareInfo.html

4. Kurzweil Educational Systems. "Kurzweil 3000 - Solutions for Struggling Readers." Accessed August 26, 2008. www.kurzweiledu.com/kurz3000.aspx

Video and Computer Courses

"No child of mine is going to spend the day in front of the television!" you may be thinking. Parents and researchers agree that too much 'screen time' in front of the television or computer screen is unhealthy. But you may find excellent video and computer programs that make a good addition to your homeschool.

What's good about video and computer programs?

- Some students with serious reading or attention problems learn better by watching and listening.
- Video instructors don't mind repeating the same explanations twenty times.
- If your child needs to drill phonics, typing, or math facts, a computer course can say, "Good job!" a hundred times a week and sound enthusiastic every time.
- Software can reward your child's ten minutes of hard work with one minute of an animated game while you are fixing dinner.
- A good animation can bring an explanation to life. When my husband and I, who both like math, watched the demonstration video for VideoText Algebra and saw a number outside the parentheses fly over to multiply itself by the numbers inside the parentheses, we agreed, the videos were a good illustration of what we see in our heads when we do these kinds of problems. Years ago, when I saw a ten-minute video on an online encyclopedia outline the battles of the American Revolution using animated maps, I grasped the flow of the war in a new way.
- A video can give you access to good teachers you could not otherwise find.
- For foreign languages, videos and software let you hear pronunciation. Better yet, some computer programs include a microphone and help assess your child's accent. Some software teaching foreign language lets you click on words to see definitions.
- Some students like the independence of working by themselves with a video.

■ Some parents liked fun educational software, such as JumpStart.[5] One mother said her children enjoyed playing easier versions, several grade levels below, which she felt gave them good review.

Not all videos and computer programs are worth your money. Some videos are exactly like being in a classroom. If the classroom didn't suit your child in real life, a video classroom may not be any better. So read reviews of computer and video programs. Watch how the courses, web pages, or workbook pages are laid out. Are the web pages easy for your child to navigate? One mother told me her child could not find his way through educational software she tried to use. Is the type large enough to read easily?

The disadvantages of good video and computer courses are, first, that some students need to be with people, not pictures. They won't settle for that anonymous voice saying, "Well done!"—they want to engage with someone. Second, an instructor on a video or software can't explain a concept a different way, or work with the child, doing half the work and asking leading questions. The instructor cannot answer questions, though some products have a customer service line that will take students' questions by phone. Also, sometimes computer courses include games, which are meant to be the reward for working hard. But if they are boring, they are no incentive, just an annoyance.

So how do you know when to buy a video or computer course? Most publishers offer demos (demonstration versions) of the computer or video series. Watch the demo, ideally with another adult.

You might have your child watch it and ask for comments. Make sure she understands it is not meant to be entertaining! Remind her it is an alternative to Mom, Dad, or a textbook. Ask what she thinks of the narrator, the animation, and the games, if any. Don't ask leading questions, like, "Did the speaker's voice bother you?" or you may plant that suggestion.

Look at the course content and compare it to other courses. As with textbooks, is the material adequate, well-organized, and clear? How much extra review is available, particularly in math courses? Some video programs have extra worksheets on their websites. Are the teacher's guides helpful? How easy is it to cheat? Even children with no interest in cheating will notice shortcuts. For instance, when all the tests were multiple choice in a high school math program, I have seen a bright student do half a problem,

5. Jumpstart World, Jumpstart Learning System, *and* Math Blaster *by Knowledge Adventure.* shop. knowledgead-venture.com/ Departments/ JumpStart-Series. aspx

eliminate several answers, and pick the right answer without doing all the work. While that is a valuable skill on timed tests such as the Scholastic Aptitude Test (SAT), a steady diet of multiple choice tests can promote a tendency to jump to conclusions rather than complete the work carefully, which is vital to success in mathematics.

Find out the company return policy. Some allow thirty-day trials. Some software is not returnable for any reason.

Investigate how good the customer support is for any video or computer class you are considering purchasing. Is there a toll-free customer service line? Do they take questions by e-mail? Ask others who have used the program about how the company has done with academic help for a confused student or with technical help, if you are installing software. Ask the company their policy on replacing defective tapes, DVDs, and CDs. For software, make sure you understand the user's license: you can probably only install the software on one computer.

Some products have online forums for users on the company websites. But if all the messages are glowing endorsements, they are not much use.

You can purchase videos and computer courses from many sources. As with textbooks, videos are a good product to examine at homeschool conventions, because the salesman there will be able to walk you through a sample lesson, and may offer you a discount. The manufacturer's website is another good place to start: How clear is the website? How easy to navigate? If you are buying videos or software secondhand, first ask the manufacturer if the customer service conveys. If it does not, you may be able to purchase customer service. Otherwise, decide whether you can do without it.

Many publishers of prepackaged curriculum now offer their courses not just as traditional textbooks, but also in video, DVD, or computer versions. Request and watch their demo and see if they are taking advantages of what video can do, or if you are just getting a video of a lecture.

Another source of good videos is your local educational television stations. I am not talking about taping *Sesame Street* and calling it school. But several families I interviewed include educational programs from public television to supplement their schooling, particularly for auditory learners and children with severe reading problems. In addition to traditional public television stations, some regions or school districts have channels that broadcast educational programs at many grade levels in many subjects, from economics to current events, biology to physics, Latin to geography. Request a printed program schedule with series descriptions. (These schedules may be online, but it is easier to skim and mark up printed listings.) Educational series can have episodes from five minutes to two hours long. They vary in quality, but it costs you nothing but a little time to record something and take a few minutes to preview it, and some are very good, such as *French In Action*. Some channels will broadcast several episodes of a series back-to-back, so you can tape them at once.

One homeschooler who incorporates all kinds of materials in her homeschool for her son said, "We use the Discovery Channel, the Learning Channel, and others. Most have websites and curriculum you can download and follow as well. Netflix has a huge selection of educational DVDs on all topics." Video can be one valuable element of your homeschool.

Other Computer Resources

In addition to purchasing software courses, a few families I interviewed reported that they used the Internet as a source of curriculum. One mother said, "We primarily use the Internet. Because my son tends to be a different grade level in each subject, and even different levels within subjects, I have to surf around for appropriate material." A few mothers found online sources of worksheets for struggling learners. Two mothers recommend online interactive curricula, purchased with monthly subscriptions.

Distance Learning
Need a teacher for one subject, but cannot find a homeschool class in your area? (Learn about homeschool classes in chapter 23.) Then look into distance learning, the twenty-first century version of a correspondence course. A teacher or company creates a course, sends you books, and posts assignments online. Your child does the work at home, and e-mails it back to the teacher, who e-mails comments back. With one program, a mother told me her son could telephone his professors. Some distance learning programs include virtual classrooms. Teachers and students log into a website at a specified time, and chat online, typing their comments.

Distance learning works well for older students who are:

- motivated,
- bright, and
- willing to e-mail or telephone the online teacher, an adult they do not know.

When shopping for a distance learning course, ask for references and talk to people who have used them. Also ask the company about the support they provide by phone and over the Internet.

Special Education Tools, Games, Kits, and Other Fun Stuff

Some special needs vendors sell all sorts of extras: from pencil grips to helps for kids with balance problems or sensory integration disorder. I list some of my favorites—homeschool catalogs, major publishing houses, and special education specialty publishers—at the end of the chapter.

Good educational games, puzzles, kits, and toys reward your child's hard work, motivate them to learn, and even make drilling more fun—or at least less painful. You can find them at toy stores and teacher supply stores. But homeschool conventions are a better place to shop for toys and kits, because you can often try them out and get help from a sales representative. That can help you weed out the junk and the products that do not suit your child. Homeschool catalogs have a better selection than traditional toy stores. Don't forget to browse the Internet. Check the library for good books about hands-on educational activities.

How to Choose

Use your lists of goals from chapter 11 to help you decide what to look for as you browse catalogs and curriculum fairs. But you also have the freedom to change goals, as you discover unexpected opportunities.

The first year of homeschooling is tough. And shopping the first time is intimidating. You can expect to purchase things you cannot use, so think carefully, but accept that you will waste some money. (But you can recoup by selling your mistakes at a used curriculum sale next year.)

In this chapter I have not mentioned children's diagnoses with their parents' curriculum preferences, because there was no correlation that I could see. For instance, the mothers quoted above who were for and against workbooks, both are homeschooling boys with autism.

Don't limit yourself to only one type of resource. Make it your goal to provide a rich educational experience at home with different kinds of materials, but don't feel you must use them all immediately. Parents I interviewed use a variety of materials. The parents who enthused about computer-based courses are also busy with 4H, reenacting, or other hands-on activities.

In chapter 5, I discussed learning styles, the way each individual learns best: by sight, sound, movement, touch. To shop for your child's school materials, you need to think about her style and also your own. Don't buy curriculum just because you love it, buy what is appropriate for your child. But you have to live with it, too.

Where to Look

Handling materials is better than reading about them online or in a catalog, so I recommend attending a homeschool convention. At a large convention, you can be sure of finding multiple vendors. Convention websites usually list the vendors ahead of time, so you can search for particular vendors before you decide whether to attend. If you are curious about material and you do not see that publisher on a convention's vendor list, you can check the publisher's website, which usually lists which conventions they will attend. If you purchase at a convention, you often receive a discount or free shipping.

Used curriculum fairs, like swap meets and yard sales, also let you handle books and can help you find bargains, but you never know what will be on sale. At many used curriculum fairs, the sellers must tend their own tables. That gives you a chance to ask other homeschoolers why they are selling, and what they liked or did not like about this or that product. Some conventions include used curriculum fairs, so you can look at new materials and shop for used bargains at the same event.

Go to a homeschool convention with a budget, and beware of impulse buying. Do your homework ahead of time online, so you have some idea of what you particularly want to examine. Wear comfortable shoes and take breaks. If you may be buying a lot, it is a good idea to bring a wheeled crate with a handle, roll-aboard luggage, or some other way to haul books without carrying them all day. Even a backpack is better than heavy bags on your arms as you try to examine more books. Some folks bring a toy wagon. I like to browse up and down all the aisles and flip through the books I am interested in. The first time I did this (at CHAP, a large convention in Pennsylvania), I was a first-year homeschooler looking for a math curriculum for our second year. It was tiring but rewarding to talk with the vendors, learn how to use the math manipulatives, and go back for a second look at my top choices. I was pleased with the results. I also brought home a bunch of catalogs, which I sorted through later. If you are looking at videos and software, you can not only watch and try samples at a convention, but take home free demonstration DVDs and CDs.

Shopping Tips

If you are settled on a particular book, you have options other than a convention or used curriculum sale. You can go directly to a publisher, an online bookseller, or the library. I saved hundreds of dollars every year by getting books from the library. If your local library does not have what you want, try an interlibrary loan. It may take weeks or months for a book to arrive from a library across the country, and you will probably only have it for two or three weeks. But that can give you time to decide if you want to own the book. For some materials, three weeks is all the time your child needs to read and enjoy it.

Remember to follow copyright laws. It is illegal to photocopy a book without permission of the copyright holder. Be a good example to your children. See homeschoolcopyright.com to learn what you can legally copy. I particularly recommend their online copyright quiz. The University of Minnesota offers a good explanation of fair use at www.lib.umn.edu/copyright/fairuse.phtml.

If you need to sleep on a decision, take the catalogs and samples home and think. Some publishers sell books and DVDs on a thirty-day trial. Do not rush into decisions, but it is courteous to reward those convention vendors who spent time helping you by purchasing from them or their websites, rather than from second-hand vendors.

Once you have made your decisions and found your materials, then sit back, put your feet up, rest, and congratulate yourself. You have your materials. You are ready to write your plans.

Resources

Curriculum Guides

There are so many curriculum choices out today no one seems able to keep track of them all. Here are two women who come close.

Cathy Duffy has written several curriculum guides. These are encyclopedias of curriculum, summarizing work from many publishers. Her older books, *The Christian Home Educators Curriculum Manuals*, in two volumes, grew and grew as she evaluated more and more work. They are still helpful guides, out of print, but available used and in libraries. Her current book is *100 Top Picks For Homeschool Curriculum: Choosing The Right Curriculum And Approach For Your Child's Learning Style*.

Joyce Herzog's book, *Choosing and Using Curriculum: Your Guide to Home Education*, (www.JoyceHerzog.com, 2004) is shorter (112 pages) and is written by a special education teacher with years of experience helping homeschooled children with special needs. It is an update of her *Choosing and Using Curriculum For Your Special Needs Child* (1996), and still has much to offer special needs children. She discusses how to choose materials and summarizes many programs and books. Her "Bonus Box" pages list her favorite resources on a variety of special needs: dyslexia, AD/HD, autism. Resources in the back include a list of more than a hundred vendors and publishers. Her Christian perspective crops up through the book. But those who do not share her convictions will still find hundreds of wise, practical tips.

A Sampling of Vendors

Critical Thinking Company
PO Box 1610
Seaside, CA 93955-1610
(800) 458-4849
www.criticalthinking.com
Aims to develop reasoning skills through puzzles and exercises in reading, writing, math and history. An excellent resource.

Educators Publishing Service
PO Box 9031
Cambridge, MA 02139-9031
(800) 435-7728
epsbooks.com
Publishes material on writing, reading comprehension, learning disabilities, math, preparation for tests, and more. Many of Dr. Mel Levine's books available here, and the popular *Explode the Code* reading series.

Most of their publications were written by teachers. Nothing flashy, but lots of good solid material, particularly for struggling learners.

Key Curriculum Press
1150 65th Street
Emeryville, CA 94608
(800) 995-MATH (6284)
(510) 595-7000
www.keypress.com
Math textbooks, workbooks, and math "courseware."
Their supplements, the Keys to… Series (such as *Keys to Fractions, Keys to Decimals,* and *Keys to Metric Measurement*) are simple, uncluttered, very inexpensive workbooks that give your child lots of practice.

Progeny Press
P.O. Box 100
Fall Creek, WI 54742
(877) 776-4369
www.progenypress.com
More than a hundred literature study guides, with plenty of white space,
many good questions in varied aspects of literature. Written from a
Christian perspective.

Rainbow Resource Center, Inc.
R. R. 1 Box 159A
50 N 500 East Road
Toulon, IL 61483
(888) 841-3456
(309) 695-3200
www.rainbowresource.com
Huge general source of books, curriculum, manipulatives, games, and other
school supplies.

Sonlight Curriculum, Ltd.
8042 South Grant Way
Littleton, CO 80122-2705
(303) 730-6292
www.sonlight.com
Good source of books, curricula, and more used by several families I
interviewed. Offers a literature- and history-based program, unusual in
its emphasis on understanding other cultures and times. Great source
for fine children's literature. Also sells fine math, science, writing. You
can purchase a complete curriculum or just a few books. Some books are
explicitly Christian.

Super Duper Publications
PO Box 24997
Greenville, SC 29616
(800) 277-8737
www.superduperinc.com
Sells a large variety of educational materials for teaching speech, language, literacy, and occupational therapy.

Time4Learning
6300 NE 1st Ave., Suite 203,
Ft Lauderdale, FL 33334
(954) 771-0914
Time4learning online curriculum is used by two families I interviewed as part of their homeschool. time4learning.com

Sources for High-Low Books (High Interest, Low Readability)
AGS Globe
5910 Rice Creek Parkway
Suite 1000
Shoreview, MN 55126
www.agsglobe.com
Produces curriculum materials, assessment tools for "middle and high school striving learners." A division of Pearson Learning.

High Noon Books
A division of Academic Therapy Publications
20 Commercial Boulevard
Novato, CA 94949
(800) 422-7249
www.highnoonbooks.com

Steck-Vaughn/Harcourt Achieve
Attn: Cust Serv. 5th Floor
6277 Sea Harbor Drive
Orlando, FL 32887
(800) 531-5015
steckvaughn.harcourtachieve.com
Primary, secondary, and adult education materials in reading, language arts, math, science, social studies, and testing preparation.

Special Needs Publishers
A.D.D. Warehouse
300 Northwest 70th Avenue, Suite 102
Plantation, FL 33317
(800) 233-9273
addwarehouse.com
"Books, Videos, and Training Programs. Resources on Attention Deficit/ Hyperactivity Disorder (AD/HD), Oppositional Defiant Disorder, Asperger's, Autism, Tourette's, and Learning Problems."

Bookshare.org
The Benetech Initiative
480 S. California Avenue
Suite 201
Palo Alto, CA 94306-1609
info@bookshare.org
Bookshare provides books and periodicals in large print, Braille, or digital files for text-to-speech synthesizers.

Integrations
PO Box 922668
Norcross, GA 30010-2668
www.integrationscatalog.com
Produces several catalogs of supplies for special education: for balance, mobility, vestibular orientation, position, sensory issues, communication, fine and gross motor development, calming and organizing, mouth and language, body readiness, daily routine, hand and eye helpers, and books to help parents with these special needs.

Kurzweil Educational Systems
(800) 547-6747
www.kurzweiledu.com
Kurzweil 3000 software aids in reading, writing, and study skills.

Recordings for the Blind and Dyslexic
(800) 211-4792
www.rfbd.org
Not just for the blind anymore, struggling readers can subscribe. Financial assistance is available.

Woodbine House
5410 Bells Mill Road
Bethesda, MD 20817
(800) 843-7323
www.woodbinehouse.com
Books on teaching a wide range of disabilities for parents and teachers.

Fun and Educational
Timberdoodle Company
1510 E Spencer Lake Rd
Shelton, WA 98584
(800) 478-0672
(360) 426-0672, hours 8-5 PST, Monday-Thursday.
This catalog is a must. Timberdoodle sells many excellent books, but it is their kits and educational toys that tempt me to blow my budget. A wide ranging assortment: from "Sewing Machine Fun," which enabled my nine-year-old to sew confidently, to Fischer Techniks, electronics kits, and DNA models, from tools as simple as Learning Wrap-Ups for drilling memory work to robotics kits, and much more.

Tobin's Lab
PO Box 725
Culpeper, VA 22701
(540) 937-7173
www.tobinslab.com
A great resource for science in all areas, kits, supplies, lab materials, dissection kits, and math manipulatives (tools for hands-on learning).

14

Adapting and Creating Materials

So you have shopped carefully, made the best choices you could, and started homeschooling. You may know from the start that the materials you have selected need adapting. Or if, after a few weeks, your child is frustrated with some program, textbook, or plan, it is time to think about adapting your materials.

In this chapter:
- Simple adaptations of curriculum
- Adapting your teaching
- Physical adaptations
- When to give up on a curriculum
- Writing your own materials

Simple Adaptations of Curriculum

Simple is a key word for this chapter. Start small. When homeschooling struggling learners, parents have limited time and resources. In this chapter, I will share many ideas, but don't try to do everything. I am describing what sixty-four different families do, for dozens of very different children—not what one father or mother should do.

Simple adaptations to a workbook or textbook:

- Enlarging the print of your child's textbook can make it easier to read. Even when the student is in high school, it is worth remembering.

- Skipping sections your child knows is one way to reduce boredom. If you think your child knows the contents of the next chapter of a textbook, let him go ahead and take the chapter test. If he has mastered the material, move on. You may finish a book in half a year. You may skip a level.

- Some books give plenty of extra problems, so your student may not have to answer every single question. A well-designed math book will not only give plenty of exercises, but they will be of gradually increasing difficulty. So don't just assign the first half of the problems. Look at how the problems are arranged: perhaps the odd numbered problems will be enough practice. For language arts and other subjects, you might choose to skip or simplify some questions.

- If you are using a book that requires your child to copy (copying a passage or a math problem), and if copying is not the important part of the exercise, then you might write for him, photocopy, or limit the amount he has to write. For instance, *Editor in Chief's* [1] workbooks have excellent editing exercises, with directions to copy over the passage, making corrections as you go. Instead, I let my son mark up corrections in the workbook with proofreaders' marks.

- If fill-in-the-blank questions are too hard for your child, write a word box, by drawing a box around a list of possible answers (and a few wrong answers). A child who has trouble finding words in his memory may recognize the answer when he sees it.

- If the material seems too hard, you may break assignments into short chunks to keep your child from becoming discouraged or restless. You may need to create more exercises for some children to get enough practice.

1. Editor in Chief *is a series of workbooks and software exercises by Critical Thinking Company, PO Box 1610, Seaside, CA 93955-1610. www.criticalthinking.com*

Adapting Your Teaching

Let's look at two examples of adapting curriculum, one that was too difficult, another that was just too boring.

Sometimes you buy curriculum that is too much for your child and have to trim it down to size. Just before my first year homeschooling, we had moved to Virginia, and I thought it would be fun to study state history. (My son, age nine, asked if we had to become Confederates.) I bought a set of Virginia history workbooks, designed for grades four to twelve. It was a good product, but not a wise choice for a dyslexic fourth grader. It was all I could find, and at that point, it did not occur to me then to try to manage without a workbook or textbook, and I did not realize how far beyond my son's abilities these books were.

But the workbooks helped me organize our year and filled in gaps in my knowledge. I read parts of the workbooks aloud, and simplified and skipped many questions. Visits to the Virginia Indian Festival, Colonial Williamsburg, Jamestown, Mount Vernon, and Gunston Hall (George Mason's home) brought our lessons to life. A visit to a restored colonial farm led to my son volunteering there once a month, working as a child re-enactor. He learned to answer tourists questions, comb flax with a hackle to help make linen, care for crops, and other eighteenth-century chores. (Bonus: I had one child-free day a month to run errands, plan, and catch my breath!) So despite a rough start, our Virginia History study went very well.

Other times the problem is not the grade level. Patty in North Carolina is a great example of adapting to her son's needs and interests:

We bring a lot of different sources into our homeschooling so things don't get boring. He doesn't always give book reports the same way or do math the same way. It's not always a workbook, or a book and pencil and paper. We use computer programs. We get in the kitchen and we cook. And with math we go to the grocery store and compare prices and use coupons. So we use a lot of real world stuff and a lot of hands on stuff. That keeps his attention really well and it also plays that trick of having him learn without realizing it. When we come back, we use books and workbooks as a skeleton, a framework,

*but then we build upon it with hands-on examples, real world
examples, and with different methods.*

*We use the tape recorder, we use the computer, we use dry erase
boards, we use chalkboards. We go out in the yard and use finger
paint. We bring so many different methods into things—anything
that suits him and very much a hands-on kind of thing. If he can
see it, touch it, feel it, taste it, smell it, hear it, he gets it a lot better.*

She later e-mailed some favorite resources:

- Magazines/newspapers/newsletters. We get everything from
  National Geographic to *Scientific American* ... also online newsletters
  (like from CHADD or 4-H) and free publications like Piedmont
  Parent (a local free publication with articles and events for
  the community).
- Government websites. Almost all have kids pages or education
  pages and links. The National Weather Service is one we have used.
- 4-H. I cannot say enough about 4-H. I would be here all day!
- Netflix: A huge selection of educational DVDs on all topics. We use
  this all the time.
- Cable TV: We use the Discovery Channel, the Learning Channel,
  etc. Most programs have websites and curriculum you can download and follow as well.

So whether the work is too hard or too easy, supplement your program with enrichment activities. Doing so can encourage the bored child,
the discouraged learner, and the gifted student—your child may be all three
at once!

Let me summarize the advice from Patty and other parents:

- Do not try to do too much. Find a sustainable pace.
- If you use a textbook or workbook or other published curriculum,
  use it as a framework. You can decide how much to add to it based
  on the time and energy you have, and how suitable it seems in itself.

- Incorporate a variety of activities. Even the child who craves routine and predictability needs to tolerate changes of activity and may discover new interests.

- Look for outdoor activities and field trips to supplement your program. See chapter 23.

- Find or make hands-on activities, kits, and projects. Simple projects can be fun. Carol Barnier's *How to Keep Your Child Off the Refrigerator and Onto Learning* tells how to make simple games.

- Simplify the way your child produces work. Along with using tape recorders, computers, whiteboards, chalkboards, and finger-paint, like Patty, at my house we also have traced spelling words in a tray of cornmeal and drawn on the sidewalk with chalk. Other families print with letter stamps and an inkpad. (Be sure it is washable ink!) Your child could answer some questions orally to you either directly or into a tape recorder, which is handy if you are homeschooling another child. You can transcribe their answers occasionally as a record of their progress. As an alternative to using a computer to type, Nafisi in Philadelphia recommended AlphaSmart, a portable word processor. It gives no Internet access and is much cheaper than a computer.

- Attractive books, such as those by Usborne and Dorling Kindersley, make good additions to social studies and science programs.

- Well-chosen videos, computer games, and interactive websites can invigorate your program.

- Projects are also a great opportunity to teach planning and research skills, and enjoy making something: a poster, diorama, model, meal, or costume.

Physical Adaptations

Other adaptations do not apply directly to the content you are teaching, but help your child learn. Several parents reported that their children could focus better if they had something to do with their hands. Some gave their children little things to fiddle with, like small erasers or squeeze balls.[2] Kneaded rubber erasers, which are flexible as putty but makes no crumbs, can keep hands busy while students listen. Anna in Maryland had to plan her options:

Because I love to read aloud and we still read aloud to our family, I came up with a list of activities he could do while we were reading aloud. Of course, coloring. He could play with clay. One of my favorites was to have the kids sort socks once a week. Just that concentration would help him focus, so he could comprehend. He could be all over the room, all over the house, but tell me verbatim what I had just read to him. So I knew he was getting it. I just had to come up with activities I could tolerate, so I could read longer!

I'd poke holes in meat trays and make letters, so he could do the stitching. In the warmer weather, we'd go out and I had them cut green beans on the table—just any little chore that could be done while I was reading.

Along with fine motor activities like these, many homeschoolers saw a benefit from incorporating large motor activities into their teaching. Chewing gum helps some children focus and be more calm. Several families use therapy balls. One remembered, when her daughter was younger, having her sit on a therapy ball during math, and letting her bounce when she got an answer right. Another mother noticed her son read better if they played with a Koosh® Ball beforehand. (These are soft balls made of thin rubber filaments that come out from a center.) Older students report similar benefits: one teenager does better with his math if he practices drums first. Another mother said her child does push-ups against a wall. Gymnastics and martial arts help some children focus. As a teen, my son found that running two miles in the morning before we started homeschool helped him settle down to work, giving him time let his mind think about other things before he worked.

Deep pressure helps calm some children. Wearing a weighted vest or holding a weighted toy in their laps can help some children settle down. One mother said her son, who has two mattresses in his room for when

2. It's important—with younger children in the home or with children who put things in their mouths—not to provide toys that can be choking hazards, or come apart into choking hazards. You can purchase small toys at a dollar store, or a bag of small, suitable items called fidgets, from www.headsupnow.com, under "Sensory Issues/Fidgeting."

friends sleep over, likes to slide himself between the two mattresses for five minutes. When stressed, he finds it soothing to lay on the floor on his stomach and hear his heart beat. Other children like to do their work lying on their stomachs on the floor, too.

When to Give Up on a Curriculum

At some point, you may decide to stop trying to adapt and simply abandon some materials and try again. You will not find a perfect product. But you don't want to be miserable, either. For each subject, I would not radically change materials more than once a school year—nor would I change in very many subjects, for two reasons. Changing materials midyear means you must reorganize and make new plans, which costs time and energy. Changing materials may unsettle, discourage, or confuse your child. Do not switch brands every new year, either, if it means big changes from your child's perspective. For some students, having to learn new ways of doing work every year can be as much trouble as learning new material. If that is hard for your child, limit unnecessary change.

If what you are using is okay but not terrific, it may be more effective to stay with it for the year. Resolve to start early on your shopping and planning for better choices for next year.

Writing Your Own Materials

Sound intimidating? Writing your own materials can be simple. For some of us, it is less work than looking for something that suits our children. Start small, by adapting what you already have. Begin by imitating what works. If your child likes Mrs. B's math puzzles or history book scavenger hunts, make up some more like hers. Studying literature? Look at some good study guides, such as those by Progeny Press or in back of the *Oxford School Shakespeare* series,[3] and if you like their approaches, imitate them, writing your own questions for other books.

If you cannot find the curriculum you need, think out what qualities you want. Look around first: patching your program together out of two or three books, websites, and trips may be faster than writing your own. But if

3. See the end of the chapter for details on these study guides.

there is nothing right for your child, writing your own curriculum may be easier than extensively adapting someone else's.

If you are writing a curriculum, after you have identified what you want, think out your goals for your child. Depending on your personality and time available, you may do this on the back of an envelope or more formally, but save it. Then do yourself and your child a favor by asking yourself how you will know when the child has met your goals. If you plan to give a test, draft it, or jot some notes. Obviously, the younger the child, the simpler this will be. Even if you are giving the test or evaluation orally, draft the test to help you think what you are aiming for. As a new school teacher, sometimes I did not write math tests until I had finished teaching the unit. Sometimes I thought of great questions that it would not have been fair to ask, because I had not given them practice in that kind of problem or in thinking outside the box.

If you are assigning a project instead of a test—a report, a talk, a model, or a poster, for example—you still need to know what you will accept. Let your child know. If you say, "Write a report on Italy," and he writes one page, when you wanted at least three pages covering geography, climate, economy, government, and culture, with a map and a picture of the flag, but you did not say so, you cannot complain.

Teachers call the set of criteria for an assignment a *rubric*. You can find many examples of rubrics. (Searching the Internet for "education rubric" produced nearly two million hits.) Judith Munday's book, *Teaching Your Special Needs Student*, and her website, www.hishelpinschool.com, can help you write more detailed rubrics. (Ordering details are at the end of the chapter. I will discuss measuring progress in the next chapter.) Of course, you can be more open-ended, making or asking for suggestions, instead of assigning project goals. It depends on your style and your child. There are several advantages to writing a rubric or other statement of what you expect for an assignment. If your child is a perfectionist, fiddling with details endlessly, your goals can help him know when to quit, or if your child is feeling rebellious, he cannot say you did not tell him what you expected. As a parent-teacher, I find the clearer I know what I expect on a test or project, the easier it is to evaluate it. And more importantly, the clearer I know what my expectations are, the better I teach.

As the parent of a struggling learner, I knew it was not fair to my son for me not to have a clear idea what I expected him to do. I did not always have clear expectations, but it helped when I did.

Conclusion

Remember not to make too much work for yourself and to keep your adaptations where you can find them for later use. A friend may thank you. Again, the goal in adapting or writing curriculum is primarily to serve your child and help him learn, not to create the most beautiful curriculum ever. But if you find you enjoy polishing it up, and it works well for your child, you may find yourself with a product. Two mothers I interviewed plan to publish curricula they have written.

Many books have been written on helping children with various learning problems, including Brock and Fernette Eide's excellent work, *The Mislabeled Child*, with tips on helping your child learn. But many books are written for teachers, rather than homeschoolers. Some are helpful; some only worth skimming. Most of these are written for the teacher with a classroom full of students and no freedom to purchase curriculum or change the schedule. Some books on teaching are hard to plow through after a long day, unclear, and time-consuming. Others are worthwhile, however; so search for books related to teaching special needs and to teaching a child with your child's particular needs. I cannot list all the good special education books, but include a few below.

Now that we have looked at adapting curriculum, in the next chapter we will turn to creating a plan for our homeschool: another project that will require revision but will benefit your child.

Resources

Four helpful books by homeschooling mothers to help you adapt your teaching
Carol Barnier is the author of *How to Get Your Child Off the Refrigerator and Onto Learning*. Lynnwood, Washington: Emerald, 2000. Don't make my mistake and think this book is just for parents of hyperactive children.

It is full of good advice creating simple, fun educational games and general advice on homeschooling struggling learners.

Also see Carol's website, sizzlebop.com, "Where Highly Distractible People are Celebrated, Encouraged & Empowered." Sign up for her "Sizzle Life" e-mails and hear her speak in person or online at opengifts.org.

Melinda Boring is a speech pathologist, homeschooler, funny, informative speaker, and the author of:

Heads Up Helping! Teaching Tips and Techniques for Working With ADD, ADHD, and Other Children with Challenges. Victoria, British Columbia: Trafford, 2002. Available from www.headsupnow.com and Amazon.com.

Adapting Curriculum for Learning Differences. Audio CD with PowerPoint and workshop outline. Available from www.headsupnow.com.

Sharon C. Hensley's book, *Home Schooling Children with Special Needs*, (Vancouver, Washington: Noble, 2001) is excellent. She has a chapter on "Choosing Teaching Methods and Techniques" and speaks out of years of experience as a homeschooling mother, special education teacher, and homeschool consultant. The director of the Almaden Valley Christian School, a support group of families serving children with special needs, she has a masters degree in special education.

Irene Baker, Kathleen Julicher and Maggie Hogan's book, *Gifted Children at Home,* is not written specifically for struggling learners. But some struggling learners are gifted. Gifted or not, many can benefit from this book's suggestions. *Gifted Children at Home: A Practical Guide for Homeschooling Families.* Cheswold, Delaware: Gifted Group, 2001.

Books by specialists knowledgeable about homeschooling
Joyce Herzog's book *Learning In Spite of Labels: Practical Teaching Tips and A Christian Perspective of Education* has good practical advice. Joyce

supports homeschoolers with her years of experience as a special education teacher and is a popular homeschool conference speaker. You may purchase some of her books at www.teach4mastery.com. She has sold her business, but you can learn more about her at www.joyceherzog.info.

Dianne Craft, a certified nutritionist, has twenty-five years experience helping bright children with learning problems and a masters in special education. She speaks at homeschool conferences on *Teaching the Right Brain Child, Smart Kids Who Hate to Write*, and other topics. You can purchase audio CDs of these talks, flashcards, and more from her website, diannecraft.com.

Judith Munday, author of *Teaching Your Special Needs Student: Strategies and Tools that Really Work* has more than twenty years experience as a special education teacher, consultant, and conference speaker. In *Teaching Your Special Needs Student*, you will find chapters on effective teaching, teaching tools, creating rubrics to evaluate performance, assistive technology, and more. Order her book [Chesapeake, Virginia: H.I.S. Place, 2007] from heav.org Visit her website, www.hishelpinschool.com/.

Joe and Connie Sutton's book, *Strategies for Struggling Learners: A Guide for the Teaching Parent*, helps parents with all kinds of special needs. Their book includes chapters on developing curriculum, program practices, modifying instruction, and teaching methods. The Suttons both hold advanced degrees in special education and have years of experience helping students and preparing special education teachers. (Simpsonville, South Carolina: Exceptional Diagnostics, 1997. Available from heav.org.)

Other helpful books on teaching children with special needs
Note: Don't reject a book just because its title includes a condition that your child does not have. Often you can glean great tips anyway.

Berk, Laura. *Awakening Children's Minds: How Parents and Teachers Can Make a Difference*. New York: Oxford, 2001. Berk's notions of "scaffolding" and the "zone of proximal development" have helped one parent I interviewed, Tammy Glaser. See Tammy's blog for more on Berk and on Tammy's homeschooling an autistic daughter, aut2bhomeincarolina. blogspot.com.

Dendy, Chris A. Zeigler. *Teaching Teens with ADD and ADHD*. Bethesda, Maryland: Woodbine, 2000.
Eide, Brock and Fernette. *The Mislabeled Child: Looking Beyond Behavior to Find the True Sources—and Solutions—for Children's Learning Challenges. .* New York: Hyperion, 2006. The end of most chapters covers strategies for helping children learn.

Kranowitz, Carol. *The Out-of-Sync Child: Recognizing and Coping with Sensory Processing Disorder,* Revised Edition. New York: Penguin, 2005.

Rief, Sandra F. *How To Reach And Teach Children with ADD/ADHD: Practical Techniques, Strategies, and Interventions*. San Francisco: Jossey-Bass, 2005.

Some vendors with tools for adapting your teaching
Heads Up Now
1308 Mulford Road
Columbus, OH 43212
www.headsupnow.com
Homeschooling family (mother is a speech pathologist) with two AD/HD children provide "expert information and products for special needs children. Our items have been selected to accommodate various learning styles and strengths, regardless of curriculum used."

Integrations
PO Box 922668
Norcross, GA 30010-2668
www.integrationscatalog.com
"Bright Solutions For Kids With Learning, Behavioral and Sensory Differences"

Pocket Full of Therapy
P.O. Box 174
Morganville, N.J. 07751
(732) 441-0404 or
(800) pfot-124
www.pfot.com
"Select Pediatric and School Based Products," founded by two
occupational therapists.

Rainbow Resource Center, Inc.
Rt. 1 Box 159A
50 N 500 East Road
Toulon, IL 61483
www.rainbowresource.com
More than 35,000 products for general homeschooling audience for
pre-K through grade 12, this catalog is 1,300 pages.

Super Duper Publications
PO Box 24997
Greenville, SC 29616
www.superduperinc.com
"Education Fun for Therapy, Home, and School"

Timberdoodle
Home Educators Resource Catalog
1510 E. Spencer Lake Road
Shelton, WA 98584
www.timberdoodle.com
This catalog is a must: books, curriculum, puzzles, games, crafts, software,
and educational toys that tempt me to blow my budget. A wide-ranging
assortment from tools as simple as Learning Wrap-Ups for drilling memory
work to software and robotics kits, and much more.

Other materials mentioned in this chapter
Editor in Chief available as books or software from:
Critical Thinking Company
PO Box 1610
Seaside, CA 93955-1610
(800) 458-4849
www.criticalthinking.com
This is another must-have catalog. Critical Thinking aims to develop reasoning skills reading, puzzles, writing, math and history.

Gill, Roma, ed. *Oxford School Shakespeare* series, Oxford: Oxford University Press. These editions of many of Shakespeare's plays are paperbacks with good summaries, project ideas, and questions. They are easier to read with their larger print and wide margins, and have good explanatory notes in the margins, alongside the text, where they are easier to find than footnotes. www.oup.co.uk/series/o/oxss/

Progeny Press publishes study guides for literature "from a Christian perspective." For some struggling learners, these study guides have too many questions and activities, so feel free to trim and modify. But the guides are well written and organized, giving you good ideas. After using a few, I felt comfortable writing my own. Try it yourself. They are looking for new guides to publish and might want yours.
Progeny Press
PO Box 100
Fall Creek, WI 54742-0100
www.progenypress.com

See also chapters 17 through 20 of this book for materials for adapting math, reading, writing, and study skills.

15

Make Your Plan

In the last chapters, you reviewed your child's progress and chosen goals, considering your teaching approach, shopped for and adapted or drafted materials. With your goals and materials in hand, you are ready to plan.

In this chapter:
- Not an IEP
- Why write a plan to address special needs?
- Remediation and accommodation
- Keep it simple
- Targets, criteria, and assessments
- Your homeschool is more than remediation
- Planning your year

Whether you have been homeschooling for years or are only starting, you are concerned with helping your child with their learning problems. So we will consider planning in two parts: first, the plan of how you will strengthen areas of weakness, and second, how you plan to teach everything else.

Not an IEP

Many parents who had children in school told me they had difficulty working with the school on planning special help for their child. Since my son's school staff was very supportive and our planning sessions went well, I was surprised by how unhappy some parents were with the process. As one mother said, "Even with the IEP (Individualized Education Plan), it just wasn't working. It was too many years of fighting with the teachers and the principal to enforce the IEP, which I had to fight to get, which they said would make all the difference in the world. I just got tired of battling." Several parents were so unhappy that even mentioning those letters seems to raise their blood pressure.

An Individualized Education Plan (IEP) is a document produced by public school staff listing academic and behavioral goals for an individual student with special needs. (A similar document addressing behavior is called an Individualized Behavior Plan, IBP.) Discussed at a series of meetings of teachers and the child's parents, the goals in the plans are set for one school year. The IEP also lists the services (such as speech therapy) and the accommodations the school will provide to help reach these goals. An IEP is a legal document, binding the school to provide remediation and setting goals for the child. The parent signs an IEP to consent to the school executing this plan and providing these services. *The parents are not bound to follow these plans if they homeschool,* just as private schools are not bound by them.

These annual goals on an IEP are listed as "behaviors," actions the student will be able to do. Each goal includes a target date and should explain how the teachers will determine when the goal is met. Goals from a sample IEP are shown in Table 15.1.

Because the IEP is a legal document irrelevant to a homeschool, some homeschoolers call their plans *Student Education Plan,* or *SEP.* Other parents call their plans IEPs or other names. Whatever parents call plans they have written for their homeschool, they are not the legal documents described above. To avoid confusion, I will refer to a plan written by homeschoolers to address a student's special needs as an SEP, and to avoid

Table 15.1
Sample goals from an IEP

IEP Annual Goals	Methods and conditions	Criterion	Projected date	Date objective achieved
Master basic subtraction facts	In classroom or resource room assignments	90% accuracy	6/08	
Solve real life problems using money	In classroom or resource room assignments	90% accuracy	6/08	
Solve real life problems using time	In classroom or resource room assignments	90% accuracy	6/08	
Use punctuation in writing	In classroom or resource room assignments	90% accuracy	6/08	
Will use periods appropriately	In classroom writing assignments	90% accuracy	6/08	
Will use capitals appropriately	In classroom writing assignments	90% accuracy	6/08	
Write complete sentences	In classroom writing assignments	90% accuracy	6/08	

confusing the general goals you set in chapter 11 with the specific ones you will create in writing plans, I will all the specific goals on your SEP *targets*.

Why Write a Plan to Address Special Needs?

When you homeschool a struggling learner, time is precious. Planning helps you crystallize your goals, focus your efforts, and assess your progress. Written plans also are evidence of your work, should you need to *document,* that is, to support with evidence, of it later.

For some, planning conjures up dreary images of paperwork, or unpleasant memories of working on educational plans with school staff. What I am proposing is neither of these. What I am urging you to do, on your own or with the help of a special education consultant, is draw up some plans that help you teach better.

Crystallize your goals, focus your teaching
Just as you limited yourself to a few goals out of thousands of possibilities in chapter 11, you need to limit the extent of your plans for one year. Focusing on a few goals can help keep you from being overwhelmed by all your child's special needs. In your SEP, you write measurable, specific targets with deadlines that help you plan. You can review it every quarter to remind yourself of your priorities.

Assessing Your Progress
The specifics of a SEP help you see how your homeschool is progressing. Once you draft plans and get started, a few months work may show you that your targets were too ambitious—mine were—or too easy. Writing goals and targets becomes easier with advice from a special education consultant and with practice. As you see what targets your child has met, that makes progress more tangible, which should encourage you.

Documenting Your Efforts and Progress
Some of you will be facing pressure from public schools to re-enroll your child. While I did not, several families I interviewed said their local schools pressured them. The Home School Legal Defense Association (HSLDA)

has an excellent section of their website on homeschooling
special needs students. There, under "The Law," they advise:

> *Our experience in defending homeschoolers and in monitoring*
> *legislation has shown us that the battlefront for homeschooling*
> *children with special learning needs is sometimes a heated one.*
>
> *In addition to complying with the homeschool laws of the state of*
> *your residence, there are two steps that we recommend our mem-*
> *bers take to help us defend their homeschools. You may also find it*
> *beneficial to take these steps. As you read through these suggestions,*
> *remember that* it is best to choose a course of action that fits the
> severity of your child's special learning needs. *[Emphasis added.]*
>
> *1. Arrange for Regular Evaluations and Document Your*
> *Child's Progress. ...*
> *2. Obtain Assistance in Meeting Your Child's Special Needs* [1]

Don't presume school systems are out to stop you homeschooling.
Aim for good relations with them. Check with HSLDA and your state
or provincial homeschooling organization to get the latest on relations
between the government and those homeschooling struggling learners.

An SEP also can document the services (such as speech or occupational therapy), remediation, and accommodations you give your child. It
provides compelling evidence that your child is receiving an appropriate
education at home, should anyone challenge you legally. Depending on the
severity of your child's needs and your state or province's legal requirements,
you may need an SEP to show others your homeschooling serves your child
well. Even missed targets can give evidence of effort and progress. (Those
of you with experience with IEPs in school know that IEP targets are often
not met there, either.) After reviewing my plans and records—and my son
certainly had not met all the targets I set for him—a pediatric neuropsychologist declared homeschooling was the best thing we could do for our
son—and others I interviewed have been told the same.

1. Home School
Legal Defense
Association.
"Two Steps for
Protecting Your
Special Needs
Homeschool."
Accessed July 26,
2008. www.
hslda.org/strug-
glinglearner/
sn_TwoSteps.asp

The chief reason to write your plan is to help you remember your priorities and meet them. It does not bind you; it is a memo to yourself. So whether you have a lot or a little time to give to it, whether you enjoy it or not, make some plan and use it to give your teaching direction.

Remediation and Accommodation

Before you plan, it is helpful to understand two terms. Special education teachers use two words frequently: remediation and accommodations. *Remediation* is activity to strengthen an area of weakness, and *accommodation* is a way to get work done despite the weakness. For example, in high school, I broke my elbow. After it had healed, my arm muscles were weak. Arm exercises were remediation; carrying books with my other arm was an accommodation.

When does your child need an accommodation? When a weakness is interfering with getting other work done. For instance, your child still may be working on third grade level spelling words at age twelve. You want her vocabulary to continue to grow, so read aloud to her. (Children can understand at a higher level than they can read.) For composition, let her type essays on a computer with a spelling checker, or you may decide to ignore spelling on certain assignments. Your plans may include both remediation (working on spelling) and accommodation (working around spelling problems). In the last chapter I gave some examples of accommodations, and will give more in chapters 17 through 20.

Keep It Simple

Since you will probably need to revise it, do not try to make your SEP overly elaborate. Guard your time—some of us are prone to spend too much time tweaking the plan. (Are we thinking, "If I write it just right, my child will succeed"?) After the first few years of homeschooling, my plans no longer included a formal SEP. But an SEP was helpful for my first years, so I will discuss how to write one. At the end of the chapter, I list sources for more help, since the kinds of targets you need to set vary with the child.

You may decide you need help planning. Three parents I interviewed work with special education consultants to create such a plan each year; one works via telephone and e-mail with a consultant across the country. As the years went on and my son made progress, I no longer wrote SEPs. I would list my goals on a few sheets of notebook paper, or a couple typed pages, in incomplete sentences, then plan the year in detail, building in special work remediating in reading, writing, and mathematics.

Not all the goals you listed from chapter 11 would go on your SEP, only the ones related to the child's special needs. Of course, the more severe your child's needs are, the more of your school time they will consume. The other goals will help you with the rest of your planning. I will discuss them later in this chapter.

Targets, Criteria, and Assessments

Write your targets so that you can tell when you have reached them. "Learn to multiply," "Read better," or even "Read at a fifth grade level" are good ideas, but vague targets. How will you know when you have succeeded? When she can multiply 9 x 9, or 243 x 57? For each target, write a *criterion*, which will show how to tell if your student has met the target. They can be as simple as, "Get four out of five two-digit multiplication problems correct," or "Write a paragraph of at least five sentences with a topic sentence and an concluding sentence."

Depending on the severity of your child's needs, and the time you have, you may spend more or less time writing *assessments*, which are short quizzes or other assignments to measure whether your child has met your targets. When writing your criteria and assessments, use your imagination to find a way to see that your child is meeting the targets. Suppose your target is for the student to capitalize the beginning of sentences. If the child finds handwriting difficult, it would be a poor assessment to require her to write a page to see if she capitalized the beginning of all the sentences. Another way would be to give her a list of sentences to capitalize, but that is not a good idea, either. She might just learn to capitalize the first word of each item on the list. Think what you want: you want her to know what a sentence is, where one begins, and to mark that with a capital letter. You can measure that by showing her a paragraph you have typed, in which you have changed some of those first letters to lower case, and see if she spots them all. That is a better way to assess if she has learned to capitalize, because it does not require so many other skills, and it is more like real life, where she must proofread something she has written. Your assessments

---

Table 15.2

Sample criterion-based test items

1. **Commas in series**
   Directions: insert commas where needed:

   Last Thursday, Meg Sam George and I went shopping. At the grocery store, we bought bananas, apples pears and pineapple for a fruit salad. Sam also bought chips pretzels and salsa for his mother. After finding the milk butter and eggs, Meg was afraid I would break the eggs, so she Sam and George carried them to the checkout line. I added cereal oatmeal bread peanut butter and jelly to the cart and we were ready to check out.

2. **Paragraph organization**
   Directions: The sentences below were in a paragraph, but they have been mixed up in the following list. One sentence was added that does not belong. Write 'T' by the paragraph's topic sentence, 'X' by the sentence that does not belong in this paragraph, and 'C' by the sentence that concludes the paragraph:

   1. Oak trees grow slowly, but they are very strong.
   2. Pine trees grow fast, and their wood is soft.
   3. There are many kinds of trees in my neighborhood.
   4. Daisies and daffodils grow in many people's yards.
   5. All the trees in my neighborhood make it a prettier place to live.
   6. Maple trees give lots of shade, and their leaves are lovely
       in October.

should test only for one target. You do not want assessments that require many other skills. Table 15.2 shows two sample assessments.

You do not need to write out all the assessments as you write the criteria, but if you think about them now as you plan, you will save time later on. You do not want to write all the assessments at the last minute.

One way to accommodate special needs on assessments is to let your child circle answers rather than writing them by hand. There are many other ways to accommodate a special need and still test for a skill. Going back to the last example of capitalizing, another accommodation would be for the child to tell you which words to capitalize. Many skills can be tested orally. (But for this to work, you have to keep a straight face and give the child no hints with your words or tone of voice.) To help a struggling reader, you could print a test in large type, or enlarge it on a copier. You might allow her to type answers. You child could point to answers instead of writing or speaking.

If you have your student tested by a reading teacher annually, you can set a target for next year's test score. Your overall criterion for reading might be, "On the Woodcock Reading Mastery Test – Revised/Normative Update (WRMT-R/NU), score at the grade equivalent 5.0 by June."

If you do not have the child tested for reading, you can still make up your goals and criteria for reading. For reading comprehension, you might say "Read a new story from _____ (choose an appropriate source) and answer questions on content," and the criterion might be "Orally answer five questions on its content, with eighty percent accuracy." See the end of chapter 18 on how to determine the reading level of a book.

Like writing, reading is a complex task, so you might have several reading targets, such as:

- "Hearing a list of twenty words, each one to three syllables long, the student will tell how many syllables long each word is, with one hundred percent accuracy."
- "Read sixty words correctly from a list of Dolch second grade sight words,"[2]
- "Given a list of ten words with three consonant clusters, [such as stream, split, strengths, first], the student will read at least nine of them aloud correctly."

2. *Dolch Sight Word Lists give the most common words in children's books, words that readers should know by sight, without having to sound them out. Available from many sources, including www. dolch-words.com.*

Objectives Help You Towards Targets

An SEP contains not only annual targets, but also short term objectives, which are milestones along the way. For instance, if one of your targets is to have subtraction facts memorized with ninety-five percent accuracy by June, your child has fifty-five facts to master. Your objectives might be to have twenty-five of those facts memorized by November 1 (including those easy ones that equal zero, like 8 - 8), thirty-five by January 1, and forty-five by March 1. Obviously, you do not stop a child who is making progress from advancing beyond the goals. You may need more time at the end for the facts your child finds hardest to master.

Sample SEP targets and objectives are shown in Table 15.3.

Table 15.3

Selected Goals from Student Education Plan for Joe Student

School year 09-10, Grade 5

LANGUAGE ARTS

Objective	Test goal	Target date	Date met
Word Analysis: Given a list of twenty blend-vowel combinations (e.g., sta-, fri-), will give correct sounds.	99%	6/10	
On hearing a 1- or 2-syllable word, will correctly indicate the number of syllables.	100%	6/10	
Writing: Accurately capitalizes beginning of sentence and first word of a direct quotation.	4/5	6/10	
Given an address and an envelope, correctly and legibly addresses the envelope using his own address as the return address.	100% accuracy	6/10	

continued next page

REFERENCE SKILLS

Objective	Test goal	Target date	Date met
Given a list of 6 words with the same first letter, alphabetizes the list.	100%	6/10	
Given a passage of 3-6 paragraphs with readability of 5th grade or below, will read the passage and outline it, identifying the topic of each paragraph.	One error or less	6/10	
Using a map and scale and ruler, finds distances.	75%	6/10	

MATHEMATICS

Objective	Test goal	Target date	Date met
Number and number sense: Identifies place value for each digit in a whole number expressed through millions.	80%	6/10	
Rounds whole numbers to nearest 10, 100, 1000, 10,000, and 100,000.	80%	6/10	
Computation: Finds the product of two whole numbers when one number is two-digits and the other is three-digits.	75%	6/10	
Subtracts 4 digit number with 3 regroupings.	75%	6/10	
Multiplies 2 digit x 1 digit with carrying.	75%	6/10	

continued next page

MATHEMATICS *(continued)*

Objective	Test goal	Target date	Date met
Divides 3 digit number by one digit number.	75%	6/10	
Computation with fractions: Converts fractions to lowest terms.	75%		
Adds unlike fractions.	75%	6/10	
Measurement: Tells time to the minute.	100%	6/10	
Recalls equivalences between units of time.	75%	6/10	
Converts between units of time expressed in one or two units of measure [e.g. hours and minutes to minutes].	75%	6/10	
Converts English units of length.	75%	6/10	

Your Homeschool is More Than Remediation

When homeschooling a special needs child, sometimes you may be tempted to spend all your energy on catching up areas of weakness, but you need to work on other areas: science, history, art, music, drama, and life skills, for instance. You won't do them all in a week or a year. You have the freedom as a homeschooler to choose what to work on this year. What you work on will be affected by the time and energy you have. (For example, did you just move, or do you have a new baby or a toddler?) Other points to consider:

- What topics did the child study in school last year?
- If you homeschooled last year, what did you not finish and why? What do you learn from this? Do you need a new approach?
- What does your child enjoy? What is she good at? If your child

loves animals, look at science, nature study, zoology. If math is her forte, use math puzzles, games, and books to do along with her regular lessons. If she loves stories, supplement your social studies with biographies and folk tales.

- Lessons in art, drama, music, or sports can be a great addition to your homeschool. They get you out of the house, they can give you a short break, and they encourage responsibility by having the child be responsible to another adult to practice, show up on time, and bring materials. See chapter 23.

- Look for unexpected opportunities that may come your way during the year. Does your spouse have a business trip somewhere you want to take the whole family? Change your studies for a few weeks and learn about where you are going.

- Perhaps a visitor from overseas can spend time in your home. You may want to spend time before or after learning about their country, trying the food, building a map out of paper mâché, or listening to stories from that country.

- Is there a special event you want to build on—a family reunion, your town's bicentennial, or a special cultural event? One homeschool family swapped homes with a New Zealand family for an unusual educational vacation.

Planning Your Year

Once you have purchased, found, or made materials and curriculum, and decided your main goals for the year, you are ready to plan the year. Rest assured you will change your plan, so don't worry about making it perfect. Also be assured this becomes much easier after the first year or two.

Check the law in your state or province for number of days of homeschool required in a year. (More on homeschooling legally in the next chapter.) Some states require 180 days. Next, look at your calendar and think what is best for your family. For our homeschool, I settled on thirty-six weeks of homeschooling (36 x 5 = 180 days). For my planning, I divided that into four quarters of nine weeks. You can divide those days differently: three twelve-week terms, or six terms of six weeks, for instance.

You can set your school calendar to start and end when you like, not necessarily September to May or June. You may want a year-round approach and take a three-week break between quarters.

Consider when to take your vacation, even if it is a "staycation" at home. Since you are in charge of your school calendar, you can vacation in the off season if you like. Some vacations are so educational you can consider them school. (If you doubt that, look at the out-of-town trips your local schools take students on.) If your child has a parent on military deployment, you will want your vacation time when that parent is home. Set your school weeks when you like.

A long summer vacation sometimes causes students to forget too much, so you may prefer to break it up with some school. Our family cut school back in the summer to about two hours a day, focusing on reading and math so my son would not lose ground. But I took my special education consultant's advice and made sure we had at least two weeks when we did not even do remedial work.

Consider the effects holidays and vacations have on your children. When he was young, my son was incapable of doing any serious work from mid-December on, for about three weeks. He was so excited about Christmas and his January birthday that he was completely distracted. I planned lighter school work for those weeks, with extra crafts (making ornaments, presents, and cards for others). We took advantage of special holiday events, like an annual model train exhibit in town. Holidays are a good time to review and practice social skills, such as being a good host and getting along with relatives. Those need to be taught explicitly and repeatedly to some children, so plan time for that.

Once you have worked out a rough idea of when you will teach, begin trying to divide the work into quarters or terms. You might divide your twelve chapters of math, for instance, into three chapters per quarter or one chapter a month year round, then review the contents and make adjustments to allow for extra time for the parts you expect will be harder, or the times you expect to be less productive.

Because you will probably want to change the plan, it will be easier to revise if you type it on a computer. You also can use a computer to set up your SEP as a table (see Table 15.1), which makes editing and completing it easier.

In public school, it was our experience that many targets (called goals on the IEP) were not met, but having them spelled out gave the staff priorities. They copied unmet targets over to the following year. You can, too.

Once you have planned the activities to work toward your SEP targets, go on to plan to meet your other goals. If you have planned, say, a year of geography, there are several ways to divide it. If you are using a textbook or workbook, you can simply divide the number of chapters. Then from that make a rough schedule, making sure to end units before vacation breaks. If you are not using a textbook, consider the content you expect to cover and resources you have, so you can divide it into chunks. For instance, if you are planning a year of state history, but you cannot find many resources on the early nineteenth century, don't spend much time on it. If you live near interesting historic sites, spend extra time on their time periods.

If you are using textbooks, remember that you may not have to cover every chapter. Some homeschoolers feel obliged to, but publishers write textbooks to satisfy the textbook requirements of different states. So they sometimes include a few extra chapters, which you might omit. If you are awarding high school credit, completing an entire book can be one way to award credit. But check with your state or provincial homeschooling organization, which can keep you abreast of the law and local homeschoolers' experiences with it.

Once you have gone through all the subjects you are planning to do in a year and divided them into quarters, divide the work again into weeks for the first quarter.

Make a rough schedule for yourself. If you aim to finish three chapters of math in nine weeks, that means about one chapter every three weeks. But be realistic. If you know already that fractions have been hard for your child, allow extra days for them. You may know you will get less done certain times of year. Allow days for testing and review and re-testing. In the next chapter, I will discuss planning your individual weeks and days.

Whatever the form of the weekly plan you create, look at your SEP and other goals every month or quarter and see how you are doing. You

may realize that three chapters a quarter in math is unrealistic, or discover
that one chapter required five weeks. You can always readjust.

Conclusion

Your plans—the SEP, the other goals, your rough schedule by quarters, and
your weekly plans—exist to serve you, not to discourage you. Now that I
have spent a chapter telling you to plan, let me urge you not to be chained
to your plan. Don't let your plans spoil the fun by pushing your harder
than you can manage or keeping you from ever stopping to take a day off
for a family outing. Be flexible. Be reasonable. Focus on helping your child
mature and enjoy learning.

Resources

Student Education Plans

- **Joe and Connie Sutton's** book, *Strategies for Struggling Learners:
  A Guide for the Teaching Parent*, helps parents with all kinds of
  special needs. (Simpsonville, South Carolina: Exceptional
  Diagnostics, 1997.) Their chapter on developing curriculum
  discusses how to write your own SEP, which they call an IEP.
  Available from heav.org.
- Visit **Judith Munday's** website for guidelines in writing your
  SEP, www.hishelpinschool.com/. For the most detailed help,
  get her book, *The Student Education Plan: A Preparation Guide.*
  Chesapeake, Virginia: H.I.S. Place, 2007. Available from heav.org
- **Sharon C. Hensley's** book, *Home Schooling Children with Special Needs*
  (Vancouver, Washington: Noble, 2001), has a chapter on "The
  Individualized Home Education Plan," reflecting her experience
  as a homeschooling mother, special education teacher, and home-
  school consultant.

IEP Guides may help you write your Student Education Plan
Although the items below are written for people creating IEPs for public
schools, you may find some ideas you would like to use.

- Office of Special Education and Rehabilitative Services, U.S. Department of Education. *A Guide to the Individualized Education Program.* July 2000. Accessed March 8, 2007. www.ed.gov/parents/ needs/speced/iepguide/index.html
- An online data bank of IEP goals is available at www.bridges4kids. org/IEP/iep.goal.bank.pdf

  "The Goal Bank has been designed to allow users to locate specific goals. … Content areas include: English, Functional Academics, Independent Living, Mathematics, Mathematics Readiness, Motor, Recreation and Leisure, Self-management and Daily Living, Social Emotional, Speech and Language, Study Skills, and Vocational/ Career Education."

16

Starting Up Your Homeschool

Before you begin homeschooling, there are some final details to arrange.

In this chapter:
- Homeschooling legally
- Documenting your child's progress
- Your personal records
- Managing time
- Tools for planning
- Managing the environment
- Leaving school
- Helping your child make the transition to homeschool
- Advice from homeschoolers for beginners

Homeschooling Legally

Before you begin homeschooling, learn how to homeschool legally.
States and provinces differ on what they require. Check the law yourself.
(Nothing written in this book should be construed as legal advice.)
Do not rely on hearsay or even on your local school district office. The
websites of the Home School Legal Defense Associations (HSLDA)—in
the United States, www.hslda.org; in Canada, www.hslda.ca—display the

legal requirements for each state and province. Your state or provincial homeschool organizations also may track changes to the law. Typically, the authorities require notification each year that you are homeschooling, and some annual indication that your child is making adequate progress.

HSLDA has special recommendations for parents of children with special needs, which I recommend you review fully. In brief, they are to "arrange for regular evaluations and document your child's progress" and "obtain assistance in meeting your child's special needs."[1] If your child has significant difficulties or had an Individualized Education Plan (IEP) in public school, this advice is especially important, but is helpful for anyone with a struggling learner. See chapters 7 and 8 on evaluation and assistance.

Showing Evidence of Your Child's Progress

How to document your child's progress depends on where you live. The most common methods required by law are to submit standardized test scores, an evaluation, or a portfolio.

Standardized Test Scores

Many states allow homeschoolers to demonstrate their children's progress by submitting scores from a standardized test approved by the state, such as the Stanford-9, California Achievement, or the Iowa Test of Basic Skills. If your state or province permits it, having your child take a standardized test is probably the easiest and cheapest method, if your child can pass. In chapter 20, I will explain how to help your child prepare for a standardized test. Make sure the test you choose is one your province or state will accept.

Some school systems will let homeschooled students take tests in a school at public expense. It may sound like a bargain, but if your child does poorly, the district still grades the tests, sees the scores, and in some cases, may put your homeschool on probation. If you have your child tested privately instead, and he does poorly, you can choose not to submit those results and find another method to demonstrate progress.

The test publishers and services that grade tests have different requirements for administering them, so inquire. Ask other homeschoolers in your area what tests they use. Ask testing services about whether your student is

1. Home School Legal Defense Association. "Two Steps for Defending Your Special Needs Homeschool." Accessed July 28, 2008. www. hslda.org/strugglinglearner/ sn_TwoSteps.asp.

eligible to receive accommodations for special needs students, such as extra time, a recorder (adult who fills the answer sheet as the student dictates), a reader to read test questions aloud, and a quiet, isolated room.

Once you receive the scores in the mail, if they meet the state requirements, you can mail them in. If not, there are other ways to show progress.

Evaluation

If your state or province permits, you may hire an education consultant to evaluate your child's progress and write a report for you to submit to the government. Find out what the law requires of an evaluator and ask your state or provincial homeschool organizations to suggest an evaluator with experience with special needs students. Talk with evaluators by phone or e-mail first to learn what to expect. An evaluator may work with your child, perhaps give some tests one-on-one and review schoolwork you have saved. If you have a special education consultant who already knows your child, that may be the person best equipped to know what constitutes good progress for your child.

Portfolio

In some states you can submit a portfolio, with samples of your child's work and perhaps "a log, made contemporaneously with the instruction, which designates by title the reading materials used,"[2] as in Pennsylvania. In some places, you must meet with a school district representative who reviews your portfolio. You may want to include copies of documentation of your child's special needs, so that his progress is appreciated in light of his difficulties. Submitting portfolios is free, but you depend on the opinion of the school employee who reviews it; while with an evaluation, you can read the evaluator's report before you send it in.

Other Options

Again, the laws vary by state and province, and they change over the years, so be sure you understand what is required. Do not rely on hearsay or the options I have listed above—they may not be legal options where you live.

In some areas, homeschoolers may enroll their children in *umbrella schools* (also called cover schools or independent study programs). These

2. Christian Homeschool Association of Pennsylvania. "Read the Law." Accessed July 28, 2008, from http://www.chapboard.org/start/law.html

organizations serve homeschoolers by helping with planning, record keeping, and meeting legal requirements.

Your Personal Records

Aside from any legal requirements, you should keep records of your child's progress. Keep some record of your instruction and some work samples, even if you do not intend to submit a portfolio or an evaluation.

Since I was never sure my son would pass the standardized tests, here is what I did. Using my old weekly plans and my calendar, I wrote a progress report, about two pages long. I wrote a paragraph on each subject, and an introduction covering anything special that did not fit into one subject and any unusual circumstances that affected my son's progress. Writing these reports made me review our accomplishments, which always looked better in hindsight, and encouraged me.

If you do not like writing, or if your state requires a log, you can keep one in different ways. One mother uses a computer spreadsheet. Check with your state or provincial homeschool organization to learn what is accepted by the authorities where you live.

To collect work samples, choose them as you go along. Again, check with your state or provincial homeschool organization, or a consultant they recommend, to see what is required. Don't make it a bigger project than needed. One way is to take a three-ring binder, label dividers for each subject, put a few samples in each section every month. Include samples of everyday work, as well as tests, reports, and creative writing. Take photos of field trips and of samples of work you cannot fit in the binder. Include programs from concerts and plays your child saw or participated in. Start at the beginning of the school year, so that you can contrast the early work with the work at the end of the year.

Managing Time

The way you manage time during your homeschool will depend on your teaching style, your personality, and your child's personality and needs. Many children do well with a structured schedule; it suits some parents better, too. It can help a child feel more comfortable, knowing what to expect, and it can help parents stay focused. One parent advised, "A schedule is important. Start with an easy one and stick to it."

I am not suggesting homeschool lessons should never run over the planned time. Many parents I interviewed said being able to change the schedule was a major advantage to homeschool. They appreciated being able to deal with behavior problems immediately, stop a lesson to re-teach material rather than "waste fifteen minutes with my daughter doing half the worksheet wrong," or just notice a child is distracted and give them "time to run, to climb a tree, or roll down a hill," as Marcia in Maryland said, adding, "I have my finger on the pulse, I can stop, repeat, and ask questions."

How do you manage the schedule for a rigidly inflexible child? I asked the parents I interviewed with children with autism spectrum disorders (ASD) how they encouraged flexibility. (Not all children with ASD have difficulty with changes in schedule.) One mother occasionally lists school assignments on paper, then cuts them into strips and puts them in a jar. Her son reaches in and pulls out a strip to find his next task. She also discovered he copes with schedule changes better if he sees them written out, such as "Doctor's appointment at two today." Two other mothers do not assign subjects to regular hours. They merely block off certain hours as "learning time" or "computer time," and within those hours, these parents regularly change the order of subjects. Parents of children who struggled with change found the best practice was to warn the child of changes ahead of time and remind them often.

Before planning your schedule, consider your child's best times of day. Selena, who homeschools two struggling learners, says for her older daughter, "We do math first, because she finds it the most stressful, and piano next because it's easy for her. The rest of the day we have two plans we follow on alternate days," covering language arts, history, sewing, and other areas, delving into new subjects as they come up. Several parents start teaching later in the day, either because their children have sleep problems or are night owls.

Consider the child's needs. You may need to schedule breaks every twenty minutes, as Lauren does (see sidebar), or as Marcia said above, you may need to watch and decide when to your child needs a break.

Flexibility and Planning

Lauren started homeschooling her son with Asperger Syndrome at age eleven. After he began his education in an elementary school that she calls "wonderful and supportive," she could not find an appropriate program for middle school. Her school district, she reported, has "a good self-contained program and large collaborative classes, but nothing for a child like mine who doesn't fit either mold." Lauren talked with me about their schedule:

For my son, there are off days when the information is not getting in. No matter what happens in the front of the classroom, his brain is not engaged. He lost out on that information when he was in the school system. Now on truly off days, we can do art, or go to the park, or study photography, and save the book work for days when his brain is ready. …

My son can be truly productive for about fifteen or twenty minutes without a break. Our day is structured, in blocks of thirty minutes: twenty minutes of instruction, and a ten minute break. …

When the current obsession takes over his brain, I have to wait until he comes to the natural conclusion before we can move on. One of the joys of homeschooling is having all day to get it done. …

We use a Day-Timer® to schedule subjects and breaks during the day, and this year, for the first time I put him in charge of planning his day.

While he is doing well with planning his days when she gives him his list of assignments, she still has to talk through any schedule changes.

As you plan a schedule, build in activities outside the home. We will discuss those activities in chapter 23, but here I will remind you to include time for them.

Try to include these five basics every day:

- Read aloud to your child.
- Have your child write something every day—something you do not correct.
- Exercise—both of you.
- Spend time outdoors.
- Make time for imaginative play. (You or a sibling may need to help your child.)

Tools for Planning

You have a choice of tools to help you plan your weeks. Like some other beginners, I began with a *teacher's planning book,* from a teaching supply store. While it made me feel professional, the main advantages were that this spiral-bound book was portable (so I could work on it at the pool, on the sidelines during soccer practice, or anywhere) and it let me see an entire week at a time, with a column for each day and a row for each subject. One problem with a teacher's planning book is changes may force you to draw lots of arrows or to erase and recopy.

For me, homemade *teacher planning pages on the computer* were a better tool. With cut and paste tools, it was easier to change or repeat activities. The downside to this was not having it bound in a book, so only this week's printout was portable, unless you own a laptop computer.

As said in the sidebar, Lauren used a *Day-Timer® weekly planner* for her son's schoolwork. When he was thirteen, she switched to giving him a list of the work to be done, and let him set the schedule. This is a great way to teach time management.

Online planners are available, too. One friend with struggling learners recently started using one at www.home-school-inc.com and writes, "I am really pleased with the tools—adding course schedules, printing out daily assignments, and blocking out vacation days."

Whatever tool you use to plan, your child should see the week's schedule. Each week I copied ours on a whiteboard, so we could see at a glance what time we needed to leave for classes or appointments. Around grade eight, we moved to a paper version.

Managing the Environment

Just as your schedule will vary with personalities, teaching styles, and your children's needs, so will the setting of your homeschool. Some families set up homeschool rooms; others teach all around the house.

Consider your child's needs. What distracts or annoys the child most at school? One homeschooling father said his daughter was distracted by "humming lights, the vacuum, the janitor mopping the floor, even the floor waxer at the other end of school." A mother said her son could not tolerate the smells. Two others said their sons need absolute silence to work. If the child is distractible, is it visual or auditory distractions that bother him most? You can help him learn what distracts him by keeping a log, as Steve and Marianne Garber and Robyn Spizman describe in their book, *Is Your Child Hyperactive? Inattentive? Impulsive? Distractible?* [3]

Here are some examples of how different families adapted their homes for homeschooling:

- Donna, who homeschools three boys, one diagnosed with ADD/ADHD and learning disabilities (LD), turned one room into their homeschool room. Setting an area for schoolwork sent the message, "We don't play here." Each boy has his own desk, turned so his siblings are not in his line of sight. While studying, the boys listen to music on headphones, which filters out distractions.
- Brandi, whose fourth-grade son needs absolute quiet, also homeschools his siblings. He could not work with them in the same room, so she explained:

  I allow him to do his schoolwork in his bedroom at his desk. I try to give him the next small assignment, and say "Please go to your room and complete it. If you need help, I'm right here." He is not allowed to go onto the next assignment until the first is completed. Then he comes back to me for the next small chunk. He is gaining

3. Gerber, Stephen W., Ph.D., Marianne Daniels Gerber, Ph.D. and Robyn Freedman Spizman. Is your Child Hyperactive? Inattentive? Impulsive? Distractible? Helping the ADD/ Hyperactive Child. *New York: Random, 1990.*

some responsibility for time management. He knows that if there is something he wants to do later that day, he's got to get the work done.

- Nafisi said:
  I took a tri-fold display board [available at office supply stores], cut it in half horizontally, connected the ends back to back, and made a cubicle for two of my sons who sit at the same table. I didn't have posters on the walls. I didn't want too much distraction for David [her son with ADHD and LD]. But I used that cubicle to post spelling lists, multiplication charts, things that he needs to refer to. But the main purpose was to limit visual distractions. One of his brothers is a year younger, but works at a more advanced pace. So the cubicle limits competition and distraction.

  I also use a CD that plays alternative-type music at an even tempo to improve concentration.

- Pat takes a different approach:
  It doesn't matter if she's bouncing on the trampoline in the middle of winter [in New York] while you're shouting words from the kitchen. As long as she's shouting the words back, you're good. Her spelling has improved seven grade levels since she left public school [three years ago]. So who cares if she's bouncing on the trampoline!

- Bonnie's homeschool is also on the move. Her teenage son has autism, sensory integration disorder, borderline mental retardation, and other conditions. She reported:
  My husband said, "You must not be homeschooling any more. I never see you at the kitchen table." Now we homeschool on recliners, on the couch, on the bed, on the rug, in the backyard, in the gazebo. Our city has a therapeutic recreation center, where my son takes cooking classes, tae kwon do, and other sports.

Visual Distractions

While Nafisi built partitions for her sons out of display board, there are other ways to prevent visual distraction. A discarded appliance carton can be cut into a cubicle. You can purchase study carrels, desks with three sides extending up from the writing surface, to shield your student from visual distractions. Or you can buy a portable study carrel made of corrugated board from several companies online.

Nafisi also limited visual distractions by limiting what was on her walls. Some homeschoolers like to create a school room lined with posters. But posters can distract. You must watch to see what distracts your child. When I started homeschooling, we used a table facing glass doors. I saw a calm forest scene, and thought, "No street, no cars, it's peaceful, it's perfect." My son looked out and saw squirrels, swaying trees, and birds. We moved to the dining room where sheer curtains screened the view.

Furniture

As I said in an earlier chapter, homeschoolers do not need to replicate school at home. But child-sized desks and chairs can be helpful. If your child is distracted by his feet not touching the floor, look for a good sturdy chair and a desk or table the right height for him. Some children like the sensory stimulation of wrapping their legs around a chair's legs. If your child is distractible or has sensory processing difficulties, you might try wrapping a bungee cord around the chair legs to give a child something to press against. Several parents I interviewed have their children sit on exercise balls instead of chairs, finding the work of balancing helps the active child settle down.

If your child is working on the floor, give him a good surface to write on, a large clipboard, a lap desk, or something else large enough to be convenient.

Storage

Homeschoolers always seem to need shelves—and not just for books. Many families organize teaching supplies in plastic bins or crates on shelves. Some families give each child one shelf. Let your child help you arrange storage of his books and supplies in a way that makes sense to him—so it will be easier for him to keep it organized. Keep supplies near where they are used. Make sure you have enough pencils, pens, and erasers. You can organize subjects by color, putting the math book in a green cover and the math papers in a green binder, for instance. You also can buy colored file folders. Use folders, file boxes, and files to keep your papers organized. It is easier to organize as you go along. Homeschool conventions often have workshops on organizing your homeschool and can help you with storage ideas.

Lighting

To avoid eyestrain, make sure the area where your child works is well lit. Watch for glare from windows or bright light reflecting off tables and paper. Earlier I mentioned fluorescent bulbs buzzing annoyingly. Some people, including some on the autism spectrum, are bothered by their flickering. Even people who don't notice a flicker may get headaches or eyestrain from fluorescent lighting. If you cannot switch to incandescent or halogen bulbs, you can lessen the effect of the flicker by switching to fluorescent lights that cycle 120 times per second (120 Hz). Or you can put an incandescent or halogen lamp on the desk or table.

Sound

If your child is distracted by sound, try earplugs or headphones. *In Heads Up Helping!*, Melinda Boring describes how foam earplugs not only help her children focus, but help her as well. They use them whenever they notice sounds are distracting them. She also suggests trying headphones or earmuffs.[4]

A few families I interviewed play music as their children work, generally calm instrumental music. Donna's boys listen to instrumental music of their own choosing on headphones. But Anna, whose son also has ADD/ADHD, had a different experience:

> *Brendan wanted to listen to music. I would have Christian music or classical music on early in the morning, and then I'd turn it off or leave it on in the background when he was doing math. He convinced me one time to do a test where we would try different types of music. With the loudest, heaviest beat, he did the best. It was*

4. See "Chapter 4, Auditory Distractibility" of Melinda L. Boring's book, Heads Up Helping! Teaching Tips and Techniques for Working with ADD, ADHD, and Other Children with Challenges. *Victoria, British Columbia: Trafford, 2002.*

*just amazing to see the difference. Total silence always produced the
worst performance. He knew what he needed.*

You, too, may need to experiment to see what helps your children.
As one mother said, "Don't think you are a bad person if they can't sit at a
desk and listen to Mozart while doing math."

Leaving School

If your child is in school, talk with him about the possibility of homeschooling. Unless you are sure he is mature enough to keep a confidence,
don't tell him too early that you have decided to homeschool—and have
him blurt it out at school months before you are ready. Wait until you are
prepared to meet the legal requirements and nearly ready to begin. You may
find it easier to finish out a school year, making your preparations while
the child is in school and not telling him your definite decision until he
is home for the summer. But several families I interviewed faced difficult
school situations and withdrew their children midyear.

Withdraw from school as cordially as possible. Though you may have
had frustrations dealing with the school and be longing to tell someone off,
there is no point in making enemies. Some homeschoolers found school
staff supported their decision to withdraw their children and homeschool.
Some school staff even provided assistance. But even if the faculty is hostile,
responding civilly to them leaves a better impression and makes it possible
for you to communicate should you ever need to.

Helping Your Child Make the Transition to Homeschool

As you are planning the transition, help your child adjust to the new idea.
It may take time. Don't expect him to be enthusiastic from the start. Even
if he knows families who homeschool, he may have no idea what to expect.
Tell him a little about it, and that there are many ways to do it. Explain
what it isn't: it is not school-at-home, and it isn't play all day, either. Don't
give your struggling learner the impression that homeschooling will solve all

the problems. While you don't want to bore him with all your research and planning, do let him know you are preparing.

Point out the advantages of homeschooling casually. One selling point for my son was that he could play with his Legos® during recess at home. After we started, he said he liked not having to wait while his teacher explained things he understood to the rest of the class. One boy whose father is an airline pilot liked being able to be home the days his father was. Parents I interviewed thought the biggest advantages were being able to customize curriculum to their children's interests and needs, adapt the schedule, take breaks when needed, incorporate movement and hands-on learning, go on more field trips, rekindle a love of learning, and be together more as a family. Some of these advantages may appeal to your child.

If your child is concerned about social life, first of all, listen—don't contradict. If you had moved, your child would need time to make friends, and in a sense, you have moved—out of the school community and into the homeschool community. Remind him it takes time to make friends. Arrange play-dates and opportunities as you can. Take him to homeschooling events, so he can meet other homeschooled children. Your child might feel lonely at his first homeschool activity and generalize: "I'm interested in _____. No one at the homeschool picnic was. Homeschooled kids are boring." Keep working at it. (See chapter 23 on developing social skills.)

If your child has become discouraged by school, several families recommend you take time to *deschool*. Deschooling is a relaxed time of transition without formal instruction, used to rekindle a love of learning. When you deschool, you arrange frequent field trips and visits to the library. You provide art supplies, music, and good books, and read stories aloud, creating a rich educational environment at home.

One parent said:

> *Go light the first year and get to know how your child learns, what are the likes and dislikes, what time of day works better for the child. Keep an open mind about learning. This is not school at home. Take it slowly and one day at a time. Avoid overloading the child. School can continue year-round. This allows for shorter days or weeks and takes care of the summer break lack-of-retention problem.*

Another recommended, "Especially when just out of school, deschool first. You can use the time to think about your philosophy, look at styles of homeschooling, then pick curriculum." A third said, "Center on what's important to the child, and truly most important to you, even if it has nothing to do with academics. Back off the first year. Develop the relationship. Make it a joy."

Advice from Homeschoolers for Beginners

As I interviewed sixty-four parents for this book, I asked them what advice they had for beginners. Despite the wide differences between their children, they agreed on many points:

"The biggest thing holding people back [from homeschooling] is wondering how to start. Fear holds them back. It's not as hard as they think. It's okay not to know everything. I have to learn and relearn things."

"Relax. Enjoy your child with all his faults, and with all his gifts and talents. Because trying to fight what is, is just going to make everyone stressed."

"The first year is going to be awful. Stick it out."

"Tell your relatives, 'Homeschooling doesn't mean we can drop everything and go wherever you want or baby-sit for you. We have obligations.' Let them know what to expect."

"People get overwhelmed very quickly. Go slow. Don't feel you have to do too much. As time goes on you realize you can do more. Keep it positive. Don't let a bad day set you back."

"It is certainly not without setbacks, failures and frustrations. But the joy on their faces when they get what you're teaching them, and helping them be who they are supposed to be in life, makes the difficulties pale."

"Don't worry what everyone else thinks. It's just like being pregnant; everybody has advice."

"Capitalize on their strengths. That's where they are wired to learn."

"Take time to play, pray, and enjoy him—he will be grown before you know it. Strive to make learning enjoyable."

"Consistency—not quantity—leads to quality. Slow and steady wins the race."

Conclusion

Now that you have arranged to homeschool legally, thought about how to document your progress, drafted your first schedule, decided what space you will use and how, and planned your transition, you are ready to begin. In the next four chapters, we will look in detail at how to help struggling learners with math, reading, writing, and study skills.

Resources

Barnier, Carol. *How to Get Your Child Off the Refrigerator and On to Learning.* Lynnwood, Washington: Emerald, 2000.

Boring, Melinda L. *Heads Up Helping! Teaching Tips and Techniques for Working with ADD, ADHD, and Other Children with Challenges.* Victoria, British Columbia: Trafford, 2002.

Home School Legal Defense Association. "Two Steps for Defending Your Special Needs Homeschool." Accessed July 28, 2008. www.hslda.org/strugglinglearner/sn_TwoSteps.asp.

HSLDA.org also lists testing services, including the one I used, below:

Seton Testing Services rents and scores the California Achievement Test-E for homeschoolers. 1-800-542-1066 www.setontesting.com/

Who dares to teach must never cease to learn.
John Cotton Dana

Part IV

Teaching at Home

17

Math Problems

I have taught regular and gifted math classes in public school and small homeschooled classes for teens. Some of my students had great ability, others had learning problems, and some had both at once. What best qualifies me to write this chapter, however, is that for grades four through twelve, I homeschooled a bright student who hated mathematics, had disabilities in reading, writing, and mathematics, and was extremely distractible. We survived. You can, too!

In this chapter:
- Symptoms of math difficulties
- What causes math difficulties?
- More severe problems
- Attitude toward math
- Tackling math facts
- General math strategies
- Accommodations
- High school options

I am indebted to Drs. Brock and Fernette Eide, authors of *The Mislabeled Child*, and to Dr. Bjorn Adler, author of *What is Dyscalculia?*, for helping me better understand symptoms and causes of math difficulties.

I recommend the Eides' book[1] to all parents of struggling learners, and Dr. Adler's[2] to anyone who wants a detailed look at math disabilities.

Symptoms of Math Difficulties

Symptoms of math difficulties can appear in early childhood, in the elementary years, in adolescence, or in adulthood.

In early childhood, most children begin to develop number sense, an idea of the meaning of number. Children begin learning numbers by rote, pretending to count: "one, two, three, five, eleventeen, twenty." As they develop number sense, they understand that "4" means this many: * * * *. Number sense is more than just knowing what the word "four" and symbol "4" mean, however. Children should be able to use their number sense in different ways.

- Counting: A child can usually count four objects by age four, and fifteen objects by age five.[3]
- Comparing and contrasting (larger/smaller, taller/shorter), and sorting objects by shape or size. A child should be able to look at groups of four hearts, four suns, and three moons, and tell which group is smaller. Children also use number sense to match number with amounts (e.g., "Which group has three things in it?").
- Distinguishing shapes by the number of sides. When my son was four, his pediatrician drew a diamond (a rhombus) and asked him to copy it. Pete drew a triangle. He could not see the difference between the three- and four-sided figures. The doctor suggested that I watch for learning problems.

For some children, symptoms of learning difficulties in math do not appear until the elementary years. Here are some symptoms of trouble:

- After the preschool years, continuing to reverse digits and symbols signals possible problems. Examples include writing or reading 6 for 9, 24 for 42, or < instead of >.
- Difficulty with number sense, such as trouble understanding the idea of quantity and place value, or trouble learning when and how to add, subtract, multiply, and divide, and how to borrow and regroup.

1. Eide, Brock, M.D., and Fernette Eide, M.D. The Mislabeled Child: Looking Beyond Behavior to Find the True Sources—and Solutions—for Children's Learning Challenges. New York: Hyperion, 2006.

2. Adler, Bjorn, Ph.D. What is Dyscalculia?, Malmö, Sweden: Cognitive Centre, 2001.

3. Eide and Eide, op. cit., p. 409.

- Trouble recognizing groups and patterns. For example, if I show you an array of spots, like this:

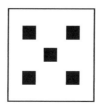

and ask you "How many spots?", you could say "Five," without stopping to count.
- Difficulty learning math facts (although this does not guarantee a learning problem).
- Very uneven performances. Is it common for your child to be able to solve a math problem one day, but to have forgotten how the next?

In *The Mislabeled Child*, Drs. Eide and Eide devote a chapter to math problems. In it, they note the following signs of difficulty:

- "Handwriting that suggests spatial impairments, such as irregularly or incorrectly formed numbers or symbols, poor spacing, or unusual spacing on the page"
- "Using inefficient strategies …, difficulty learning … new strategies"
- "A tendency to get lost in the middle of a problem"
- "Problems with pacing, working either too fast and inaccurately or too slowly to complete"
- "A tendency to ignore or skip problems without noticing"
- "Trouble showing work, either because of handwriting problems or because, 'I don't know *how* I know the answer—I just know it.'" [4]

Sometimes symptoms of learning problems in math only appear in teens and adults. If a teen has been muddling along without a good grasp of math facts, getting by with secretly counting or adding, her problem may become obvious only when she moves on to advanced math. She may have trouble grasping the math vocabulary she needs. In addition, secondary school success in math requires the ability to follow algorithms, which are step-by-step sets of instructions. (One example of an algorithm students learn early is long division.) Beginning in algebra, students are expected to

4. *Ibid., pp. 409-411.*

learn many more algorithms quickly. Having trouble learning or showing the steps of a complex process can be disastrous in high school math.

Some students may find it hard to visualize patterns or to identify relevant parts of problems. For example, suppose they learn that a linear equation can be written $y = mx + b$. When different variables or numbers are used (such as $y = ax + b$, or $y = 3x + -2$, or $y = x/2 + 7$), they may have difficulty seeing that the pattern is the same. Problems can also arise when the left and right sides are switched, as in $3x + -2 = y$.

What Causes Math Difficulties?

Not all problems in math are caused by a learning disability in mathematics. As I describe difficulties, think about what is hard for your children in order to find the best strategy to help them. You may need to observe your child and ask her questions about doing math. For more serious difficulties, you should have your child tested for learning disabilities, so you understand better what is hard for her and get advice on how to help her. Some causes of math disabilities are:

- *Long-term memory problems* cause trouble learning and remembering math facts, such as $7 \times 6 = 42$, formulas like $a^2 + b^2 = c^2$, or steps in a process, such as how to simplify a fraction.
- *Trouble understanding math concepts and the language of mathematics* make it hard to interpret a problem, deciding whether to add, subtract, multiply, or divide, or which formula to apply. Some children have trouble grasping the most basic ideas, when they should reason, "Ten men got on the bus; six got off—oh! That's subtraction."
- *Difficulties in planning* cause students to get lost in a math process, (such as long division, or learning to tell time), or to try one approach, fail, and get stuck. Some children find it hard to organize what they need on paper. Having trouble keeping track of the relevant parts of the problem and the method to use may mean the student has a problem with executive function or working memory.
- *Trouble keeping a sequence of steps in order* can make procedures such as changing fractions to decimals or factoring a polynomial harder.

- *Lack of good teaching* makes some children seem to have a math disability.
- *Trouble processing language* makes it hard to understand directions. But it is interesting that some children can work around language processing in math because they may understand a process by following examples. For some, math symbols and mathematical patterns are easier than words.
- *Trouble reading* leads to trouble understanding written directions.
- *Trouble with visual-spatial relationships* makes it hard to see size, shape, relationship, telling a pentagon from an octagon, recognizing which is the numerator and which is the denominator, and so on.

A learning disability specifically in mathematics is sometimes called dyscalculia. Danish neuropsychologist Bjorn Adler, author of *What is Dyscalculia?*, defines it as "a group of related and highly specific mathematical learning difficulties."[5] According to Adler, most children who have dyscalculia have pure dyscalculia, but twenty to thirty percent also have dyslexia. He says children with dyscalculia have normal intelligence, but may have "spectacularly uneven results in intelligence tests."[6]

Adler has another useful category. He defines pseudo-dyscalculia as inability in math arising from "emotional blocking"[7]—a mental block. The student has experienced so much failure that she is convinced she cannot do math.

More Severe Problems

Some difficulties in math, such as continued difficulty mastering counting, are beyond the scope of this chapter. See the resources at the end of the chapter.

Attitude Toward Math

So how do you bear with tackling math facts again, when your child didn't get them for the last four years? First, work on your attitude. You are not a failure because she did not get them and neither is she! For her to learn to be patient with herself, you must demonstrate patience. Keep perspective:

5. *Adler*, op. cit, *p. 12.*

6. *Ibid.*

7. *Ibid., p. 13.*

when my son was in third grade, I was sometimes tempted to panic: "He can't count change. Not even McDonalds will hire him!" But there are gainfully employed people who need calculators. More importantly, life is more than math facts. Review chapter 5 to help you adjust your attitudes and assumptions.

Next, work on your child's attitude. Listen to how she talks about herself in math.

Lots of people hate math or find it painful. But for people with learning disabilities in math, it can be a source of terror, despair, and a sense of worthlessness. Remind her of prior successes. Praise the way she does not quit, which is a quality that will serve her well all her life. See chapter 24 on encouraging your child.

Tackling Math Facts

Now, down to the business of working on those math facts: addition, subtraction, multiplication, and division:

- Find the time of day that is best to drill.
- Limit the practice time to about five or ten minutes a day.
- Choose activities that involve different senses.
- Present several ways to practice and let the child pick which way to drill that day.
- If you are giving a worksheet, make it challenging, but something at which she can succeed. Don't exhaust the struggling learner. Rather than assigning a whole page, let her do half, to finish three rows, or to work for a set number of minutes. But do not make it a race, and do not make the time limit so short it is stressful.
- Many struggling learners do better if the printed problems are enlarged.
- Remember that one of the hallmarks of learning problems is uneven performance, so take the slower days philosophically.

Here are some ways to drill:

- *Flash cards* can be bought or hand-made. You do not have to get though the whole deck every day. You can let the child win the cards she answers correctly, and when you are through today's part of the deck, go back for a second chance to win those tougher cards.

- Triangular flash cards let you practice both addition and subtraction. For example, the triangular card for 3 + 7 = 10 would have 3, 7 and 10 each in a different corner. (If you make these, you might write the sum, 10, in a different color.) Cover the 10 with your hand to practice 3 + 7, and cover the 3 to practice 10 – 7, and cover the 7 to practice 10 – 3. Sometimes seeing these "fact family" numbers together helps children learn the related facts: 3 + 7 = 10, 7 + 3 = 10, 10 – 7 = 3, and 10 – 3 = 7.

- *Learning Wrap-ups* [8] are products that let children match problems with answers by wrapping a string around a plastic strip. This makes a great hands-on drill, which children can check themselves. The same company makes *Learning Palette*, another hands-on way for children to drill and check themselves, but one which requires less hand-eye coordination than Wrap-ups.

- Modest prizes such as M&Ms® or Skittles® can be an occasional reward for good work. (These are rewards, not bribes. It is not bribery if it is given for something they are supposed to do.)

- *Simple, homemade board games.* You will need two ten- or twelve-sided dice, preferably each die a different color. (You can get these at a game store.) Draw or type a grid of one hundred squares, ten by ten, labeling each square with one number, one to one hundred, with one through ten on the first row, eleven through twenty on the second, and so on. (If you type this "hundred chart" on the computer, save the file; you can use it again.)

  This chart becomes your playing board. Each player has a token to move, starting from number one. The object is to get to one hundred first. When it is your turn, roll the dice, add the two numbers aloud, and move that many spaces forward. When it is not your turn, check your opponent's math as she adds. Variations of this game include subtracting instead of adding, and, later on, letting one of the dice represent negative numbers.

- Your child can also practice math facts with flash cards while bouncing on a trampoline or jumping rope. Do not do this if the movement adds to the tension.

- Math computer games and online games let your child practice drilling. Some of these games also will produce worksheets you

8. www. learningwrapups. com

can print. One mother I interviewed recommended *Flashmaster*, a hand-held game for drilling math that her sons enjoyed.

- Before you teach multiplication (and as you review it), practice skip counting. Skip counting is counting by fives (5, 10, 15, 20, …), threes, fours, or any other number. Start with skip counting by twos and fives. Count up to ten times the original number, then skip count backwards. For instance, counting backwards by nines would be: 90, 81, 72, 63, 54, 45, 36, 27, 18, 9, 0. There are several ways to make this more fun. Our favorite was to march around the house, taking larger steps for larger factors, like eight and nine, baby steps for skip counting by twos, and walking backwards as we skip-counted backwards. Some other ways to practice skip counting are to sing along with skip-counting tapes, produced by several different companies.

- Print some more of your hundred charts and have your child circle the multiples of five one color, four another color, and so on. Talk about the patterns.

- RightStart Mathematics makes a versatile set called the Math Card Games Kit, with three hundred games in one box. One mother told me, "RightStart stays fresh and interesting, and it amazes me how much more the kids retain in the games!"

- Stories are an effective way for some children to learn math facts. My first exposure to this was the book, *Addition the Fun Way*, by City Creek Press, (citycreek.com). Numbers are characters in a story. For example, one story ends, "When 5 is with 6, remember Five-Who-Drives takes Six-Who-is-Sick to buy an 11-Popsicle."[9] City Creek also makes *Times Tables the Fun Way*, and other related products. Other programs that links math facts with stories are from Dianne Craft: *Visual Number Cards for Teaching Addition* and *Right Brain Multiplication Cards*.

- Parents have told me their children love to make up and illustrate their own silly stories or songs to remember math facts.

- Finger math appeals to some children. One example is Chisanbop, the Korean method, which is explained in several websites and books. Some of you may know an example of simpler finger math:

9. Rodriguez, Judy. Addition the Fun Way. Minneapolis: City Creek, 1996. p. 58. citycreek.com.

the nines trick. To do this, put both hands palms down on a table. To multiply nine by four, start at your left pinky finger and count over four fingers, to your left pointer finger. Fold that finger down and you will see you have three fingers to the left of it, six to the right of it (your left thumb and all five fingers on your right hand). That "three-six" means the answer is thirty-six.

Experiment and see what methods your child likes. If none are fun for her, at least find the drilling methods that are least painful or stressful.

General Math Strategies

What about the rest of elementary mathematics? How do you keep your child going? Remind her of the objectives you are working on and what the big picture is. You might help her make a transition to new material this way: "So far we have been adding fractions and subtracting fractions with the same denominator, but sometimes we need to add fractions that have different denominators. First we are going to learn how to transform them so they have the same denominator, then we are going to add them." You may need to say that every day as you build a new skill.

If you give pretests, explain why: "This is so I know where to start teaching." To ease the pressure, tell her to give her best guess. When you give tests afterwards, explain why.

If the curriculum you are using does not seem to work for your child, consider using one of these curricula: RightStart Mathematics, Moving with Math, Making Math Meaningful, or Math-U-See. These programs incorporate many hands-on activities. Details on where to find these materials are at the end of the chapter.

Another approach is to take your child back two or three grade levels as you switch curricula. A homeschooling friend says moving down a few levels relieved her children, because it made math easy enough that they stopped hating it. It gave them a better foundation and filled in gaps. They were able to do a year's worth of math in a few months and now have advanced to their current grade level.

One of your math goals should be to ease your child's anxiety to help her succeed. If we are anxious, we cannot learn. So play math games every day. Enjoy patterns—play with pattern blocks and look at the Fibonacci sequence, the Golden Rectangle, perspective and scale drawings and enlargements, and the drawings of Escher. See the end of the chapter for a few resources. These same resources can help you fight boredom by breaking up your math lesson.

When possible, make math multi-sensory, full of hands-on activities. Here are some examples.

- We always practiced money math with real change—much more exciting.
- When I first taught integers, positive numbers were navy beans, negative numbers were pinto beans. Positive and negative numbers cancel each other out, "like matter and anti-matter," as Harold Jacobs says.[10] This is sometimes an excuse for dramatic sound effects when I teach. So positive 5 (students sets out 5 "positive" beans) plus negative 3 (pause for the student to pair off 3 of the positive beans with 3 negative ones, making 3 small pretend explosions as the pairs cancel each other out and are swept away) leaves positive 2.
- Sometimes we used the staircase as a number line to add and subtract integers on: stairs to the basement were negative; the stairs going up to the bedrooms were positive.
- Supplement fraction work with hands-on materials like fraction circles and fraction bars to help children see what a third of a circle looks like, or that five-tenths equals one half.[11]
- To teach multiplication and area, buy one-inch square ceramic tiles or make some out of cardboard. Then draw a three by five inch rectangle and let her see by counting that it takes fifteen squares to cover the entire surface. Let her keep practicing with different-sized rectangles, and gradually move her towards seeing that those three rows of five make fifteen, that three times five equals fifteen, and that length times width equals area.

Does your child feel overwhelmed by a page of problems? Cover up half the problems with a piece of cardboard. Alternatively, cut a window in a piece of paper that allows her to see only one problem at a time.

Watch for and explain sources of confusion. For example, the numerals 2 and 4 can be written different ways, and fractions can be written with a

10. Jacobs, Harold. Elementary Algebra. *New York: Freeman, 1979. p. 121.*

11. *These are circles or strips of plastic or cardboard, divided and shaded to illustrate many fractions, everything from halves, to tenths or twelfths. They are available in some teacher supply stores and from rainbowresource. com*

diagonal fraction bar (like ½) or with a horizontal one. Arithmetic problems can be written vertically or horizontally. These two decimals are equal: 0.5 = .5. Watch for other differences in notation.

Sometimes when your child is struggling, you try a different math book. If you do so, watch carefully for changes in terms that may confuse your child. For any change in terminology, stop and explain and give a few examples. For instance, if you use *Video Text Algebra*, and your child already knows what a variable is, you need to say, "In *Video Text*, variables are called 'placeholders.'"

You may need to spend more time teaching estimating than most math books do. For example, "Dividing a number by a whole number makes it smaller. So 8/2 = 9 is not a reasonable answer, because we started with eight, but got a larger number. Half of 8 can't be 9."

Teach rounding and practice it often. For example, ask "Want 3 t-shirts at $11.99? That is about $12 each. Don't know your twelves tables? Three times ten is thirty, so the shirts will cost more than $30."

If a child does not see that 3 + 5 = 8 and 5 + 3 = 8 are related, point out that saying "Mom and Dad" and "Dad and Mom" means the same thing. Reinforce this principle, called the commutative property, every time you practice. When teaching multiplication, use tokens or counters to show the commutative property: three rows of four equals four rows of three, for instance.

Once you have taught a concept in a way they understand, repeat it often with the same words: "Subtracting a number is the same as adding its opposite." Sometimes I use nonsense words to stress patterns: "The inverse of three-fourths is four-thirds, the inverse of nine-tenths is ten-ninths, and the inverse of blip-blopths is blop-blipths."

If you are using a textbook or computer-based instruction, make sure that the child can follow the flow of the text or website easily. Beware of programs that require a lot of reading. You may want to read directions aloud to your child, or have her read them aloud to you, and discuss what the directions mean.

Teach math vocabulary clearly and review it often. I call this learning to speak "Mathlish."

Accommodations

How can you move beyond the times tables when your child has not mastered them? For a learning disabled child, you should not spend five years working only on arithmetic facts. Many children who struggle with math facts can work more sophisticated problems. Some people with doctorates in math and sciences have trouble with subtraction, but not with calculus or writing proofs. Math is not merely arithmetic. Here are some accommodations, ways to work around areas of weakness to get the job done.

If your student struggles with math facts, give her a times table or an addition table. Drill daily, but when she is not drilling, let her look up the answers to help her do other math. Some parents report their children learned the facts by looking them up repeatedly. It is also less stressful than agonizing over one fact for two minutes. Some people like to cross out the answers they no longer need to see. You can make a pocket-sized version for the older child. Some parents laminate the chart.

Teachers (and parents) disagree about using calculators. Some feel it prevents children from learning facts, or that there is a stigma associated with needing a calculator. The fact that calculators are allowed on college entrance exams ought to have lessened the stigma. One option is to let a student who has had long-standing trouble learning math facts use a calculator to help only with simple arithmetic. For example, a student can use a calculator for each step of long division or algebra, rather than typing in the complete problem. Examples are on my website at www.LearnDifferently.com.

For the child with planning problems, who has difficulty remembering how to solve something she could do last week, or who gets lost in a sequence, it is best for the child to write her own math manual.[12] Every time she masters something that was hard for her, whether it is adding two fractions, changing fractions to decimals, or any new process, have her write out a page or two for her math manual. This will be a memo to herself about how to solve this kind of problem. Discuss with her what ought to be on the page. Make sure she includes enough information so that it will make sense when she refers to it, even months later. Have her illustrate her directions to herself with one or two examples. Store these directions she

12. I am indebted to special education consultant Lynn Kuitems Henk for this suggestion.

has written in a special loose-leaf binder, her math manual. The beauty of this is that she can read an explanation that makes sense to her and reminds her that she can do it. It will boost her morale.

Memory aids, called mnemonics, can also help a child learn these processes and other math tricks. Mnemonics can be rhymes like, *"To multiply 2 fractions, it's easy if you've got'em. Just multiply the top, then multiply the bottom."*[13] Search the Internet for "math mnemonics," and you will find other useful aids, including how to sing the quadratic formula to the tune of *Pop Goes the Weasel.*

Train your child to watch for reversals. I know dyslexic adults who are successful computer network administrators and accountants. They know what kind of mistakes they are prone to and they have trained themselves to proofread carefully.

If your child has writing and organizing problems, buy graph paper, make large print graph paper with your word processor, or turn regular notebook paper sideways and use the lines to keep the columns of digits aligned.

Provide plenty of review. Look for curricula with lots of practice and frequent review sections, preferably daily reviews. *The Key To …* series of math booklets are a good supplement to your math program and are very inexpensive. Their measuring and geometry books are especially good for children with fine motor difficulties. My son worked through all their geometry booklets before taking high school geometry. I am convinced that is why he had no difficulty with any of the constructions (bisecting angles, constructing an equilateral triangle without a protractor, and so on) that befuddled my other students. *Blueprint for Geometry* is also a good preparation for high school geometry.

Whatever curriculum you use, you may still need to prepare some daily review to fill in some gaps. I wrote index cards for my son for elementary math. We would work through ten or twenty cards a day in five or ten minutes. One card asked him about how many days there were in three different months, another card asked about the freezing and boiling points of water in Fahrenheit and Celsius, another asked him to use a calendar to figure out what the date would be six weeks from now and four weeks ago, and another asked what time it would be in forty-five minutes, in two

13. Barnier, Carol. "Rhythms that Work—Day Three." Sizzle Life e-mail, November 26, 2006. To subscribe, visit sizzlebop.com.

hours, and so on. Make cards to cover whatever areas your child most needs help in that are not covered in your other math materials.[14]

High School Options

For struggling learners, your first thought for high school may be consumer math. Everyone should learn how to keep and balance a checkbook, pay taxes, figure tips, pay bills, calculate discounts, and choose insurance. Resources for teaching these are at the end of the chapter.

While considering those worthy goals, consider that some people who struggle with arithmetic can handle higher mathematics such as geometry, algebra, and calculus. Here are some other suggestions for high school math:

- Harold Jacobs' books, *Elementary Algebra; Geometry: Seeing, Doing Understanding;* and *Mathematics: A Human Endeavor* include review in every lesson, plenty of exercises, humor, and puzzles that require creative thinking. *Mathematics: A Human Endeavor,* subtitled, *A Book for Those Who Think They Don't Like the Subject,* is an excellent book not only for struggling learners, but gifted students, too. Covering logarithms, permutations, probability, statistics, and topology, this unusual book is designed to help readers "understand and enjoy mathematics, without having to find square roots, or memorize the quadratic formula, or prove geometric facts."[15] After a few weeks in this book, my son announced, "I thought I hated math, but I don't. Math is cool. I just hate algebra."

- Consider video courses. Animations can be helpful. Videos don't mind repeating themselves dozens of times, and they may help your child be independent of you, but a video cannot reword the explanation when your child does not understand.

Five courses to look into are *VideoText, Math-U-See, Great Courses, D.I.V.E.,* which coordinates with *Saxon Mathematics,* and *Ask Dr. Callahan,* which coordinates with Jacobs' algebra and geometry books. Watch their demonstrations online, or order the demonstration DVDs. Talk with the companies about your child's specific difficulties before you invest. Also look at the tests provided.

14. Courtesy
Lynn Kuitems
Henk.

15. Jacobs,
Harold.
Mathematics:
A Human
Endeavor. *New
York:* Freeman,
1994, p. xii.

Multiple choice tests are easy to grade, but they can encourage students to guess, rather than to complete the problems.

- *The Geometer's Sketchpad* is software developed by Key Curriculum that allows students and teachers to easily create various geometric figures and observe properties. The software can be used to teach not only geometry with the textbook *Discovering Geometry: An Investigative Approach*, but also with Key Curriculum's entire program, from Algebra I to Calculus. While the activities are designed for groups, the tools in *Geometer's Sketchbook* can help hands-on learners understand concepts.
- *Saxon Mathematics*, a program for grades K-12, includes regular review and is well organized and comprehensive. Its approach appeals to some students who like predictability and structure.

Other accommodations for high school are available, including continued use of a calculator or multiplication tables. Remember your child does not have to do every problem in the book. (Textbook authors include lots of problems for students who need extra practice.)

You might hire a tutor to give your child a new voice and perspective from which to learn. If you do, keep your distance so that the tutor can develop rapport with your child. Sometimes your child's frustration may come partly from her awareness that she is disappointing her parents. A tutor can give her a fresh start with a difficult subject. When a friend of mine offered to teach my son from *Mathematics: A Human Endeavor* while she taught her son, it gave us both a break. That led to his success in my geometry class the following year.

Conclusion

Math difficulties have a variety of causes, so you must determine what exactly is hard for your child. Testing can help. Watch your attitude and your child's. Keep the workload manageable and help both of you reduce stress so she can relax enough to learn. Praise perseverance, be creative, and have fun with the patterns and beauty of mathematics.

Resources

For Further Reading
Brock and Fernette Eide's book, *The Mislabeled Child* has an excellent chapter on difficulties with math. (New York: Hyperion, 2006.)

Dr. Bjorn Adler's book, *What is Dyscalculia?*, is available free as an e-book from www.dyscalculiainfo.org. (Malmö, Sweden: Cognitive Centre, 2001.)

Mastering Math Facts
- *Learning Wrap-Ups* and *Learning Palette* from www.learningwrap-ups.com.
- *FlashMaster*, a handheld electronic device for practicing math facts, available from Sonlightcurriculum.com

Math Programs
- *RightStart Mathematics*, by Activities for Learning, makes K-3 curriculum and the Math Card Games Kit, a versatile set of 300 math games in one box. www.ALabacus.com
- *Moving with Math*, grades 1-8, www.movingwithmath.com
- *Math-U-See*, Steve Demme's K-12 series, mathusee.com
- *Making Math Meaningful*, by David Quine, Cornerstone Curriculum, K-6, plus algebra and geometry. www.cornerstonecurriculum.com/Curriculum/MMM/MMM.htm
- *Saxon Mathematics*. K-12. saxonhomeschool.harcourtachieve.com

Other Helps
- *Math on Call: A Mathematics Handbook* by Andrew Kaplan *et al.* (Wilmington, Massachusetts: Great Source, 2004), is a helpful reference book, not as good as making your own math manual, but handy and comprehensive.

- *Keys To … series (Keys to Metric Measurement, Keys to Decimals, Keys to Geometry*, etc.) provides simple, clear, inexpensive workbooks for review. These are good and inexpensive supplements. Do not

confuse these with Key Curriculum's high school algebra or geometry, listed below. Both are available from www.keypress.com

For Those With More Severe Difficulties

- TouchMath, by Innovative Learning Concepts,
  www.touchmath.com
- Semple Math, www.semplemath.com
- DeAnna Horstmeier's book series and related materials, *Teaching
  Math to People with Down Syndrome and Other Hands-On Learners*,
  (Bethesda, Maryland: Woodbine House, 2008).
  woodbinehouse.com

Fun Stuff

- Critical Thinking Books and Software, www.criticalthinking.com
- Any book of M.C. Escher's drawings is fun to look at and try to
  copy or take inspiration from.
- Carol Barnier writes regular e-mails with tips for parents of
  distractible learners; I quoted a rhyme from one in this chapter.
  To subscribe, visit sizzlebop.com
- Ellen Braun's free coloring book of 3-D patterns, *Twenty-Four Hours
  of Peace and Quiet*, an e-book available from www.raisingsmallsouls.
  com/coloring.html
- Harold Jacobs' *Mathematics: A Human Endeavor*. New York:
  Freeman, 1994.
- Games and pattern blocks are available from Timberdoodle,
  www.timberdoodle.com

Consumer Math Resources:

- www.mymoney.gov, basics about financial education.
- www.federalreserve.gov, "Publications and Education Resources"
  section.
- choosetosave.org
- irs.gov Search for "Teachers" or go to this link for lesson plans &
  resources on understanding taxes: how they work (application) and
  why (history) www.irs.gov/app/understandingTaxes/jsp/teacher_
  home.jsp

- Boy Scouts of America. *Personal Management* merit badge pamphlet. Available at libraries and from scoutstuff.org, under literature, see "merit badge pamphlets."
- Larry Burkett. *Money Matters for Kids, New Edition*, and *Money Matters for Teens, New Edition*. Chicago: Moody. 2001.
- Mary Hunt. *Debt-Proof Your Kids*. Los Angeles, DPL Press, 2007.
- Christine Field. *Life Skills For Kids*. Colorado Springs, Colorado: Shaw, 2000. See chapter 8.

Secondary Mathematics:

- Harold Jacobs' math books:
  Elementary Algebra. New York: Freeman, 1979.
  Geometry: Seeing, Doing, Understanding. New York: Freeman, 2003.
  Mathematics: A Human Endeavor. New York: Freeman. 1994.
- *Discovering* series of math textbooks and *The Geometer's Sketchpad* software, from Key Curriculum, www.keypress.com (800) 995-6284. Homeschoolers can buy a single student edition for less than $40.
- One parent recommended Algebra Lab Gear, a set of manipulatives for algebra. See author Henri Picciotto's website: www.picciotto.org/math-ed/index.html for details on what to order. Order from Creative Wright Group / McGraw-Hill by phone at (800) 648-2970 or online at www.wrightgroup.com/index.php/programcomp?isbn=0076033449
- D.I.V.E. www.diveintomath.com, 936-372-9216. These DVDs coordinate with Saxon Mathematics, listed above under "Math Programs."

- *Algebra I* and *Algebra II* in the series, *The Great Courses*, from The Teaching Company. One homeschooling parent wrote, "I am loving this because it doesn't focus so much on symbol manipulation as much as on understanding concepts. It teaches kids to use the graphing calculator."
  The Teaching Company
  4151 Lafayette Center Drive, Suite 100
  Chantilly, VA 20151-1232
  (800) TEACH-12
  www.teach12.com
- Dale and Lea Callahan's Ask Dr. Callahan series covers Algebra 1 through Calculus. www.askdrcallahan.com. The Algebra 1 and Geometry DVDs coordinate with Jacobs' *Elementary Algebra and Geometry: Seeing, Doing, Understanding*, described in this chapter.
- Also see *Math-U-See* and *Saxon Mathematics*, listed above under "Math Programs."

18

Reading Difficulties

For some children, learning to read was so easy that it seemed natural. For others, one-on-one help, practice, and time are the keys to success. When working with other students, however, "teaching reading is rocket science," as reading expert Dr. Louisa C. Moats writes.[1] Much has been written about reading, and I make no claims to expertise. In this chapter I lay out a few basics and point you toward the experts.

In this chapter:
- Components of reading
- What could be the matter?
- General reading tips
- Reading programs and therapies
- More help for the struggling learner: a multi-sensory approach

---

Components of Reading

Why is reading so hard for some students? We might ask why it is so easy for others, since reading is a complex task. To read we must do many things, including:

- Be aware of phonemes. Phonemes are meaningful units of sound in a particular language. (For example, in English, /l/ and /r/ are

From preceding page:
1. Moats, Louisa C., Ed.D. "Teaching Reading Is Rocket Science: What Expert Teachers of Reading Should Know and Be Able to Do." Washington, D.C.: American Federation of Teachers, June 1999. Dr. Moats is head of the Washington, D.C., site of the Early Interventions Project of the National Institute of Child Health and Human Development (NICHD), and clinical associate professor of pediatrics, at University of Texas, Houston, Health Sciences Center.

2. Wolf, Maryanne, Ed.D. Proust and the Squid: The Story and Science of the Reading Brain. New York: HarperCollins, 2007.

distinct phonemes, but in Japanese they are considered the same sound, and so native speakers of Japanese must learn to distinguish them when learning English.) Phonemic awareness is the ability to hear the difference between phonemes: both vowels (pin and pun) and consonants (numb and nun), singly and in clusters (stuck and struck, stark and stalk).

- Recognize letters: upper case, lower case, cursive, print, in different fonts.
- Recall the common sounds of letters. For example, when seeing the word "civil" for the first time, readers must recall the possible sounds associated with each letter or group of letters, beginning with c, which can either indicate the sound /k/ or /s/.
- Blend sounds into words, trying different possible combinations of sounds together, like this— /Kivil/? /Sivil/?—until the reader recognizes the second as a known word.
- Determine the meaning of individual words. If a word has two meanings, decide which is correct, as in "He couldn't bear to shoot the bear."
- Interpret idioms and figures of speech, such as "Jon let him have it," "Megan is taking Allyson under her wing," or "Stephen is up to his eyeballs in work."
- Read fluently, that is, with speed and expression.
- Read with comprehension. Readers must remember the first word of the sentence when reaching the last, hold all the words and their meanings together, and follow the thought of the author. Not only that, they must remember the flow of the paragraph, and the article or book of which it is a part.

I have scratched only the surface of what is involved in reading. For those interested in learning how we read from the standpoint of neurology and psychology, Tufts University Professor of Child Development Dr. Maryanne Wolf has written *Proust and the Squid: The Story and Science of the Reading Brain.*[2]

What Could Be the Matter?

Children have trouble learning to read for different reasons. Some children just develop more slowly than others. A few children read before age five. Others are not interested until age eight or nine. As discussed in chapter 7, late-blooming readers are not as common as some homeschoolers think.

Vision problems can cause reading problems. The early elementary years are often the time parents and teachers identify vision problems, and some children get their first pair of eyeglasses. Some parents become concerned with their children's ability to coordinate eye movements, tracking across the printed page from left to right. They may take their children to vision therapy (also called vision training), where some children are greatly helped (one I know personally), but others not at all. Even those who have benefited personally from vision therapy, like special educator Joyce Herzog, say that vision therapy will not help all the people who take it, and that there is no way to know who will benefit.[3] And vision therapy is expensive. The American Academy of Ophthalmology concluded:

> *To date, there appears to be no consistent scientific evidence that supports behavioral vision therapy, orthoptic vision therapy, or colored overlays and lenses as effective treatments for learning disabilities. It seems intuitive that oculomotor [eye movement] abilities and visual perception play a role in learning skills such as reading and writing. However, several studies in the literature demonstrate that eye movements and visual perception are not critical factors in the reading impairment found in dyslexia, but that brain processing of language plays a greater role.[4]*

That conclusion overlooks the possibility of vision therapy retraining and improving that brain processing. As with any alternative treatment, it is wise to wait for definitive, replicated research to be published. However, parents of struggling learners may want to experiment with alternative treatments. See chapter 9 for a discussion of how to evaluate them wisely.

Though some reading problems may stem from vision problems, others may spring from difficulty paying attention, from ADD/ADHD

3. Herzog, Joyce. "Rx For Special Needs." Indiana Association of Home Educators Convention, Indianapolis. March 23, 2007.

4. The American Academy of Ophthalmology. "Complementary Therapy Assessment. Vision Therapy for Learning Disabilities." September 2001. Accessed March 24, 2008. one. aao.org/asset. axd?id=ad1eb06f-b51b-4025-917c-7e2f25d55af9

or other causes. Sleep disorders and other health problems also can hinder reading. Learning disabilities, developmental delays, and other neuro-developmental problems can make reading a challenge, too.

If your child is having trouble reading, what do you try first?

General Reading Tips

Here are some common-sense suggestions popular with many homeschoolers and other parents.

Read aloud to your child daily. Before he can follow a story, you can read simple picture books. Ask him to point to objects in the book. Read rhymes. Enjoy language play and tongue twisters.

Keep reading as he grows. If he cannot sit still, don't make him. Let him stand, lie down, or wiggle. Homeschooling in California, Lois discovered that if her son "wants to listen to me reading his history, [while] standing on his head, that's perfectly fine. … This child answers my questions better if I let him play with his Legos® and read to him than if I make him sit still." Other parents provide quiet activities their children are allowed to do while being read to.

Read good literature to children. Their comprehension level is above their reading level, so do not limit yourself to their current reading level. Reading good literature builds their vocabulary. It stretches their imagination and helps them think from another's point of view. It exposes them to the world and universal truths.

Don't stop reading to them once they can read. Reading aloud is a great way to have family time together. You can help them improve their reading fluency by having them read along silently as you read aloud. (At one homeschooler's home, I spotted four or five copies of a dozen different books on her shelves. She collected them from used book stores, so several family members can read along when one reads aloud.) Discuss what you read to develop comprehension.

When you can't read aloud to your children, let them listen to a book on tape. Sometimes your child can read along, which also will help improve his fluency. Reading the same passage repeatedly while listening to it also helps.

Along with reading to your child daily, your child should read to you each day. I liked to vary between having my son read something that challenged him and passages that were comfortable for him to read. You can alternate reading paragraphs to each other, or even alternate sentences, which I did to force my son to focus and read along. Your child can read aloud to younger children who cannot read, or read the same passage to you several times, over several days, to build fluency. Your goal in this practice is to be encouraging and positive as they read, not to correct every error.

Many games have been invented to develop reading skills. Phonics cards can help you review common sounds. Carol Barnier's book, *How To Get Your Child Off the Refrigerator And On To Learning* (see the end of the chapter), has games that are simple, fun, and expandable. A simple home-made matching game can help your child learn the Dolch word list. This list of 220 words that should be learned early, compiled by Edward Dolch, includes many words that cannot be sounded out easily, like "said" and "blue." You can make a simple memory matching game by choosing five or ten of these words, writing each word on two cards, and arranging the cards, face down, in rows. You and your children can each turn two cards up at a time, and compete to find matching pairs, reviewing the words as you go.

Reading Programs and Therapies

I cannot possibly summarize or even list all the reading programs and therapies available, and if I did, the list would be out of date immediately. Ask your homeschooling friends what they have used. Read Joyce Herzog's and Cathy Duffy's lists, given at the end of the chapter.

With reading training and reading therapies, beware of charlatans. As one homeschooling parent told me, "Learning disabilities are big business." Every reading program will have stories of people who experience success, so consider the sources. Anyone can publish so-called research and give it an official sounding title. See chapter 9 on newer treatments and therapies, and look for approaches with results backed by independently verified research.

More Help for the Struggling Learner: Multi-Sensory Approaches

Suppose you have tried a traditional reading program or two, without success, and you suspect a reading problem. When you have your child tested, choose a psychologist who can refer you to local reading experts not only willing to help your child, but willing to help you teach your child. (See chapter 8 on choosing professionals.)

What kind of help does your child need? The National Institute of Child Health and Human Development (NICHD) of the U.S. National Institutes of Health recommends that children at risk for reading failure be identified early and "provided with systematic, explicit, and intensive instruction in phonemic awareness, phonics, reading fluency, vocabulary, and reading comprehension strategies."[5]

To understand this style of instruction better, the International Dyslexia Association (IDA) is a good source of information. The IDA includes professionals, dyslexics (people with a learning disability in reading), and their families. Its purpose is "to pursue and provide … information and services that address the full scope of dyslexia and related difficulties in learning to read and write."[6]

The IDA provides excellent information about effective instruction for dyslexics in two fact sheets, "Multisensory Teaching" and "Orton-Gillingham Based and/or Multisensory Structured Language Approaches." You will find both, and many others, at the IDA website, www.interdys.org; under "Information," click on "Fact Sheets." Here is an excerpt of the former:

> There is a growing body of evidence supporting multisensory teaching. … Young children in structured, sequential, multisensory intervention programs, who were also trained in phonemic awareness, made significant gains in decoding skills. These multisensory approaches used direct, explicit teaching of letter-sound relationships, syllable patterns, and meaning word parts. Studies in clinical settings showed similar results for a wide range of ages and abilities.[7]

5. Lyon, G. Reid, Ph.D. "Reading Disabilities: Why Do Some Children Have Difficulty Learning to Read? What Can Be Done About It?" Perspectives (The International Dyslexia Association's quarterly), Spring 2003, Volume 29, No. 2.

6. International Dyslexia Association. "About The International Dyslexia Association (IDA)." Accessed March 27, 2008. www.interdys.org/whoweare.htm

What do the experts mean by multisensory teaching? The same fact sheet explains:

Multisensory teaching is simultaneously visual, auditory, and kinesthetic-tactile to enhance memory and learning. Links are consistently made between the visual [what we see], auditory [what we hear], and kinesthetic-tactile [what we feel] pathways in learning to read and spell.

Margaret Byrd Rawson, a former President of The Orton Dyslexia Society (the precursor to The International Dyslexia Association), said it well:

Dyslexic students need a different approach to learning language from that employed in most classrooms. They need to be taught, slowly and thoroughly, the basic elements of their language—the sounds and the letters which represent them—and how to put these together and take them apart. They have to have lots of practice in having their writing hands, eyes, ears, and voices working together for the conscious organization and retention of their learning.[8]

A true multisensory approach is based on the pioneering work of neuropsychiatrist Dr. Samuel Orton, and educator and psychologist Anna Gillingham. Many programs quote IDA and NICHD materials and claim to be multi-sensory and Orton-Gillingham (OG) based. And some are, but others are not.

What kind of help your child needs depends on the severity of his difficulties. As I said above, some children respond well to individualized instruction at home using a traditional reading program. If that does not work, there are several OG-based programs you can use at home without prolonged training:

- *Alphabetic Phonics* by Aylett Royall Cox. Cox developed this from research with dyslexic children at the Texas Scottish Rite Hospital in Dallas. "Materials include a basic manual outlining lesson plans and procedures, a series of workbooks based on the lesson plans,

7. "*Multisensory Teaching.*" *Baltimore, Maryland: International Dyslexia Association, 2000. Fact Sheet #69-01/00. Accessed March 27, 2008. www.interdys. org/ewebedit-pro5/upload/ Multisensory_ Teaching.pdf*

8. *Ibid.*

tests for evaluating performance at each level, teacher reference books, drill cards, wall cards, and teacher's manuals."[9] You can download an overview from Educators Publishing Service, the publisher. Their website is epsbooks.com.

- Educators Publishing Service also offers an online course in the Orton-Gillingham approach. See epsbooks.com.
- *Reading Reflex* by Carmen and Geoffrey McGuinness. This mother and son team also provides a week-long training in their PhonoGraphix method through trainers around the country. ReadAmerica.net is their website. One parent I interviewed reported that her son's tutor uses the PhonoGraphix method and they have seen him make great progress.
- Barton Reading System. Susan Barton's program includes tutor training on DVDs and tutor manuals with complete, scripted lesson plans. See www.brightsolutions.us.

I have not used most of these programs, and have done no graduate work in teaching reading, so I urge you to investigate them further and consult with experts in your area. These programs will not help everyone; in fact, the professional who evaluates your child may advise you to move directly into programs that require more teacher training. You can hire a tutor to work with your child, hire a tutor willing to train you to conduct some of the training at home, or become a certified tutor yourself. A tutor's willingness to train you will depend partly on how well you follow directions, because these are complex methods.

There are several of these more intensive, multisensory, OG-based reading programs, including Slingerland, Lindamood-Bell, (used by one family I interviewed, but see the note at the end of the chapter), the Association Method (used by one family I interviewed, and used and studied at the University of Southern Mississippi DuBard School for Language Disorders), Wilson Reading System, and Multisensory Structured Language, which are described below.

These programs are expensive in time and money. I include them not only because parents I interviewed have seen them work, but also because I am seeing my adult son benefit from them now, and I wish he had started earlier. If your child has serious reading problems, you should not compare

9. "Alphabetic Phonics." Accessed August 27, 2008. epsbooks.com/ dynamic/catalog/series. asp?seriesonly=400M

the cost of your reading program to a traditional reading curriculum, but to the cost of enrolling your child in a private school designed for children with learning disabilities, or the cost of weekly or bi-weekly sessions with someone trained in one of these methods. As academic therapist Marilyn Zecher pointed out, some parents may want "drive-by training," an easy way to teach reading that they can learn in a two- or three-hour workshop and apply for the whole year. "But it really is rocket science. ... Homeschool parents have to think of themselves as professionals," Zecher explained.[10] Even one thirty to forty-five hour class doesn't give parents—or student teachers—the practice or experience equivalent to a fully trained reading expert. But with time and good training, parents can learn and become expert.

One program is the *Wilson Reading System*, a multisensory, OG-based approach. Wilson moves the student through twelve steps. You may find a Wilson tutor by contacting Wilson Language through their website, wilsonlanguage.com. You also can be trained as a Wilson tutor yourself, at either Level I, which qualifies you to teach the first six steps, or at Level II to be qualified to teach the complete program. To be certified, you must first complete a fifteen-hour introductory workshop on applied methods, then complete both online and seminar instruction, and finally a practicum of at least sixty lessons in which you work with a student under the supervision and observation of a Wilson trainer. Four of the parents I interviewed had completed Wilson training, and found it helpful, including Lily, who said:

> I had homeschooled because both public and private schools could not teach my son how to read. And I figured I could do no worse. He was nine years old and wasn't able to read at all. In one year's time he went from not being able to read to reading on the fourth grade level. You can teach a child to read if you can find the right things to do with him.

Wilson is no cure-all; that "right thing" varies with the child. Another option is a Multisensory Structured Language Education (MSLE) approach. (The International Dyslexia Association defined MSLE as "a generic designation of the shared characteristics of well-known Orton-Gillingham-based

10. Zecher, Marilyn M.A., CALT, Instructor, Atlantic Seaboard Dyslexia Education Center. Telephone interview. November 29, 2007.

approaches to teaching reading and language skills."[11]) Certified tutors are called academic therapists (AT). They have completed the equivalent of at least nine graduate credits in MSLE and the psychology of dyslexia. They also must complete one hundred hours of supervised instruction before they can take paying students. ATs have completed training at a center certified by the International Multisensory Structured Language Education Council (IMSLEC, see www.imslec.org). With additional study and supervised tutoring and a passing score on the national exam, academic therapists may become Certified Academic Language Therapists (CALT) and members of the Academic Language Therapy Association (ALTA).

I asked Marilyn Zecher how academic therapy differs from other structured reading programs. One key difference is that the approach "provides much more oral repetition, is more sensitive to a child's needs and sound production, and integrates input and output, not just reading, but writing."[12] Other differences are that rules are taught explicitly but incrementally, and reinforced until they become automatic. "We go as fast as we can, but as slow as we must," she explained.

You can locate an academic therapist by contacting altaread.org, or visit imslec.org to find an IMSLEC-certified training center near you. There you also can train to become an academic therapist yourself. Two of the homeschoolers I interviewed trained at Masonic Learning Centers for Children, which are IMSLEC-certified, and are located around the country.

Conclusion

Some children with reading problems will respond well to individualized attention at home, but others will need more explicit instruction. Teaching reading can be easy or extremely difficult. We may need sophisticated help, but we can get it.

All teachers—not just homeschoolers—who help children with severe reading problems need sophisticated instruction. In her 1999 paper *Teaching Reading is Rocket Science*, Dr. Louisa Moats explains why teaching practice has failed so many dyslexic students:

11. IMSLEC. "Questions often asked about IMSLEC." Accessed September 17, 2008. www.imslec. org/questions.html

12. Zecher, op. cit.

What drives the mind of the reader is neither self-evident nor easy to grasp, and, consequently, many years of scientific inquiry have been necessary to expose the mechanisms of reading acquisition. Only recently has basic research allowed the community of reading scientists and educators to agree on what needs to be done.

The demands of competent reading instruction, and the training experiences necessary to learn it, have been seriously underestimated by universities and by those who have approved licensing programs. The consequences for teachers and students alike have been disastrous. ...

This new information about language, reading, and writing is just beginning to shape teacher preparation and instructional programs. This knowledge must also form the basis of in-service professional development for practicing teachers.

The knowledge base for teaching reading is hidden, extensive, and complex.[13]

Since this approach is only beginning to shape teacher instruction, many students who need this multisensory, systematic reading instruction get it after school or not at all. One benefit of homeschooling is not having to cram it in after a long school day. Homeschooling gives parents the flexibility to make reading instruction based on the latest research the core of their homeschool.

Resources

Determining the Reading Level of Material
To learn the reading level of books your child can read or enjoys reading, you can use several approaches. One is the SMOG readability formula, another is the Flesch-Kincaid Grade Level Index. Microsoft® Word will calculate this as part of its grammar check function. To learn more about either SMOG or Flesch-Kincaid, see either www.hsph.harvard.

13. Moats, *op. cit.*

edu/healthliteracy/how_to/smog_2.pdf or uuhsc.utah.edu/pated/authors/
readability.html, which is adapted from McLaughlin, G. "SMOG grading:
A new readability formula." *Journal of Reading*. (1969), 12 (8) 639-646.

To Learn About Reading and Reading Problems
International Dyslexia Association, www.interdys.org, is a great source
of information. See the fact sheets: "Why Home School a Dyslexic
Child?" "Multisensory Teaching," and "Orton-Gillingham Based and/or
Multisensory Structured Language."

LDonline.org has many excellent articles.

Wolf, Maryanne, Ed.D. *Proust and the Squid: The Story and Science of
the Reading Brain*. New York: HarperCollins, 2007.

Tools to Help You Teach Reading at Home
Barnier, Carol. *How To Get Your Child Off the Refrigerator And On To
Learning*. Lynnwood, Washington: Emerald, 2000.

Educators Publishing Service, epsbooks.com, publishes excellent resources
including: *Alphabetic Phonics* program by Aylett Royall Cox, developed
from research with dyslexic children at the Texas Scottish Rite Hospital
in Dallas; *Explode the Code* workbook series by Nancy Hall, with their
amusing cartoons; and *Reasoning and Reading* by Joanne Carlisle.

Edward B. Fry has written two sets of workbooks, *Skimming and Scanning*
for teaching those sometimes-neglected skills and *Reading Drills* for
improving speed. (New York: Glencoe/McGraw Hill, 1999.)

Verticy Learning Academy Program is a homeschool curriculum for
children with language-based learning disabilities (LLD), developed by
The Calvert School, who have served homeschooling families for over one
hundred years, and The Jemicy School, which serves children with LLD.
www.verticylearning.org

Teaching Reading Comprehension

Goodman, Burton, *The Reader As Detective* series. New York: Amsco School Publications, 1994. www.amscopub.com

Critical Thinking Books and Software publishes excellent activity books in many subjects, including the *Reading Detective* series.

Progeny Press produces nearly a hundred different study guides for literature for kindergarten through high school, ranging from *Frog and Toad Together, Charlotte's Web,* and *In the Year of the Boar and Jackie Robinson* to *Hamlet, The Scarlet Letter*, and *Heart of Darkness.* These study guides are written from a Christian perspective. www.progenypress.com

General Guides to Choosing Curriculum

Duffy, Cathy. *100 Top Picks For Homeschool Curriculum: Choosing The Right Curriculum And Approach For Your Child's Learning Style.* Nashville, Tennessee: Broadman and Holman, 2005.

Herzog, Joyce. *Choosing and Using Curriculum.* JoyceHerzog.com, 2004.

To learn more about specific reading programs:

LDOnline.org has an excellent overview, "Multisensory Structured Language Programs: Content and Principles of Instruction," (1995), www.ldonline.org/article/6332

International Dyslexia Association, interdys.org, for a good, impartial overview of many programs and for help finding therapists and tutors.

International Multisensory Structured Language Education Council, www.IMSLEC.org, can help you find places to be trained as an academic therapist. Or you can contact the center nearest you to find a therapist.

The Academic Language Therapy Association, altaread.org, also can help you find academic therapists and training centers.

Wilson Language Training, www.wilsonlanguage.com, describes the program, how to train in it, and how to contact them to find a Wilson tutor in your area.

Lindamood-Bell publishes several excellent books and programs including *Lindamood Phonemic Sequencing® (LiPS®) for Reading, Spelling and Speech*, by Patricia Lindamood and Phyllis Lindamood; *Visualizing and Verbalizing*, and *Seeing Stars®: Symbol Imagery for Phonemic Awareness, Sight Words and Spelling*, both by Nanci Bell. One family I interviewed is using this method at home, based on these books. However, Lindamood Bell recommends you not do this at home without training, nor that you hire any tutor not affiliated with one of their learning centers. www.lindamoodbell.com

Barton Reading System: Brightsolutions.us. This website includes several videos by founder Susan Barton.

Other Resources for Students with Reading Problems
Franklin Electronic Publishers makes electronic dictionaries, the size of calculators, which help people who cannot spell to look up words. See www.franklin.com or chapter 20.

Kurzweil 3000 software reads text aloud. See www.kurzweiledu.com or chapter 13.

Bookshare.org and RFBD.org provide recorded books for those with disabilities. See chapter 13 for details.

Read: Outloud text-to-speech software and study aids. See www.donjohnston.com

19

Struggles With Writing

Writing is a complex task. Handwriting requires visual-motor processing and fine motor skills. Composing a sentence requires skills in spelling, mechanics (capitalizing the first word of a sentence, what to do with commas, and more), and grammar. Writing a longer passage—a paragraph, story, or essay—requires more organization. Whether your child has difficulty with handwriting, composing, or both, your approach should be two-pronged: *remediate* and *accommodate*. Remediation strengthens areas of weakness. Accommodations work around a weakness. You should do both.

In this chapter:
- Causes of writing problems
- Handwriting tips
- Accommodations for handwriting problems
- Bad penmanship, bad spelling, good writing
- Spelling, vocabulary, and grammar
- Writing tips
- Writing programs
- Accommodations for poor spellers

Causes of Writing Problems

Your child may struggle with handwriting for many reasons. It might just be that the child develops more slowly than her peers. A child with Asperger Syndrome may struggle to write neatly. It could be a vision problem or any number of learning disabilities: trouble with visual-motor processing, with fine motor output, or with recalling how to form each letter.

If the child has a problem with composing, it could arise from several causes. Learning disabilities in expressive language can make it hard to find words, to retrieve the right words from one's memory, or to construct a grammatical sentence. Some children with autism spectrum disorders may prefer writing to verbal communication, yet at the same time they may struggle with perfectionism, berating themselves for grammatical errors. An attention problem could make it hard for a student to organize her thoughts. A problem with working memory can make it hard to plan a paper. Even writing one paragraph requires that you keep in mind what the paragraph is about, what you just said, and what you are going to say. Some students have great difficulty remembering how to spell each word, even after many hours of drill. Other learning problems can make writing hard, too.

Handwriting Tips

Daily handwriting practice is important. How the child holds her pencil matters. The direction the pencil strokes are formed also matters. Praise her efforts. Let her see you write. If your young child is not interested in writing, you can develop weak fine motor skills by encouraging drawing. Having markers, colored pencils, or crayons, and decent paper can help. You can learn to teach drawing from Mona Brookes' *Drawing with Children,* or use books such as *Draw Write Now.*

If your child needs aid with handwriting, there are many programs to help. Families have recommended to me *Handwriting Without Tears* more than any other program. *Loops and Other Groups* is recommended by several occupational therapists. See the end of this chapter for details on these programs.

Should your child learn the standard vertical manuscript taught in most elementary schools, or a slanted alphabet, such as D'Nealian, which is a modified italic alphabet? D'Nealian is recommended by some parents and educators as being half-way to cursive, easing the transition later from print to cursive writing. But *ERIC Educational Reports* summarized research in 1997, in "Six Questions Educators Should Ask before Choosing a Handwriting Program,"[1] observing that:

Slanted (modified italic) letters are harder to write, using very complicated strokes for young children, requiring twelve different strokes, while vertical manuscript requires only four strokes.

Vertical letters are easier to read, and more closely resemble printed text.

There is no published research supporting the claim that learning to write a slanted alphabet actually eases the transition to cursive.

On the other hand, children who tend to reverse letters when printing may find learning D'Nealian or cursive eases those problems. For example, since the cursive "b" and "d" are formed very differently, the theory is that it is harder to confuse them.

Knowing more about handwriting development can help you see if your child needs help from an occupational therapist (OT). According to pediatric occupational therapist Laurie Chuba, the "skills necessary for writing readiness are:

- A consistent dominant hand.
- Able to use two hands together effectively.
- Separate shoulder movement from hand movement.
- Able to separate thumb and finger movement.
- Able to twiddle thumbs.
- Can turn over a line of pennies easily."[2]

The four stages of writing are "imitation (preschool), graphic presentation (ability to write letters, grades one and two), incorporation (writing without a model, grades two to three), and automatization (writing as an

1. "Six Questions Educators Should Ask before Choosing a Handwriting Program". ERIC Educational Reports. Accessed April 3, 2008. FindArticles.com. findarticles.com/p/articles/mi_pric/is_199700/ai_1090105665

2. Chuba, Laurie, OTR/L, "Learning to Writing and Writing to Learn," workshop handout, 2007. Learning Integrations. www.Learningintegrations.com

effective tool to be used to present other things, grades four to seven.)"[3] If your child is not meeting these benchmarks, an OT can diagnose handwriting problems and recommend exercises. Follow his or her instructions carefully. Look for an OT who does not think she or he is the only one who can provide therapy, but an expert willing to train you to be an assistant therapist at home.

Accommodations For Handwriting Problems

While your child should practice handwriting daily, a handwriting problem need not hold the rest of your language arts hostage, much less the rest of your homeschool. You can give some quizzes and tests orally, rather than adding the stress of handwriting to every subject. You child can tell her stories and assignments into a tape recorder; a parent or older sibling can transcribe them later. You can and should teach your child to type; there are several decent software programs available. *Dragon Naturally Speaking* dictation software will type for your child as she speaks into a microphone. As students type using *Kurzweil* 3000 software, the program speaks what is typed, to help the student spot mistakes. More software is listed at the end of the chapter.

Bad Penmanship, Bad Spelling, Good Writing

Handwriting and spelling problems don't need to stop your child from becoming a good writer. When I taught composition to a small group of homeschooled teens, one student hated to write. This puzzled me, because she was very articulate, loved to learn, and enjoyed expressing her opinions. Handwriting was what she actually hated, after she had been teased about her poor penmanship in a private school. After a lot of hard work, in a few months she decided she enjoyed writing—provided she could type.

The story of good writers overcoming difficulties is repeated over and over. Academic therapist Marilyn Zecher told me about novelist William Faulkner's writing practices:

3. *Ibid.*

He used to plot out his novels on three-by-five cards and pin them to the wall. And then he would take a card down each day and write that section. He couldn't spell anything. His secretary transcribed all of his work, because he couldn't spell. But look at the first two pages of his short story "The Bear," and you'll see sentences that go on for a paragraph, and they are grammatically correct.[4]

Faulkner was one America's great writers. Fine motor problems, spelling struggles, and organization troubles have nothing to do with whether someone has something to say and can learn to say it well.

Spelling, Vocabulary, and Grammar

There are many products for teaching spelling and vocabulary. One good spelling program for grades K-12 is *Spelling Power* by Beverly Adams-Gordon. Another parent recommended iSpellWell software, which speaks the words while teaching their spelling. A third uses *Sequential Spelling*, written by a dyslexic for other dyslexics. (See the end of the chapter.)

Some struggling learners are helped by a study of the Greek and Latin roots of words. Several publishers produce flashcards and workbooks to teach them. (I had thought this was too complex for my son with LD and ADD, but I was wrong. Now his academic therapist is teaching them to him. He loves it and enjoys explaining it to me.)

There are many vocabulary workbooks available. Educators Publishing Service produces a good series called *Wordly Wise*. Struggling learners may enjoy and benefit from *Vocabulary Cartoons: SAT Word Power* by Sam, Max, and Bryan Burchers, which uses cartoons, humor, and rhyme to teach vocabulary.

What about the child who does all the workbook exercises, but can't apply that knowledge to her reading? Reading and writing are excellent ways to improve spelling and vocabulary. Janet Allen's book, *Words, Words, Words: Teaching Vocabulary in Grades 4-12*, convinced me, by reviewing academic research, that the best way to make vocabulary stick is to teach it through the literature your child is studying.[5] In her book she shows how.

4. Telephone interview with Marilyn Zecher, M.A., CALT, Instructor, Atlantic Seaboard Dyslexia Education Center, Thursday, November 29, 2007.

5. Allen, Janet, Words, Words, Words: Teaching Vocabulary in Grades 4-12. Portland, Maine: Stenhouse, 1999. www.stenhouse.com

Like vocabulary, grammar seems best mastered when it is tied to the writing process, as in the *Writer's Workshop* approach described later. But an excellent foundation is provided in Paul R. Ervin's *Winston Grammar* series. It is a clear, hands-on way to teach the elements of grammar. Colored cards represent different parts of speech. Work with your child slowly through both the basic and advanced levels. Spend at least a year on each level. See www.winstongrammar.com for details.

Writing Tips

First, your child should practice writing daily. She should write something each day which is not corrected, just for the practice—and, I hope, the joy—of expressing herself. She can write in a diary about her day or her dreams, tell a story, tell or describe what she wishes would happen.

If she needs inspiration, appeal to her personality and her interests: let her write about her favorite hobbies or her friends. Let her be creative, telling the story of her day from the point of view of her cat, her shoes, or her pencil. Let her rewrite a scene in a favorite book from another point of view. If she struggles with point of view, as some children on the autism spectrum do, and has a passion for one subject, let her write on that subject. Harness her passion to help her practice.

Second, reading is one of the best ways to improve one's writing. Reading good literature exposes readers to new vocabulary, correct spelling, good grammar, and clear organization. It also helps readers appreciate a well-turned phrase, a vivid description, an apt metaphor. It stretches the mind. Your child's involvement in literature should tie directly back into her writing. Have her write about what she has read. Both the classical and Charlotte Mason approaches to education begin with copying well-written work, both as a handwriting exercise and to develop an appreciation for good writing. You may want to start there.

Third, be positive and encouraging as you review your child's written work.

Some homeschooling parents like me recall their own school essays coming back from their English teachers bleeding red ink, every mistake circled on the page, and comments written in the margins: "Wordy,"

"Vague," "Unsupported—give examples." Some parents worry that if they do not correct every mistake, then either their child will not learn, or the parent will be negligent. Neither is true, and a paper covered in red ink can make the child want to quit.

I thought if my son did not see all his errors uncorrected, he would continue in them. After years of working with my son and his learning disabilities, I realized that a few uncorrected mistakes are not going to reinforce bad habits: his reading problems are severe enough that seeing an uncorrected, misspelled word isn't going to ruin him. That freed me to be more selective about what I correct. Don't give your child forty-seven areas to improve in: she won't remember them all, and you will have trouble keeping track of whether she's improved in any. If she has much to learn, pick one or two glaring errors and focus on them.

To critique effectively, let the positive comments outnumber the negative ones. Find specific aspects of the writing to praise. Whatever they have written, you can find something to praise: an unusual perspective, legible handwriting, good choice of an adjective, a strong verb—something. Praise should be specific. Don't just write "Good job!" on the paper, say "Vivid description" or "Well-organized paragraph."

Encourage a positive attitude to rewriting. Some children imagine that books come straight out of an author's pen in final form. They have no idea of how much rewriting and editing most writing goes through. So they look at their first drafts and despair. "I can't write," they think. If, however, you emphasize that writing is largely rewriting and praise the improvements rather than expect every work to be perfect, you can help your child become a writer.

Writing Programs

Homeschoolers use a variety of writing programs. Here I will focus on a few.

To begin with the books that cover the basics, Diana Hanbury King has written the *Writing Skills* series, books that include handwriting and writing for grades two through adult. Based on her years of work with dyslexic students, she teaches systematically, ranging from pre-writing skills—like making lists and brainstorming—to parts of speech, kinds of sentences, and paragraph construction. See also Darlene Mannix's *Writing Skills Activities for Special Children*, which moves from writing words to sentences to paragraphs to longer projects.

Frode Jensen's book, *Jensen's Format Writing*, is also very structured, both in its format and in the format it proposes for students. Note that Jensen assumes the student can write sentences. He emphasizes organization even more than King and moves on to longer writing projects. Jensen begins with some good exercises on continuity and explores seven different kinds *(formats)* of paragraphs: example, classification, definition, process, analogy, cause and effect, and comparison. Jensen elaborates these formats much more than King. He gives examples of each sort and tells students how to organize them.

Jensen's approach is cut and dried, not exciting, but easy to follow. For each assignment, even for paragraphs, students write an outline. By outlining, writing and rewriting three to five of each of these, my son and his classmates in a small homeschool composition class mastered the formats. That work enabled them to move on to what I consider the core of Jensen's book, five paragraph essays, and proceed through the seven formats of essays in the same way. Each week my students were writing a first draft of one essay, revising last week's and outlining next week's. We met one hour a week, and they e-mailed some work to me midway between meetings. My son benefited from seeing that I was assigning all his classmates all this writing, and they all responded well. Jensen's book also gives good instruction on business writing, condensing, and writing major papers. I found this a helpful way to teach teens.

The principles of Jensen's approach apply to longer writing projects. Jensen tells the story of a former student who became a technical writer for Boeing. He found that writing books was "just more of the same but bigger. Once mastered, these writing techniques can be adapted to a variety of tasks no matter what the size or occasion."[6]

I know two homeschoolers with struggling learners who use the *Institute for Excellence in Writing* (IEW) program by Andrew Pudewa. Pudewa wrote the program for his son, who has learning disabilities. This program teaches parents how to teach writing; it is not a curriculum in

6. Frode Jensen. Jensen's Format Writing. *Grants Pass, Oregon: Wordsmiths. 2002. p. 116.*

that there are no workbooks for each grade level. Parents should begin by attending the IEW seminar *Teaching Writing: Structure & Style* or watching it on DVD; www.excellenceinwriting.com has details.

A fourth approach to teaching writing is the Writer's Workshop model, used in classrooms around the country, but easily adaptable for any age, and to the homeschool or homeschool group class. This approach is not a program you can buy, and its principles can be applied to other programs, so I will describe it in more detail. The philosophy of Writer's Workshop (WW) is that children are treated as writers more than as students. The student chooses the topic she will write on, which increases her interest. (I used this approach when teaching with Jensen, and whenever possible.) The WW approach is very encouraging and targets instruction to areas of need. It incorporates lots of revision. The emphasis is more on the process than the finished product.

The WW approach should be used at least four times a week, about an hour each time. It begins with a mini-lesson, a five- or ten-minute lesson on a point of grammar, mechanics (such as punctuation or capitalization), or composition with which your children struggle. This is an approach that lends itself to working with children of different ages. You might use a grammar book such as *The Little, Brown Handbook, Write Source 2000,* or *Writers Inc.* as a basis for these mini-lessons. Use a good grammar workbook to give your child practice with the rule you have just taught.

Next comes a quick check of your children's projects to see where in the writing process they are. The stages are prewriting (brainstorming), writing first draft, first conference, revising, second conference, student edit, teacher edit, and final.

Then the children write or revise for about ten to sixty minutes, depending on their ages. The parent or teacher meets with any students who need to confer. Conferences enable the adult to help the student assess her own progress, with guiding question such as, "What were you trying to say?" "What would make this a better paragraph?" "Can you think of a stronger verb to use here?" A conference takes only a few minutes. Teachers praise improvements and good techniques. If they make suggestions it is only one or two ideas, at the end of the conference.

Writer's Workshop in a classroom ends with "Share time." If you are teaching more than one child, give them each a moment to discuss their stories and their progress.

Because WW emphasizes the process more than the product, it develops good attitudes in writing and allows some freedom. A child may decide not to complete a project. Younger students may make illustrated covers for their books. A child or a teacher may want more than two rewrites. Students may have peer conferences instead of teacher conferences, giving them practice critiquing each other's work. For peer conferences, I grade the child who does the critiquing. I don't grade her on whether she found every mistake, but on whether she had constructive criticism and found something positive to say.

I learned this approach from Diana L. Thomas, who now teaches writing in live, online classes via the Potter's School (www.pottersschool.org). She writes,

> One of my favorite "how to write" authors is Ralph Fletcher. How Writers Work *and* A Writer's Notebook *are terrific resources for students and teachers—short and easily accessible. He has also written a book on WW. It's called* Writing Workshop— The Essential Guide.[7]

Accommodations for Poor Spellers

If your child struggles with spelling, there are several easy ways to help her continue to work without her spelling interfering. It is good to work on spelling, but like a handwriting problem, spelling should not hijack your writing program.

- Spelling dictionaries: While most of us think a dictionary is the place to learn how to spell a word, spelling dictionaries are easier to search through, since they don't contain definitions. Several publishers make children's versions, including *My Word Book* and *Words I Use When I Write*, available from Educators Publishing Service.

7. Thomas, Diana L., e-mail to the author, June 2, 2008.

Encouraging the Struggling Writer

Whether you use WW or not, imitate their practice of praising, teaching students to edit their own work, and seeing rewriting as essential and a good process, not a sign of failure. Denise, homeschooling three children in Florida, gets help from Brave Writer Online Writing Services (Bravewriter.com), the website of Julie Bogart, which offers books, online classes, and other help for parents teaching writing at home. Denise writes about one way she has encouraged her children to write:

> *Food for thought—one of the things I've noticed from Bravewriter. com is the amazing power of food. Bravewriter suggests tea time for poetry reading each week. It is expanded for us. Now we have "tea time," or snacks, with copywork [copying passages by good writers] and freewriting as well. My kids so look forward to this time each day, that they practically beg to write—and this was the area of most resistance for us! The subject we do at tea time is one we do at the table during snack, which for us includes chocolate milk and cookies. They love to write and read poetry now! Its made a positive connection to something they like. … not offered as a bribe to do their work, but as a time of day they look forward to. I think the distinction is important, because my earlier attempts to reward cooperation never worked, but this does.*

As explained by Bogart, freewriting is a term from Peter Elbow, author of *Writing with Power* (New York: Oxford, 1998). It is a writing exercise in which the parent sets a timer for ten minutes and everyone, including the parents, must write continuously, about anything, for the entire time, without editing. Each writer reads her work to the others, then marks her own mistakes. Like WW, the emphasis is on learning to enjoy writing and on looking for strengths. See bravewriter.com/Exercises/free-writing.html for details.

- Spell-check software: Students who learn to type not only can write faster and more legibly, they can have software check their spelling. The problem is when the software guesses wrong. Teach your child to check words that are commonly confused, like "there," "their," and "they're." *Writers Inc.*, or the other guide books from The Write Source, and *The Little, Brown Handbook* list such words, and provide many other valuable writing tools.

- Electronic dictionaries: A wonderful resource for the older student, these look like a a calculator. They are better than print or online dictionaries for struggling learners. One problem with dictionaries is that to look up a word you have to be able to spell it, or at least get the first few letters right. Even worse, some students find it hard to remember alphabetical order, and so looking up words can be slow. With an electronic dictionary, though, you type in your guess of the spelling and several possible words appear on the dictionary's screen. You select one to check its definition. My son bought a *Franklin Talking Collegiate Dictionary* that can pronounce unfamiliar words to him. He is delighted with it.

Teaching writing is important, not only because it teaches students to communicate clearly, but also because it requires them to organize their thoughts. How many of us have tried to write a letter or paper and realized we had nothing to say, or that the idea that seemed so clever isn't so well-thought out as we believed? A struggling learner, like most learners, needs to be explicitly taught to organize her thoughts on paper before she writes.

As we teach organization, we must watch out if our children want everything prescribed. Composition requires flexibility and creativity. There is no set number of sentences a paragraph should have. All sentences in an essay should not have an identical structure. The form of our writing flows out of the content. When teaching, I find it helpful to set ranges, such as "a paragraph of five to eight sentences," or "four to six pages, double-spaced, twelve point type."

When you aren't sure in which order to put the facts of ideas of your essay, one helpful technique is webbing. Webbing is the process of jotting down ideas across a page and drawing lines to connect them, to help the writer see how the ideas relate. For example, when I was preparing to outline chapter 6 of this book, part of my web looked like this:

Software such as *Inspiration* and *Kidspiration* helps writers create webs and organize information for writing or note-taking. *Kidspiration* is designed for grades kindergarten through five; *Inspiration* is for grades six to adult. The software also helps the student convert their web to a more structured outline, and aids in formatting and adding notes to the outline, linking to files and websites. See their website, www.inspiration.com.

Writers Inc. and other books from The Write Source have helpful sections on organizing, as does *The Little, Brown Handbook*. There are several study skills books that teach some of these organizing skills, which I'll discuss in the next chapter.

Conclusion

Reading, math, and writing are three of the most daunting skills to teach. With a child who has expressive language difficulties, fine motor difficulties, attention problems, or other learning problems, teaching writing sounds intimidating. Nevertheless, working at home allows you to customize your curriculum, give your child one-on-one attention, and work at her pace. You can encourage her without her being distracted by a classroom of peers performing far above her level. There are many good resources, and the professionals described in chapter 8 can help you, train you, and provide you resources for more training. Our children can make great gains in these basic areas as we homeschool. One of our goals is to raise thoughtful, creative citizens. Teaching them to write clearly serves that goal.

Resources

Books Explaining Causes of Writing Problems
Eide, Brock, M.D., and Fernette Eide, M.D. *The Mislabeled Child: Looking Beyond Behavior to Find the True Sources—and Solutions—for Children's Learning Challenges.* New York: Hyperion, 2006.

Silver, Larry, M.D. *The Misunderstood Child.* New York: Three Rivers, 2006.

Curricula Related to Handwriting

Benbow, Mary D., M.S., OTR/L. *Loops and Other Groups: A Kinesthetic Writing System.* San Antonio: Therapy Skill Builders (Pearson), 1999. Available from www.otideas.com or phone 1-877-768-4332.

Brookes, Mona. *Drawing With Children.* New York: Tarcher, 1996. One way to remediate fine-motor difficulties is by teaching drawing.

Hablitzel, Marie, and Kim Stitzer. *Draw Write Now, Books 1-8.* Poulsbo, Washington: Barker Creek, 1994. The series is designed for primary grades, but may be used for older or younger students. Book numbers do not correspond to grade level. www.drawyourworld.com

Olsen, Jan. *Handwriting Without Tears* series. Cabin John, Maryland: Handwriting Without Tears, 2008. HWT also provides workshops in teaching handwriting; see www.hwtears.com.

Teaching Spelling and Vocabulary

Adams-Gordon, Beverly. *Spelling Power*. Lynnwood, Washington: Castle-Moyle Books. 1997. www.castlemoyle.com.

Allen, Janet. *Words, Words, Words: Teaching Vocabulary in Grades 4-12*. Portland, Maine: Stenhouse, 1999. www.stenhouse.com.

Burchers, Sam, Max Burchers, and Bryan Burchers. *Vocabulary Cartoons: SAT Word Power*. Punta Gorda, Florida: New Monic Books, 1997.

Hodkinson, Kenneth, *et. al. Wordly Wise* vocabulary series. Cambridge, Massachusetts: Educators Publishing Service, 2007. Visit epsbooks.com for details.

iSpellWell software. www.ispellwell.com.

McCabe, Don. *Sequential Spelling* series. Birch Run, Michigan: AVKO, 1990-2006. See www.sonlight.com, the website of Sonlight Curriculum, for details.

SpellingCity.com offers free online instruction, practice games, and tests, using your own list of words.

Writing Programs

Bogart, Julie. Bravewriter.com offers help to parents teaching writing.

Hanbury King, Diana. *Writing Skills*. Cambridge, Massachusetts: Educators Publishing Service, 2004. epsbooks.com provides more information.

Jensen, Frode. *Jensen's Format Writing*. Grants Pass, Oregon: Wordsmiths, 2002. Get the second edition, which has examples of each format.

Pudewa, Andrew. *Institute for Excellence in Writing* program. See www.excellenceinwriting.com

Writer's Workshop Resources

Fletcher, Ralph. *A Writers Notebook: Unlocking the Writer in You*. New York: HarperTrophy, 1996.

_____. *How Writers Work: Finding a Process That Works For You*. New York: HarperTrophy, 2000.

_____. *Writing Workshop: The Essential Guide*. Portsmouth, New Hampshire: Heinemann, 2001.

Accommodations

Dragon Naturally Speaking takes dictation from your student. See www.Nuance.com for details and a demonstration.

Kurzweil Educational Systems reads aloud what your child types. See www.kurzweiledu.com for details.

Spelling dictionaries are available from many publishers, including Educators Publishing Service, which carries *My Word Book, Words I Use When I Write,* and *My Content Words*. Visit epsbooks.com/dynamic/catalog/subject.asp?subject=68S to see sample pages.

Franklin handheld electronic dictionaries can be seen at www.franklin.com There are children's talking dictionaries, bilingual dictionaries—many kinds. For high schoolers, I recommend the *Speaking Merriam-Webster's Collegiate® Dictionary*. It won't read you the definition of a word, but it will tell you how to pronounce the word.

Write: Outloud and *Co-Writer* software from wwwdonjohnston.com. *Write: Outloud* reads aloud as you write and helps you edit; *Co-Writer* predicts the next word you will type, assisting with spelling and composition.

Other Resources

Handbooks, such as *Write Source 2000* or *Writers Inc.* by Patrick Sebranek, Dave Kemper, and Verne Meyer, are something for every child to have on her desk. They cover grammar, mechanics, and organization tips in an easy-to-use layout. For struggling learners, purchase a book listed for a lower grade than your child. The material is similar, but the upper grade editions have smaller print and more detail. www.thewritesource.com

Fowler, H. Ramsey, and Jane E. Aaron. *The Little, Brown Handbook*. New York: Pearson Longman, 2008. This is another excellent desk reference for high school. The font is smaller than the Write Source books, but the pages are plainer, which will appeal to some struggling learners.

Mannix, Darlene. *Writing Skills Activities for Special Children*. San Francisco: Jossey-Bass, 2004, was recommended by a parent and covers elementary writing skills.

Verticy Learning Academy Program is a homeschool curriculum for children with language-based learning disabilities (LLD), developed by The Calvert School, who have served homeschooling families for over one hundred years, and The Jemicy School, which serves children with LLD. www.verticylearning.org

Erwin, Paul R. *Winston Grammar*. Battleground, Washington: Precious Memories Educational Resources, 1992. You will need one complete kit, plus a card set and a workbook for each additional student. www.winstongrammar.com or ChristianBook.com

.

20

Study Skills and Test-Taking Skills

Traditionally the three R's—reading, writing, and 'rithmetic—are known as the core of education. Learning how to study, how to manage time, and how to take tests are just as crucial. While many students pick up these skills quickly and with little or no instruction, struggling learners need explicit, clear, regular instruction in these basic skills. It is easy to get discouraged teaching these skills, because they can take a long time to learn, but they are essential. In this chapter I will discuss goals as you teach these skills. Since so much has been written on these areas for a typical student, I will not repeat what others have said better. At the end of this chapter, I will list some resources.

In this chapter:
- Study skills
- Time management
- Why teach test taking skills?
- Preparing for standardized tests
- Preparing for college-level standardized tests

Study Skills

Students with good study skills have practiced *meta-cognitive skills*, that is, they have been thinking about how they think, learning how they learn. Struggling learners often have trouble becoming aware of themselves, so we should teach study skills repeatedly, perhaps every year. You can teach these skills either in regular short sessions through the year, or in a more intensive period over a few weeks, possibly in a small group class. Help the student pick one or two areas to focus on throughout the year, with the goal of building one good habit at a time. We should teach these skills very explicitly, not just saying "take good notes,"
or "prioritize this week's work," but walking them through the process.

Begin by showing your child how you do it, and gradually give him more and more responsibility as he grows older, gradually withdrawing your help. For example, in organizing academic work, when my son was in the primary grades, I told him what to do each day. When he reached grade seven, each week I made a list on the computer of all the work I had assigned. Then I had him read me the assignments his homeschool class teachers gave him, and I typed them on my list. We put due dates by everything, then using cut and paste on the computer, he helped me sort them by due date. As we went on, I did less, and he did more.

If your child continues to have trouble with organizing work, taking notes, or other study skills, see the books listed at the end of the chapter or other study skills books to find alternatives to the methods you have been using. As Claudine Wirths and Mary Bowman-Kruhm remind their young readers in *Where's My Other Sock?*, "Find a way of organizing that is right for you. No two people organize exactly the same way."[1]

1. Wirths, Claudine G. and Mary Bowman-Kruhm. Where's My Other Sock? How to Get Organized and Drive Your Parents and Teachers Crazy. New York: Crowell, 1989.

Here are three goals as you teach study skills:

- Students should choose ways to organize their time, work, and materials that make sense to them, not just do it a parent's way. When a child plans how to organize his work or possessions, he is more likely to remember the plan than if it is imposed on him. Finding a method that suits him may take some experimenting; we bought a different kind of calendar or planner each year for years. The goal is for the student is to claim the method as his own.

- Students should learn how they learn best and what is hard for them, and work accordingly.
- As much as possible, students should become independent learners. We want to teach them how to find information on their own, and how to ask politely and confidently for help when they need it. We must, therefore, teach those social skills, as well. For example, we should not help them out without being asked.

Study skills to teach:

- Reference skills: using the phone book, dictionary, an index, a glossary; practicing in finding items on an alphabetized list; reading a map, determining which information on the Internet is reliable (see end of this chapter).
- Note-taking from textbook and lecture. Like organizing, note-taking can be done several ways. Your student may need to experiment. (Some students with auditory processing problems or handwriting problems may have great trouble taking notes while listening. For them, discuss using a recorder or arranging for a classmate to take notes.)
- Reading comprehension. See resources at the end of the chapter.
- Organization: to-do lists, organizing school materials, cleaning out backpacks and desks, filing, breaking larger assignments into smaller parts.
- Study environment. Students need to learn what is best for them: desk, table, or floor; lighting; and sound (music, earplugs, headphones). See the resources at the end of this chapter and chapter 16.

Time Management

Teaching distractible students time management can seem like a hopeless task, but work steadily at it, and do not expect quick results. Think long term. Here are some skills to cover:

- Prioritizing, deciding when to do the hardest work, not neglecting the urgent, not neglecting the important. See Stephen Covey's book, *The 7 Habits Of Highly Effective Teens*, page 107-112, on not letting the urgent tasks crowd out the important ones.

- Budgeting time and estimating how long it will take to complete the work.
- Taking breaks—when to take them, getting back to work, learning when they need them.
- Tools—wall and pocket calendars, planners, handheld and wristwatch personal digital assistants.

Also see chapter 16 for more on different scheduling methods.

Why Teach Test-Taking Skills?

One measure of a student's study skills is how he performs on tests. Some people say they do not test well; it is true some bright people do not do well on standardized tests. But like it or not, standardized tests are a fact of modern life in North America. In the U.S., many states require homeschoolers to submit evidence of academic progress. Some homeschoolers choose to submit test scores, partly because standardized tests are usually the cheapest way to show progress. But even if we do not need test scores for our homeschool, our children will face standardized tests someday. Whether they will be mechanics, doctors, or simply licensed drivers, they will need to pass standardized tests. And some children will want to study in colleges or universities that require standardized test scores, for instance, the SAT or ACT college entrance exams.

Preparing for Standardized Tests

Struggling learners do not always pick up details as quickly as equally bright children, so prepare them ahead of time for standardized tests.

- Parents, don't panic. Don't communicate anxiety as you practice. Set a serious tone, but be matter-of-fact. Treat it as a game to win.
- If your child is taking the test away from home, tell him what to expect. Practice at home. The proctor will not allow talking during the test or even the appearance of looking at another child's paper, so discuss what to do if your child a) has to go to the bathroom, b) breaks both his pencils, c) is sure that there is a mistake on the test and wants to tell the proctor about it, d) feels sick, or e) notices

the child next to him has dropped his scratch paper. (Picking it up and saying, "Here's your paper," can get him in trouble.) Also discuss f) what to do when one of the above happens to the child next to him.

- If your child has not taken many multiple choice tests before, teach some strategies. If he does not know an answer, can he at least eliminate some answers as wrong, improving his odds of success? Does he know to pace himself, moving on calmly if he does not know one answer, not spending ten minutes agonizing over it?
- Take your time helping him prepare for a test. If test-taking skills are hard for your child, do not cram all your test preparation into a week or two. Short daily sessions over several weeks will be less stressful.
- See what types of problems are on the test and practice some of each.
- Your child may have never seen a computer-readable answer sheet before nor shaded in the circles to fill out his name or mark his answers. It is not hard, but your child should not have to learn how on test day.

For standardized tests to submit to local school authorities as evidence of progress, you may need to work through a good test preparation book, such as McGraw Hill's *Spectrum Test Prep* series or *Scoring High*, which comes in different versions for different grades and different standardized tests.

For driver's license tests, check your department of motor vehicles website for sample questions and tests. Drill for a short period daily. Have your student bring something quiet and entertaining to pass the time while waiting to take the test.

If the driver's license test or other tests (like the GRE) are given on a computer, practicing on the computer with multiple choice questions is very helpful. You may request a written version of the test if your child finds the online version too frustrating. (Here in Virginia, the online test shows one question at a time on the screen, with no chance to go back and change your mind. I know several struggling learners who have found this excruciating.)

On The Day of the Test

- Make sure your child is well rested and eats a good breakfast.
- If you are giving tests at home, pick days and times when your child is more alert. Follow the lead of the local public schools in my area, which no longer give standardized tests on Mondays or Fridays, because students perform worse those days. They give tests in the morning, when their students are freshest, and assign little work the rest of the day.
- Set a serious, calm tone if you are giving the test at home.
- Plan pleasant, but not exhausting, afternoon activities.

Preparing for College-Level Standardized Tests

Here again you need to balance the child's abilities, disabilities, and aspirations. If your child has a diagnosed learning problem and may be college-bound, prepare him for college exams.

There are two major organizations producing college entrance exams. ACT (formerly American College Testing) produces the ACT exam and the COMPASS college placement exams. The College Board makes the SAT (Scholastic Aptitude Test), the SAT Subject Tests, the AP (Advanced Placement) exams, and the CLEP (College Level Examination Program). Generally, colleges require applicants to take the ACT or SAT. The SAT Subject Tests are one-hour exams in individual subjects, and required by some colleges. Also written for individual subjects, the AP and CLEP exams give students the chance to be exempted from some college classes or to earn college credit.

Start with the official websites, www.collegeboard.com or www.act.org. Read about how to apply, and look at sample questions, particularly the sample writing questions. Help your student decide which exams to take. Some think the ACT is more friendly to struggling learners than the SAT. If your student plans to take the SAT, be sure to have him take the PSAT because it is a similar format and good practice. If your child takes it as an eleventh grader, it also determines eligibility for National Merit Scholarships and other scholarships. The PSAT is only offered in October.

Some colleges require more standardized tests from homeschooled students. Look at the websites of the colleges you are interested in. If your child is taking tests in a single subject, such as the SAT Subject Tests, AP, or CLEP, he should take them when he finishes those courses, not a year or two later.

Involve your student; have him log in to the official test websites and look around. Perhaps you will have him register for an exam as you look over his shoulder.

Get a current edition of good test preparation book, such as the Princeton Review. You may prefer the computer version on CD. Have your student work on it a little each day for several months before the test. A test prep course may help. If he is taking any test including a timed essay, he should practice taking timed essays at home. Require him to outline before he writes, and let him practice pacing himself. Practice helps tremendously.

Accommodations

Accommodations should level the playing field, enabling a struggling learner to better demonstrate his ability. They will not make taking a college entrance exam easy. (The current policy for both organizations is send tests scores to colleges without disclosing which students received accommodations.)

If you think your student needs accommodations for these tests, first go to the ACT and College Board websites to read about their "Services for students with disabilities." Services include providing various accommodations, such as fifty or a hundred percent extra time (not unlimited), a larger print copy of the test, use of a computer for dysgraphic students, and more. I will not discuss those services in detail here, because they continue to change. Start reading the official test websites early, a year or two before you expect your child to take any exams, to get an overview of the process and how long it will take for them to determine if your student is eligible for these services. E-mail the ACT and the College Board if you have questions.

Both organizations require that disabilities be documented by a qualified professional. The diagnosis must be made or reconfirmed within three years of your request for accommodations. So schedule your child's next psycho-educational battery or neuro-psychological evaluation accordingly, because they are expensive. We wanted my son's evaluation to be accepted not only by the College Board but by our son's college. Colleges and universities also want evaluations that are less than three years old. For that reason, we postponed our son's evaluation one year, because we expected he would want to take a year off before college. He was tested the summer after tenth grade, and we immediately submitted those scores to the College Board. When he applied for college two years later, his test results were still less than three years old, and we saved the cost of another evaluation.

When your child is re-evaluated for special needs, choose a professional with experience with college-level accommodations. You want someone to evaluate your student who knows the correct terminology to use in his or her report, someone who has kept up with the ACT and College Board requirements. Talk to a few professionals or their office managers by phone before you choose. After your child's evaluation is complete, ask this professional which accommodations would enable your student to do his best, and ask to have these specific accommodations included in the final report. Check the report as soon as you receive it. Do not wait six months to discover the accommodations you expected are not mentioned.

This is a changing area, so check with the test provider (www.collegeboard.com or www.act.org), others who are homeschooling children with special needs, and homeschool message boards before your follow-up meeting with the professional.

Conclusion

Though often overlooked, study skills are vital to your child's success as a life-long learner, responsible employee, and independent adult. Passing standardized tests is the key to qualifying to drive a car and enter many careers. For the college-bound student, preparing for college entrance exams and other college-level tests takes time. Don't leave these skills out of your homeschool. Investigate the resources below. Be diligent and be patient as you help your child acquire these skills.

Resources

As you choose resources, refer to the guidance on choosing textbooks in chapter 13, and on adapting materials in chapter 14. There are many books on study skills, time management, and organization; these are just a few.

Study Skills

Ervin, Jane. *Reading Comprehension in Varied Subject Matter*. Cambridge, Massachusetts: Educators Publishing Service. This series of books for grades two through eleven gives short passages to read and exercises to answer. www.epsbooks.com

Franklin Electronic Publishers, One Franklin Plaza, Burlington, NJ 08016-4907. www.franklin.com

Ever have trouble finding a word in the dictionary because you did not know how to spell it? An electronic dictionary can help. Franklin produces electronic dictionaries, about the size of a calculator. One version even pronounces words for you. They also make a Spanish/English dictionary and other add-ons. Available on line and in office supply stores.

Frender, Gloria. *Learning to Learn: Strengthening Study Skills and Brain Power*. Nashville: Incentive Publications, 2004. There are many workbooks on study skills; this is my favorite.

Gold, Mimi. *Help for the Struggling Student: Ready-to-Use Strategies and Lessons to Build Attention, Memory, and Organizational Skills*. San Francisco: Jossey-Bass, 2003.

Mel Levine's books *All Kinds of Minds* (for grades three to six) and *Keeping A Head in School* (for grades four through twelve) are not study skills books, but help your child learn about his learning problems, which can help him study more effectively. Cambridge, Massachusetts: Educators Publishing Service, 1995 and 1999, www.epsbooks.com.

Several strategies for taking notes from textbooks are covered by study skills books and websites. For example, the SQ3R approach stands for Skim (look over the whole chapter, headings, subheads, review questions), Question (ask yourself what question the author is answering), Read (each section thoughtfully, considering its main point), Recite (in your own words, summarize the main points of each section, orally or in writing), Review (the whole chapter). Other strategies, such as the similar PQRST (Preview, Question, Read, Study, Test) and KWL Tables (what we Know, what we Want to know, and what we Learned), are explained in various study skills books and websites.

Teaching Students to Evaluate Internet Sites

For younger students:

Health Development Agency, National Health Service. "The Quality Information Checklist." May 15, 2000. Accessed September 18, 2008. www.quick.org.uk

For older students:

Germain, Carol Anne, and Laura Horn. Albany University. "Evaluating Internet Websites 101!" January 2007. Accessed September 18, 2008. library.albany.edu/usered/webeval/

Kelly, Tina. "Whales in the Minnesota River?" New York Times. March 4, 1999, accessed September 18, 2008. descy.50megs.com/mankato/NYT/nyt34.html

Tyburski, Genie. "Teaching Internet Research Skills." October 11, 2001, accessed September 18, 2008. www.virtualchase.com/researchskills/quality3.html

University of California. "Evaluating Web Pages: Techniques to Apply & Questions to Ask." July 13, 2008, accessed September 18, 2008. www.lib.berkeley.edu/TeachingLib/Guides/Internet/Evaluate.html

Time Management
Covey, Sean. *The 7 Habits Of Highly Effective Teens*. New York: Simon & Schuster, 2003.

The late Randy Pausch, professor at Carnegie Mellon University, famous for his "Last Lecture" on achieving your childhood dreams, also gave a popular lecture on time management. Like the "Last Lecture," this includes a few swear words, so I do not recommend it for younger students. He borrows from Covey and others. For the student who prefers a video to a book, it is a helpful talk. See download.srv.cs.cmu.edu/~pausch/ His slides for the talk can be seen better here: www.alice.org/Randy/timetalk.htm

Time Management Tools
The Time Timer is a visual timer that can be set for up to sixty minutes by sliding a red disk to fill all or part of a circle labeled zero to sixty. (For example, fifteen minutes is a quarter circle.) As time passes, the red portion shrinks, enabling users to see time passing. Timetimer.com has a demonstration online. This is great for folks who have trouble noticing the passage of time. It comes in silent and audible versions, in various sizes.

The Timex Men's *Ironman Data Link USB Watch* is a personal digital assistant on your wrist. It comes with a cord and software to work with a computer. You type in and schedule messages which scroll across the watch face.

Two struggling learners I know use *DayTimer*® planners. www.daytimer. com has many kinds.

On Preparing to Take a Standardized Test
Critical Thinking Books and Software has many products, and links their titles to particular tests. www.criticalthinking.com

Spectrum Test Prep series, at different grade levels, is sold at bookstores, www.schoolspecialtypublishing.com, and Amazon.com. Grand Rapids: School Specialty Publishing, 2006.

Scoring High, which comes in different versions for different grades and different tests (the Stanford-9, ITBS and CAT), is available from hsrc.com.

SAT and Other Standardized Tests
Be sure to get the newest editions.
Cracking the SAT. Princeton: Princeton Review, 2007.

The Official SAT Study Guide. New York: College Board, 2004.

Books on Organization
Goldberg, Donna, and Jennifer Zwiebel. *The Organized Student: Teaching Children the Skills for Success in School and Beyond.* New York: Fireside, 2005.

Moss, Samantha, and Lesley Schwartz. *Where's My Stuff?: The Ultimate Teen Organizing Guide.* San Francisco: Orange Avenue, 2007.

Nadeau, Kathleen and Judith Kolberg. *ADD-Friendly Ways to Organize Your Life.* New York: Brunner-Routledge, 2002. (This book not just for folks with ADD/ADHD.)

Wirths, Claudine G. and Mary Bowman-Kruhm. *Where's My Other Sock? How to Get Organized and Drive Your Parents and Teachers Crazy.* New York: Crowell, 1989.

21

How to Write Tests

Several homeschooling parents I interviewed reported that one benefit of homeschooling was the freedom not to have to focus on meeting the school system's benchmarks and pass state-mandated tests, but to set their own goals and timelines for their struggling learners.

Why then, if some of us homeschool to get away from tests, should you write tests for your homeschool? Once we have our goals, we need a way to see if we have reached them. Tests are not the only way, but they are one way to assess our children's progress. Since children differ, I'll describe how to write several kinds of tests. Don't let this chapter make you think you need to write more tests than you want.

In this chapter:
- Testing a student with learning problems
- How to write tests
- What kind of questions
- Preview your test

Testing a Student With Learning Problems

Before you begin to write a test, think about your child's learning problems. For example, if your child has an auditory processing disorder, you will want to make sure the child understands how to complete the test and what is expected. Clearly written test directions and written study goals can help her. If your child has an expressive language disorder, you may want to provide multiple choice or a word bank (a list of possible answers). If your child has a reading problem, short clear directions and larger print with extra white space can help. You can hire a special education teacher as a consultant to review your child's psychological evaluation and give you ideas of how best to test her.

Here are some other ideas for testing accommodations—the helps that give a child with disabilities the chance to do the best work she can. Allow your student to:

- Take her tests untimed.
- Take tests in a room free of distractions.
- Type essay answers on a computer.
- Use spelling software, dictation software, an electronic dictionary, or a calculator.

Students do not have to write answers to tests. You have many ways to test, or assess, your child's progress, including:

- Giving an oral exam. Be sure to record your child's answers on paper with the test questions and the date, so you have a record of her progress if you may later need to submit a portfolio. (See chapter 16 on portfolios.)

  This can be an informal discussion. "Tell me about sharks. … Okay, now tell me about their skeletons. … How do they behave?" and so on.

- Assign an oral presentation. Your child can write a complete speech or an outline, rehearse with parents, and then present her report to relatives, your homeschool group or co-op. Document the oral presentation with your written comments.

  I prepared a simple grading sheet for oral presentations to help my son know what I was grading on and to help me keep track of everything. I graded on content, making it clear in advance what I expected my son to cover. I also graded on voice (appropriate volume, tone, and speed) and physical elements (good use of gesture, good eye contact). When I began teaching a group of three teenagers, each student used the form to evaluate the others' performances.

- Have your child prepare a poster or tri-fold display.

There are many more possibilities. For his final English project at Landmark College, David Cole, author of *Learning Outside the Lines*,[1] was told to "Explicate Your Writing Process." He submitted a steel sculpture to instead of a paper. When he applied to Brown University, he took the sculpture, *Process*, to the admissions office. He was admitted and later graduated at the top of his class. Your child may need to create a project rather than take a test. Be creative.

How to Write Tests

Sometimes you may need to write a test. In chapter 15, you planned to fulfill specific criteria as part of your student education plan. Once you have written those criteria, writing tests for them is straightforward.

You need a way to measure progress in other areas, apart from those criteria, so let's consider how. If you are teaching specific skills, such as writing a well-organized paragraph or multiplying fractions, or knowledge, whether spelling words or the life cycle of a butterfly, a test is one way to see if your child has learned them. You may have few or many tests as you homeschool, but you will need to write some, even if you give many of them orally.

One hallmark of learning and attention problems is uneven performance. When my son was learning long division, he would have it one day and forget it another, for about a year. The first time he did it correctly on a quiz, it would have been ridiculous for me to say he had mastered it. Brace yourself for these setbacks and include regular review in your work and in your quizzes. Don't be discouraged if you have to write several quizzes or tests on the same material before your child masters it. Children with learning disabilities are intelligent: once they learn something they can go far with it, but mastering the concepts, facts, and skills can take time.

Writing tests can be interesting because there are many ways to assess progress. Here are a few tips to consider. To write a good test, you need to:

1. Jonathan Mooney & David Cole. Learning Outside the Lines: Two Ivy League Students With Learning Disabilities And ADHD Give You The Tools for Academic Success and Educational Revolution. *New York: Simon and Schuster, 2000, p. 58 and back cover.*

- Know what you want your students to learn before you begin
  to teach.
- Communicate your objectives before the lesson and review them
  before you test. For younger children, you can ask questions and
  give problems similar to the ones you will give on a quiz or test.
  For older students, you might create a study guide, helping them
  know what they need to learn. Later you can help them to make
  the study guide themselves; this is an excellent study strategy. As
  students mature and their comprehension improves, you also will
  ask harder kinds of questions, moving from simple questions of fact
  to interpretation, generalizations, and abstractions.
- Make sure you are testing for the knowledge and skills for which
  you mean to test. If your child struggles to write a complete
  sentence, requiring complete sentence answers won't be the best
  way to find out what she knows about history. Instead, you might
  give fill-in-the-blank, multiple-choice, oral, or some other format. If
  you want her to practice sentence writing on a history test because
  you decide that is an important skill, be aware of what you are
  doing. You might give one test two grades: one for history and one
  for language arts or English.
- Write your questions ahead of time, ideally before you start
  teaching the material. I confess that I don't always practice this.
  Sometimes while writing a test after teaching a topic, I have had
  great ideas that I could not use because they required skills I had
  not taught. As children mature, we expect them to be able to apply
  knowledge to new situations, but sometimes these leaps of application are too far to be fair assessments. With practice, parents, like
  teachers, get a sense of how far their students can apply their knowledge and skills to new situations.
- It is best to decide in advance how you will grade your child's
  work. Will spelling count? How about handwriting? For younger
  students, you might choose only to count spelling, grammar, and
  usage on language arts assignments. For college-bound teens, on the
  other hand, you should use a higher standard. Regardless of your

child's age, if you can't read her work and she is capable of writing legibly, it is reasonable to have her rewrite or type it. For tests or other assessments, such as written assignments, you need a clear idea how you are going to evaluate them, what form of feedback you will give, and what your criteria are. The feedback might be a letter grade, a percentage, a number of points, or written comments. To make criteria clear, some teachers create a rubric, a list of what is required to get an particular letter grade, or an explanation of how much spelling, grammar, content, or other elements will count for essay questions. Don't tell your child one rubric or standard, and then switch once you start grading. Sometimes you will realize you left something important out of your standards, but play fair; don't "move the goal posts." With trial and error you will improve.

- Decide if you are testing only on the current objective or reviewing earlier material. With a struggling learner, review is important, so you should give some test questions that build on earlier material.
- Don't be unnecessarily elaborate. Keep the rubric simple and clear. I give lots of advice here, but do what you have time for.

What Kind of Questions

Writing tests can be creative. Usually, the longer it takes to write the test, the quicker it is to grade. For example, multiple choice questions take more time to write than fill-in-the-blank questions, but they are the easiest to grade. Essay questions are easier to write, but harder to judge. If you take the time to write out a rubric in advance for essays, the grading will be faster.

Different students find different kinds of tests harder. For example, I always thought multiple choice tests were the easiest, because the correct answer was visible to refresh my memory. Other people find them very difficult; in particular, some creative thinkers can come up with justifications for every choice, and sometimes cannot tell which answer the test writer intended.

Some common formats for test questions are: true or false, matching, multiple choice, fill-in-the-blank, short answer, and essay. Each has advantages and disadvantages, so it's best to include several kinds of questions in your test.

True or false questions can be easy or hard to answer, depending on how long and complicated the statements are. A long, complicated statement is a difficult exercise in reading comprehension, so it tests for that skill in addition to assessing mastery of the material. A dyslexic reader can overlook one word easily and fail the question, while she might do fine if she had been quizzed orally on the same material. Another drawback of true or false questions is that your student has a fifty-fifty chance of being correct by guessing. True or false questions are easy to grade, once you announce a simple rule. Ts must not look like Fs, as they may in cursive. On true or false questions, make sure the answers are divided fairly evenly.

Multiple choice questions are easy to grade if they have been written clearly. Some of our children would make good lawyers and are prepared to argue exceptions that might justify their answers, so make sure your questions have only one correct answer. Don't give the game away by writing correct answers that are much longer or shorter than the others. Look over your answers and make sure the correct answers are randomly place among the others; one of my education professors told our class that "B" is the most popular answer. Realize that if there are four possible answers, random guessing should get your student right about twenty-five percent of the time, so that does not mean they know one-fourth of the material. Give at least four answers, because if you give fewer, it becomes too easy to guess. If you have trouble coming up with four possible answers, resist the temptation to be trivial or ridiculous. If you must have three, random guessing will give them a score of thirty-three percent, so raise your expectations. Do not cram your answer choices into a narrow space; make them easy to read.

Matching questions are given as two lists, usually items and definitions, or events and significance. Students pair up items from each list. These are easy to write and grade. But if a student makes one pairing wrong, she may have used up the correct answer to another question, cascading into more mistakes. Another difficulty is that, the last questions may be answered by a process of elimination.

Fill-in-the-blank questions are harder to guess. They are hard for students with retrieval or spelling problems, so you may wish to include a word bank on the test. A word bank is a box listing the possible answers. To avoid guessing by elimination, include a few extra likely-sounding answers in your word bank. If you use a word bank and one word is the answer to two questions, be sure to state that answers may be used more than once. Make sure the length of your blanks does not give a hint as to the answer. Your grammar can be a giveaway, too, so watch your articles and whether your verbs are singular or plural in number. If I write "An _____ is a subatomic particle with a negative charge," my student does not have to remember the difference between protons, neutrons and electrons. I have given away the answer by starting with "an" instead of "a." It is better to write "_____ are subatomic particles with a negative charge."

Short answer questions are hard to guess, too. Be sure to leave enough space for the answers. Many struggling learners write more easily if you provide widely spaced lines for them to write on.

For math and science problems, give plenty of room to work math and science problems. Avoid requiring the students copy problems onto another page; it can lead to transposing digits and other mistakes.

Essay questions require answers of one or more paragraphs. Be sure to explain in advance what you want: for instance, a topic sentence for each paragraph, supporting details, as well as a thesis and a conclusion for longer essays. If your child has not succeeded with essay questions before, let them write some practice essay answers before you give a test. If the student is college-bound, give them practice with timed essays. Most beginners find them very intimidating, but practice helps tremendously. Teach them to take the time to outline and help them practice pacing themselves.

Preview Your Test

A day or two after you write your test, preview it for errors. Read your directions slowly. Check to make sure you stayed with the content you intended to cover. Tests that require mind reading are not fair; your child should be able to answer your questions if she has learned the material you taught. Make sure questions don't give away answers to other questions.

("Huckleberry Finn helps _____ escape." And later, "What kept Jim and Huck from traveling up the Ohio River?")

Make sure there is enough white space and room for your child to fill in the answers comfortably. Any test is harder for a struggling learner if she has to copy the problem or answer onto a separate page. It's too easy to transpose digits or make other errors before she begins to answer. Unless they are practicing for a standardized tests or answering an essay question, let your child answer on same page as the questions.

For longer quizzes and tests, make a copy for yourself and take the test. Check how long it takes you to complete the test. Your child will need more time, perhaps four times as much, or more. I recommend that tests be untimed; however, make sure your test isn't so lengthy that it overwhelms your child.

Once you've taken the test, save it as your answer key. If you might use it again for a younger child or lend it to a friend, file away your answer key. In a few years, you may be glad to have it.

Conclusion

There are many factors to think about when measuring your child's progress. You need to consider what your goals are, how you'll know when your child has met them, and how you'll measure her progress. Make your tests and assessments clear. I have discussed many ways to write them. As your child grows, your tests will change as you keep them appropriate for her and the material she is learning.

Homeschooling Through High School

When I started homeschooling, if you had told that me I would homeschool through twelfth grade, I don't think I would have started. Homeschooling a struggling learner sounded hard, and homeschooling one in high school sounded terrifying. There were times I wanted to quit. Whenever we weighed the other options though, homeschooling seemed best for us. He graduated in 2006, and I am glad we kept going.

Whether you are homeschooling already and wondering whether to keep on through grade twelve, or if you are considering beginning to home-school when your child is a teen, you face many of the same concerns.

In this chapter:

- How can your teen learn what you cannot teach?
- Shouldn't my teen be in school?
- Your teen's goals and future
- Planning and transcripts
- Transition to college or work
- Social skills and relationships

How Can Your Teen Learn What You Cannot Teach?

You may be thinking, "I cannot teach French," "I don't remember biology," or "I hate trigonometry." But your teen still can learn them under your supervision. You have many resources: homeschool group classes, community college, tutors, online courses, and instruction via video or computer software. I will consider those first three options below. In chapter 13, I discussed online, video, and computer classes.

With any of these options, if you have been doing all the teaching in your homeschool, you may be tempted either to intervene too much or not to supervise the work at all. Think of these as training for college and work. You should set a time each week to go over what the assignments are (not in the car on the way to class!), look at work the teacher has returned, and see if any tests or projects are due soon. Soon you will see how much monitoring your student needs during the week. See chapter 20 on teaching your student to plan.

Train your child to communicate with his teachers. Talk with him about what to say, and how to respond. Get involved by e-mail or phone if you need to, but try to give your student practice in working things out on his own with another adult. Be courteous with the instructors; explain your student's needs early but briefly.

Consider the time of day the class is offered. Pay attention to your teenager's opinion and to your observations of him. My son thought one local math teacher was excellent, but she taught at five in the evening. He knew that was the hardest time for him to concentrate, so we found another class.

Homeschool Group Classes

Group classes often form when homeschoolers pool their expertise. Group classes usually meet once or twice a week for lecture, discussion, and lab. Teachers provide schedules, quizzes, tests, and accountability. Parents supervise work at home, as students complete reading, written assignments, and sometimes exams. Group classes can be part of an umbrella school, a co-op in which parents share the work, or a paid service.

Homeschool group classes have some advantages. Group classes are usually taught by other homeschoolers, who understand and support homeschooling. They are smaller than community college classes, move at a slower pace, and, in my experience, are less intimidating. When I taught a homeschool class including my son, he stopped complaining about deadlines because he saw everyone else had to meet them, too. He worked faster to keep up. In other subjects, it was good for him to be accountable to someone else, to help him distinguish between me as parent and me as teacher. He learned some practical tips about answering to a boss. One teacher taught him a lesson I had been trying to teach for years. "I've figured out something," my son announced one day. "If you haven't done the work and you come to Mr. Powell with excuses, he gives you a hard time and won't help. But if you admit you messed up and ask, then he'll help." Small classes are helpful in developing speaking skills, too. One student I taught in a small class has auditory processing problems and anxiety disorder. He felt more relaxed speaking in a small class than he had in larger classes in school.

What are the disadvantages of homeschool group classes? The teacher cannot slow the pace for your child if he gets behind, as you could at home. If you are considering a group class, look over the material early. Ask about the pace. If you are not sure your teen can keep up, talk with the teachers before you sign up.

Another disadvantage is the teachers may have no experience with struggling learners. (This can be a problem in community college, too.) Tell the instructors about your student's special needs and discuss how they might adapt assignments for him. For instance, you might ask that your student be allowed to:

- Type work, allowing him to use spell checking software or dictation software,
- Use a calculator in math classes,
- Complete shorter assignments than his classmates,
- Receive printed homework schedules. Or if the teacher prefers, you could require your student to record his assignments and have the teacher check and initial them after class. The mother of one of my

students said, "No TV if the list isn't initialed," and he never failed
to have me check it.

With group classes, you still may owe them the year's tuition even
if your child must drop out mid-year, because the group must pay their
teachers. Discuss this in advance.

Community Colleges

Community colleges are an asset to struggling learners. Some are not ready
for community college, and those that are should start with one class,
carefully chosen, so success can encourage them that college is possible.

To determine whether your student is ready for college-level classes
at a community college, visit the college website, and then stop by their
counseling office with your child. Ask about services for students with
disabilities and how to qualify. To be sure your child has a disability, the
college will want to see documentation—a medical or neuropsychological
evaluation less than three years old.

You may award high school credit for college courses your student
takes; high schools also do this. Students who take college classes while in
high school are called dual-enrolled. Generally, a three credit, one semester
class in college is equivalent to a year-long, one credit high school course.
See the Home School Legal Defense Association's excellent website on high
school, at www.hslda.org/highschool/, for more on dual enrollment and
other topics.

To choose classes, start with a general education requirement—a
required course—or an introductory class in a favorite subject. Stop in the
college bookstore to see the class's textbooks. If you are still not sure the
class is appropriate, look at the department website or talk to staff in the
department offering the class, and get a syllabus. It can change with the
instructor, but any version will give you an idea of what is expected.

Tutoring

Another way for your student to complete a high school class is with a
tutor. Tutors can be expensive. If you cannot find a good one by referral,
ask at your local schools. Some teachers tutor in their free time. University
campuses sometimes have bulletin boards or other arrangements to link

college students with families needing tutors. Remember when you hire a tutor that expertise does not mean someone knows how to teach or knows how to teach a struggling learner. Meet with prospective tutors before you begin, or interview them by phone. Ask about their training, references, experience in teaching, and experience with teaching those with learning problems. Describe your student's difficulties, progress, and goals. Discuss their plans: what materials do they plan to use? Are they opposed to homeschooling?

From a distance, observe the tutor's first session with your teen—but do not interrupt. (Ideally, you might listen in from another room where you cannot be seen.) When I have tutored, I have seen students cringe as their mothers felt obliged to step in and explain to me what was their child's problem. Tutors can figure some of this out themselves, and the parental interruptions makes it hard to develop a rapport with the student. Some parents discourage their teens by referring to old problems as if they would never be overcome: "We have been working on long division for five years, and he never keeps the numbers in straight rows." It is better to have those discussions with the tutor privately. Don't feel you must justify your child's lack of progress to the tutor.

Driver's Education

One particular course some parents do not feel prepared to teach is driver's education. Check with your state department of motor vehicles or provincial licensing authority to see what they approve. Some homeschool teens enroll in private driving schools; others study video- or text-based curricula at home. Make sure the program you choose meets your government's and your insurance company's requirements for driver education. Ask other homeschoolers in your area what they are doing.

Visit patient advocacy organization websites to learn about helping a student with your child's learning problems master driving. Search for information; for example, search the Internet for "ADHD driving." If possible, start teaching and practicing the mechanics of driving very early so that they become automatic before you allow your child to drive in traffic. Talk with your teen about avoiding distractions. For the first year our children held licenses, we did not allow them to take passengers without us, talk on the phone, or even listen to music. Don't just say "Turn left" to your learning disabled driver-in-training, but point left out toward the windshield, so he can see your hand. (You might even put "L" and "R" in grease pencil on the corners of the windshield.) A driving instructor suggested I buy a large convex rear view mirror to put on the passenger side sun visor, to help me help my son judge lane changes. (They can be purchased from boating supply companies; boaters use them to watch the water skiers they tow.) A magnetic "STUDENT DRIVER" bumper sticker seemed to cut down on our getting honked at. Some teens hate these, but I think they should be mandatory for all new drivers.

Once he is driving alone, I would recommend having your teen carry a cell phone so he can call you when he is lost or late. I would keep talking about distractions and make your teen pay for car insurance. A talking GPS navigation device, such as by *Garmin, TomTom,* or *Magellan,* is a big help for anyone who tends to get lost.

Shouldn't My Teen Be In School?

If you are not sure about homeschool for high school, consider your alternatives. Chapter 3 discussed other options generally; let's look at that question on the high school level. There may be a few private high school options, but distance and cost rule them out for many of us, so I will focus on public school.

What Programs Do Your Secondary Schools Offer?

As a former public school teacher, I appreciate that schools serve the community by educating the population. To teach thousands of students on a tight budget, schools must be efficient. So teachers chiefly lecture and demonstrate, and students learn primarily by taking notes, asking questions, and reading textbooks.

Public education in America is not one-size-fits-all, but there are often only a few options: gifted (GT) or Advanced Placement (AP) classes, regular classrooms, and special education classes. In the GT or AP classes, most students push themselves and have excellent study skills. In the regular and special education classrooms, there are students who want to learn and those who do not, students who struggle to learn and some who have given up and are waiting until they can drop out. And they don't always wait quietly. None of these possibilities may be a good fit for your child. He may need a custom-made program. Few schools have that flexibility.

Two parents in different cities told me they had decided to homeschool after their sons with autism spectrum disorders started middle school. Both boys received good help at their elementary schools, but in middle school the parents found no placement suitable for these bright but struggling learners. Public schools have limited resources, students with many different needs, and increased pressure to improve their students' performance on standardized tests. One homeschooler with a foster daughter in a high school special education classroom told me that her classmates had such varied needs that the teachers had to teach at the level of the lowest.

Regardless of which classroom students are assigned, the high school routine is highly structured, which affects struggling learners particularly. High schools begin very early. Every fifty or one hundred minutes, the students leave a classroom, walk through hectic, crowded corridors, and into another room with a different teacher. This teacher may not be as interesting as what happened in the hallway, and likely has different expectations and methods than the last teacher. Mr. A may hand out a schedule of assignments every month, while Ms. B writes assignments on the board, and expects your child to copy them. Changes like this can be hard for struggling learners to manage.

Consider the School Environment

But high school is more than teaching methods, mounds of work, a bell schedule, and classrooms. High school has a culture of its own. How does that culture affect the struggling learner?

High school is an intensely social time. Teens in school spend most of their day either with or communicating with their peers. That rapidly changing world—what's cool to wear, who's dating, and who's in trouble—is fuel for distraction and frustration as the struggling learner labors to interpret social cues.

Few adults spend nearly so much time with others their exact age. Segregation by age is relatively new; it began in the last century with the development of comprehensive high schools. Before that, most people started work at age fourteen. Our culture encourages teens to be preoccupied with their peers, instead of preparing them for the adult world they are soon to join.

That teen culture does not help the struggling learner, who needs to spend more time than the average teen learning everything: not only the academics, but time management and life skills. That culture is a loud, flashy, busy world that appeals to distractible people, like a *Sesame Street* episode attracts a preschooler. It focuses on appearance, change, and excitement. Teen culture promotes youth, being cool, being impulsive, not the responsibility or forethought struggling learners need to embrace.

Teen society often is unforgiving. A freshman's gaffe still can label him as a senior. So can being assigned to a special education program. And while everyone should be able to handle unkind remarks, you need to consider how well your child will cope, based on their temperament and maturity. They may need an environment that offers more support and that encourages them to mature.

Your Teen's Goals and Future

As you ponder homeschooling through high school, you need to consider your student's goals. Does he want to go to college, to work, or is he not sure? What do you, his parents, think he can or should do? If you are going to homeschool, you need to decide what kind of high school program you want to develop. Do you want to plan a college preparatory program, a general program, a vocational program, or is he still mastering basic skills? Whatever you plan, your goals may change as you work through high school.

If your teen cannot manage a college preparatory program, a community college may be a good choice to follow his education at home. You can aim for that by doing as much of a college preparatory program as possible before you graduate him from high school.

Whatever program you develop, with a struggling learner you will need to spend more time teaching him study skills and skills for independent living, such as social skills, responsibility, hygiene, money management, diet, job-keeping skills, such as how to treat a boss and resolve a disagreement. You can create high school level courses in these areas.

We have to focus on character, too. We want our children to develop their talents, become independent, and support themselves. But we also want them to obey the law, stay out of jail, and to be honest, just, dependable, caring people. Being with them, you have more opportunities to talk about what is important, and to praise honesty and perseverance.

Planning and Transcripts

Another concern parents have about homeschooling for high school can be about content: how to design a program, keep track of it all, and create a transcript. How do you know what the standards are? Several good books can help you map out a high school program. The Home School Legal Defense Association provides excellent material. I have listed books and websites at the end of this chapter.

Let's first consider the student who is or might be college bound. Look at the websites of colleges your child might attend. What do they want to see on a high school transcript? Probably several years of foreign language, and more math and science than the minimal program suggested below. Check with colleges to be sure. The biggest mistake I made planning high school was not looking carefully enough at what was required and by whom.

More colleges are seeking homeschooled students; some have web pages for homeschoolers. Some have special requirements or suggestions, such as more standardized test scores. For example, my alma mater, William and Mary, recommends that homeschooled students take SAT II subject tests.

For a general diploma, the requirements are less strenuous than for a college preparatory program, and include:
- four years of English language and literature,
- three years of math,
- two years of science
- two of social studies,
- two of foreign language,
- one or two years of physical education and health,

- one or two years of fine arts (art, music, drama, speech)
- electives, such as technology, computer courses, life skills, or photography.

Credits and Transcripts

Courses are measured in credits and half-credits. Credits are also sometimes called Carnegie Units. HSLDA has an article on evaluating credits that I recommend. It describes several ways to earn a credit:[1] either by completing a high school textbook from a reputable publisher, (not necessarily every problem), or 120 to 180 hours of work depending on the subject, or taking one semester of a community college class.

Three important tips on high school records are: to learn how to create them before high school begins, to keep them up as you go, and to write brief course descriptions of each class. Include the basic content of the course and the books used. If lab work was done for science classes, say so.

Transition to College or Work

Whether your child goes to college or work after high school, you want to help him make a good transition. You may feel inadequate and want to hand that task off to professionals. But there is no guarantee that putting our children in school will solve those problems.

Whether he is going to college or to work, you will need to prepare your student for a transition. He will need to decide if and how to discuss his disability with others and whether to ask for accommodations. Whether he formally applies for accommodations or not, work with him on self-advocacy, the ability to ask for necessary help. Resources on this are at the end of the chapter.

College Bound or Not?

If your child is heading to college, look for colleges with good services for students with learning problems. Check their websites and compare them. When you go to campuses, visit the centers for students with disabilities. Have your teen talk with staff. See how well-staffed and organized these offices are. Some campuses also provide support groups and mentoring for

1. Home School Legal Defense Association. "Evaluation of High School Credits." Accessed September 18, 2008. www. hslda.org/ highschool/docs/ EvaluatingCredits .asp

students with special needs. Your student's learning problems may qualify him for a single room in the dorm. Off-campus organizations may also provide support with studies, social life, and managing the college system. Some students hire a life coach to help them keep organized.

Don't think everyone must start college at age eighteen and finish in four years. Many students are taking longer and combining work and study. The Attention Deficit Disorder Association reports that forty to sixty percent of college freshmen with AD/HD return home before freshman year is over.[2] Going to community college or attending a local college part time while living at home can be a smarter way to begin for struggling learners.

The struggling learner is often emotionally a few years behind his peers. Do you foresee him tempted by underage drinking in a dorm? Can you count on him to keep track of all his work by age eighteen? Will his dorm room be condemned as unhealthy, even by lax freshman dorm standards? If he is taking medication, will he remember to take it?

When my son was about eleven, Lynn Kuitems Henk, our special education consultant, asked me whether I intended him to learn to live on his own first, or go to college first. It was a good question. One of her points was that trying to learn two things at once—how to earn a degree and how to live independently—could be too much.

Perhaps your teen should work six months or even a few years after graduation to mature and to decide if college is worth the effort. There is nothing like long hours and low wages to sober a young adult.

Work and Entrepreneur Opportunities

On the other hand, a teen's job may lead to a career, as it did for Nancy's son. (See next page.) One advantage of homeschooling teens is that you can free up more time for them to pursue passions that may lead to careers. Often these can begin as small businesses at home.

If a teen is going to work while in homeschool, check on child labor laws. Even then, consider what is best for him long term. To help him succeed academically, limit work hours.

When your teenager is fourteen to sixteen, you may not see how his interests will lead him. You may not know if he will attend college, but be open to alternatives after graduation.

2. Attention Deficit Disorder Association. ADD: Transition to College— Passport to Success. *Video. Silver Spring, Maryland: ADDvance Seminars, 2001. www.add.org.*

Third grade failure becomes successful businessman

Nancy, whose oldest son is now twenty-three, recalls their journey. In chapter 5, I quoted her describing him before homeschooling: "I had a third grader who couldn't read, had zero self-esteem, was so full of anger, and just hated everything and cried all the time." Here's the rest of her story.

Dyslexia runs in our family—I have uncles that never learned to read and a niece diagnosed with dyslexia. God led me, kicking and screaming, to homeschool. We were in a real small town; my kids were the fourth generation to go [the local] school. We were the first homeschoolers in the county. [My son] was the poster child for the child who slips through the cracks in public school, then does excellently.

After beginning homeschooling in fourth grade, he entered the Daughters of the Texas Revolution essay contest. My dyslexic learner won first locally, then regionally, and then for the state. A year after we started homeschooling, my child who could not read stood in front of two hundred people in formal dress at a banquet in El Paso and read his essay. That was a God thing.

I don't know where he'd be today without homeschooling. I look at him, my twenty-three year old who's run his own business since he was fourteen. He is one of the largest livestock buyers in this area. He ships sheep and goats all over the United States.

I asked her the main advantages of homeschooling a struggling learner. She replied, "My twenty-three year old calls or visits daily. Closeness develops in a family when you homeschool."

Entering the Workforce

If you know your student will not be heading to college, you have different concerns and options. If he has a particular interest, look into related apprenticeships and mentoring, described below. If not, you may want to make investigating different careers a part of his education. Getting out in the community, as described in the next chapter, can lead to opportunities. Summer jobs or part-time work during the school year can teach valuable lessons—punctuality, honesty, reliability, and courteous customer service, among others. These jobs may lead to long-term work. Even bad jobs can teach your teen useful lessons.

One concern your teen will face will be whether or not to disclose his special needs with his employer. As Dale Brown says in *Learning a Living*, "Although discrimination on the basis of a disability is illegal, disclosure at an early stage can lead to your being screened out."[3] She outlines three good reasons to disclose a disability:

> *You need reasonable accommodation to do the job. …*

> *Keeping your disability hidden makes it difficult for you to maintain your integrity.*

> *The way your disability manifests itself is causing a problem for other people. You think they deserve an explanation.*[4]

If your child is going to disclose a disability, check with your state disability services to see what transition and job placement services they offer.

Apprenticeships

If your teen wants to learn a trade, investigate apprenticeships. "The eligible starting age can be no less than 16 years of age; however, individuals must usually be 18 to be an apprentice in hazardous occupations," says the U.S. Department of Labor's Education and Training Administration. They add, "Program sponsors may also identify additional minimum qualifications and credentials to apply, *e.g.*, education, ability to physically perform the essential functions of the occupation, proof of age." [5]

3. Brown, Dale S. Learning a Living. Bethesda, Maryland: Woodbine House, 2000, p. 147.

4. Ibid. p. 267.

5. Employment and Training Administration, U.S. Department of Labor. "Eligibility and Requirements: Apprenticeship Website." Accessed February 13, 2007. www.doleta.gov/OA/req.cfm.

Begin by talking with workers in various trades or calling a union office. Some workers may let your teen follow them for a day. (This is sometimes called *shadowing*.) Remind your teen that no job is exciting all the time. Tell him that one day may not give him a good sense of what a job is like, but have him shadow a few people in trades that interest him. As with anyone your child will spend time with, you will want to know about the person's character. So personal references from people you respect are best. Your teen will be learning from this person's work ethic, manners, and integrity.

Mentoring

Mentoring is an informal relationship in which a person who is successful in a career or trade helps a less experienced person (in this case, your teen) advance in his field. This is something for which your child could earn a high school credit, but the guidance may be so helpful that I include it here. A mentor gives advice on how to proceed in training and developing in a career, meeting occasionally for encouragement and advice, in person or by phone. Family and family friends may be the best source of mentors, but it doesn't hurt to ask anyone you respect if they are successful in a field of deep interest to your teen. Be sure to explain to your young adult that the mentor has a limited amount of time, and monitor his contacts with the mentor to be sure he is not being a nuisance. In the next chapter, see how Rob's interests have led to his being mentored by a professor at a nearby university.

Social Skills and Relationships

Parents may worry that children who lack social skills will miss valuable practice by being homeschooled. It is a legitimate concern, but it's not a black-and-white choice. One mother said she preferred that her son not have to learn social skills and academics at the same time. Going to high school doesn't guarantee learning good social skills. Who will your child spend time with? If you are thinking of putting your child in high school, visit your local high school and check out the atmosphere in the lunch room, the special education classroom, and in the halls between classes. This may not be the socialization you are looking for.

Realize that for some of our struggling learners social skills are going to take time to learn, whether they are homeschooled or not. If you homeschool, you will probably work harder to find and arrange social opportunities, but you may know your child's friends better. My experience is that homeschooled teens are more comfortable having conversations with adults than public-schooled teens, who tend to relate to me more formally and superficially. Balancing homework, other responsibilities, and social activities is a challenge, wherever your child is educated.

Some parents wonder whether they can get along with their teens well enough to homeschool through high school. But as your children grow in maturity, they work more independently, even when they have special needs—few of us need to sit with our students all day.

Children grow up. For twelve years, Cathy has homeschooled her daughters, including Rachel who has ADHD and anxiety disorder. I asked Cathy about the difficulties of homeschooling. She replied, "Being together all the time was just hard. But when I'd consider my options—we did look at private schools—I just didn't think that would work. We persevered and now homeschooling has worked." I asked when it started to get easier. She replied:

> I've told some friends that have younger kids, "Hang in there," because there was this day, two years ago, when Rachel was almost fourteen. We were starting math, and I was thinking "Oh, here we go again." She just looked at me and said, "Mom, I've decided I'm just going to do the math." And for her that meant, "I'm not going to resist, I'm not going to freak out, I'm just going to do the math." I nearly fell off my chair. She has matured.

As we homeschool, we work to nurture independence, teaching them to manage their time and workload. Several parents told me they homeschool to deepen family relationships. While the teen years are a time teens crave independence, they also want their parents' love and guidance.

My husband has been a good father, especially through the teen years. He gave advice and correction—to me and our son. He sought out time to talk with our teens individually, taking them to events they would enjoy. He took our son on camping and backpacking trips with the Boy Scouts, which gave mother and son a breather. Regular time apart is helpful in homeschooling through high school, if not with Scouting, through some other activity outside the home.

The next section of this book gives advice on getting out and other ways to keep on homeschooling.

Conclusion

I am not saying all special needs students should be homeschooled for high school. Each family has to make their own decision. But homeschooling a struggling learner through high school can be successful and rewarding. I certainly made mistakes. But homeschooling seemed the best way to nurture our son's strengths, keep him on as academically rigorous course as he could follow, and preserve time for activities he loved. For us, it was the right choice.

Resources

General Resources on Homeschooling Through High School
Begin with www.hslda.org/highschool/ for information on planning, transcripts, resources, vocations, extracurricular activities, and much more.

Howard and Susan Richman have written several helpful articles. www.home-school.com/Articles/#Richman

Planning High School and Transcripts
Campbell, Janice, *Transcripts Made Easy*. Ashland, Virginia: Everyday Education, 2002. For the bright student, also see Campbell's *Get a Jump Start on College!*, 2006. Visit everydayeducation.com to purchase them in paperback, or you may download them as e-books at a discount.

Cannon, Inge, *Transcript Boot Camp* Seminar on DVD. Available from www.homeschooltranscripts.com/, which also sells *TranscriptPro* transcript producing software.

Transition to College

If your teen is college-bound, see also "Transition to Work," below.

- Attention Deficit Disorder Association. *ADD: Transition to College—Passport for Success.* Video. Silver Spring, Maryland: ADDvance Seminars, 2001. At www.addvance.com/bookstore/young.html you can purchase this video.
- Kravets, M. and I. Wax. *The K & W Guide to Colleges for the Learning Disabled.* New York: Harper Collins, 2002.
- Mangrum Charles T. II, Ed.D., and Stephen S. Strichart, Ph.D., eds. *Peterson's Colleges with Programs for Students with Learning Disabilities or Attention Deficit Disorders*, seventh edition. Lawrenceville, New Jersey: Peterson, 2003.
- National Resource Center on ADHD. "Succeeding in College." *What We Know* information sheet series. www.help4adhd.org/en/education/college/WWK13
- Reiff, Henry B., Ph.D. *Self-Advocacy Skills for Students with Learning Disabilities: Making It Happen in College and Beyond.* Port Chester, New York: National Professional Resources, Inc., 2007.
- Yahoo! Groups: Two good online groups for parents are homeschool2college and conservativehs2c, where homeschooling parents can discuss preparing their students for the transition to college. What homeschool2college says is true for both groups:

Posts can include but are not limited to preparing the child for high school course work, selecting books or curricula or programs, reviews of any particular curriculum and how it helped (or failed to help) your child, extracurricular activities including sports and music and driver's ed, identifying potential colleges, how particular colleges treat homeschoolers, college applications, preparing for and taking the PSAT/SAT/SAT II/PLAN/ACT and AP tests, preparing and submitting transcripts, financial aid—and now we're being blessed by reports from homeschooled students who have made the transition to college.

Two-Year Colleges for Struggling Learners
Landmark College in Vermont
(802) 387-6718
www.landmark.edu

Louisburg College in North Carolina
www.louisburg.edu
(919) 497-3236

Transition to Work
ADDitude magazine's website has a section on adults with ADD/LD.
www.additudemag.com/channel/adult-add-adhd/index.html

Brown, Dale S. *Learning a Living: A Guide to Planning Your Career and Finding a Job for People with Learning Disabilities, Attention Deficit Disorder, and Dyslexia.* Bethesda, Maryland: Woodbine House, 2000.

Grandin, Temple, Ph.D., and Kate Duffy. *Developing Talents.* Shawnee Mission, Kansas: Autism Asperger Publishing, 2004.

The Learning Disabilities Association of America website has a series of articles on workplace issues. www.ldaamerica.org/aboutld/adults/index.asp

LDonline has useful articles available from their *Transition: School to Work* page, including "College or Training Programs: How to Decide," "Building the Bridge Between Community College and Work For Students with Learning Disabilities," and "Transition and Self-Advocacy." www.ldonline.org/indepth/transition

National Resource Center on ADHD, has several articles accessible from "Living with ADHD: Workplace Issues." help4adhd.org/en/living/workplace

By perseverance the snail reached the ark.

Charles H. Spurgeon

Part V

Keeping Going

23

Homeschooling Doesn't Mean We Stay Home

Homeschooling doesn't mean you stay home. For my son, a good day means getting out of the house. If we stayed inside all day, he grew restless. If we stayed home two days, we both got restless. Not everyone does. Some families enjoy being home. But everyone needs to stir from home, and it gives us more opportunities to learn.

In this chapter:
- Fresh air and exercise
- Social advantages of homeschooling
- Developing social skills
- Hanging out with homeschoolers
- Mistakes to avoid when choosing activities
- Different kinds of activities
- Homeschool group or community group?
- Choosing activities

Fresh Air and Exercise

In his book *Last Child in the Woods: Saving Our Children From Nature Deficit Disorder*, Richard Louv makes the case for having our children play outdoors on their own. He outlines the reasons why children do this less and less: parents' fears for their safety, increasing development and regulation of land, and children's busy schedules. Louv discusses the value of letting children putter about in fields and woods, exploring and observing nature, pretending, and building tree forts. He cites studies that show these kinds of play help our children feel less stressed, more independent, and more in control of their environment.

The soccer mom mentality makes us feel we are inadequate parents if we don't keep the children busy. When we homeschool, we may feel obliged to fill up their schedules so no one can say we are neglecting their social lives. But this is bad for the children. They need time on their own. My children explored the woods behind our house, inventing stories and naming places along the creek. They played Pooh sticks, dropping sticks in the water to race against each other. When there was no time to go into the woods, they constructed miniature towns and forts in the yard. To you, it would look like some twigs, pebbles, and acorns; to them, it was a story.

Exercise also is vital for us and our children. It helps distracted people burn excess energy and focus. It can help children on the autistic spectrum calm down. Dr. Temple Grandin says, "Another thing that people need to do is plenty of exercise. I do a hundred sit ups every night. I hate every single one of them. But I'm sleeping better when I'm doing it."[1]

Exercise relieves stress. It helps everyone feel healthier and have more energy. My son and other teenagers whose mothers I interviewed reported being able to focus better after starting the day with exercise. When he was younger, on rainy days my son would jump rope, bounce on a mini-trampoline in the garage, or—his favorite—go out and jump in puddles.

Social Advantages of Homeschooling

"What about socialization?" is the question every homeschooler is asked. How will your child develop social skills?

By homeschooling, you can help your child avoid some of the social problems of school. Have you walked in a school hallway between classes recently? It can be deafening, crowded, and extremely distracting. During one tough part of tenth grade at home, I wondered if my son ought to finish at the local high school. A public school teacher who knew Pete well

1. Grandin, Temple, Ph.D. My Experience with Autism. *2007 Distinguished Lecturer Series, University of California-Davis M.I.N.D. Institute. February 14, 2007. Accessed September 18, 2008. www. ucdmc.ucdavis. edu/mindinsti-tute/events/dls_ recorded_events. html*

said he could imagine him spending the first twenty minutes of every class with his mind still back on what happened in the hallways.

It's not just the corridors and classrooms. Youth culture is self-absorbed, and now younger children are invited to join in and call themselves preteens. The teen culture emphasizes the immediate, the wild, and the crazy, which can be powerfully dangerous attractions for the impulsive personality. Homeschooling lets you pry children from that culture a little. They are not immersed in it eight hours a day.

Homeschooled children not only miss distractions, but other social problems. They miss bullying, nastiness, and ridicule. Marcia began homeschooling her son partly because, "there was a lot of ridicule, even in a Christian setting. Kids are kids—they picked up on the fact that he was a struggling learner and could be pretty unkind." Kate in Alberta said her son is "not being singled out on a daily basis as someone who needs special help, somebody who's different from the rest. So he hasn't had any self-esteem or self-image issues or depression, which … can be common for children who have difficulty in school." Isolation at school is a problem for others. Don said his daughter with high functioning autism had very little social interaction in sixth grade at school.

Homeschooling gives families have more time together. People who meet my son are sometimes surprised by how much he enjoys his parents. We disagree, as all families do, but we all enjoy talking together. Nancy in Texas commented, "Closeness develops in family when you homeschool. My twenty-three year old and my twenty-one year old call daily." Talking of her family, Patti in North Carolina reported, "Everybody is happier." When parents are around and in conversation more, we can find the best moments to utter our pearls of wisdom, or better yet, to gently ask the right questions. We can coach children through upcoming social events, preview difficult situations, and discuss afterwards how they went. We have more natural opportunities to help our children develop social skills.

Homeschooled students have opportunities to work with a wider range of people of all ages, simply because they are not in school all day with hundreds of their age-mates. Socialization in school is artificial, because it is segregated by age. In no other stage of life are all your peers

exactly your age. Compulsory education is only about one hundred years old in the United States; before that young teens had more opportunities to work for and with people of all ages. But homeschooled children spend more time with older and younger children, as did earlier generations of Americans, who were taught at home or in one-room schoolhouses. By volunteering, homeschooled students work with and for adults in adult day care, recreation centers, and other volunteer services. Homeschooled students also have more opportunities
to be with people of all ages in their classes, whether they are older teens taking classes at a community college, or younger teens joining in with adults in daytime exercise classes. Pat reported her hyperactive daughter thrived in a women's daytime cardio-kickboxing class. As the only teen in the class, she rose to the challenge of having to behave well with her adult classmates.

Developing Social Skills

Despite these advantages, socialization is a concern for homeschoolers. Homeschoolers have to put more effort into helping their children plan a social life. Many of our children want friends their age, in their circumstances.

Some of our children need extra coaching to develop social skills and manners. Children with autism spectrum disorders (ASD) or attention problems may miss social cues, and need more training and reinforcement to learn the lessons than the typical child does. Children with auditory processing disorder (APD) may have trouble following a conversation and responding quickly enough not to disturb the flow of the conversation. We all have the experience of thinking of something to say and not working it into the conversation. Our children with ASD, ADD/ADHD, and APD either may regularly not join in conversations, or speak when they should not, because they may not notice that it is not appropriate to speak.

As homeschoolers, we can build social skills lessons into our day, as we go through the day, and also in explicit social skills lessons. At the end of the chapter, I will list some helpful books on this subject. For some children, you may want to see a social worker or an occupational therapist for help. Some of them organize social skills classes.

Or you may want to read one of the books listed, and then advertise and organize your own social skills class. I know parents who have set up a club based around some interest, knowing that they are really running the club for the sake of helping their child develop social skills. Dr. Sam Goldstein said that an important indicator of future success for a child with ASD and ADD/ADHD is simply whether or not she has one friend.[2]

Hanging Out With Homeschoolers

If you have not begun to homeschool, you may wonder what homeschoolers are like. We don't all have twelve children, grind our own wheat, or make all our clothing! Homeschoolers vary tremendously in their beliefs, priorities, and politics. What most of us have in common are traits shared with many other parents:

- We care deeply about our children's education.
- We are pragmatic: we want to know what works for each child.
- We tend to be frugal. (At one meeting for homeschoolers, a guest speaker/therapist accidentally brought the house down by saying, "You don't want to spend your hard-earned paychecks on this therapy unless you know it will work." We laughed, and told her, "We gave up our hard-earned paychecks to homeschool.")
- We like to help others, especially new homeschoolers.
- Many of us have opinions and some of us like to talk about them. If we were indecisive, we never would have started homeschooling.
- We like being with our children—hormones and other factors not withstanding!

Mistakes to Avoid When Choosing Activities

As you choose activities for your child, watch for these mistakes:

- Don't isolate yourselves. Give your children opportunities to learn how to relate to others. As parents of struggling learners, we have a special duty to equip our children with the life skills they need to support themselves, including the ability to communicate and get along with others. Our children often need more help and practice than a typical child to develop basic social skills.

2. Goldstein, Sam, Ph.D. "AD/HD, Autism and Asperger's Disorder: Understanding, Evaluating and Treating a Complex Comorbidity." *Children & Adults with Attention-Deficit/Hyperactivity Disorder* 19th Annual International Conference Pre-conference Symposium. Arlington, Virginia. November 7, 2007.

- Don't overbook your children, exhausting the family as you drive from lessons to classes to practices. Everyone needs time to think, reflect, and rest. Cathi Cohen observes that many social skills cannot be developed in extracurricular activities, but are learned in unstructured activities, like playing with the neighbor children or having a friend over.[3] You cannot do that if you are too busy.

- Don't conceal your child's special needs from teachers and leaders if their learning problems will affect their activity significantly. We do not want to make too much of our children's problems, but a few words to a leader can make life easier for everyone. Be brief. All the leaders need is a brief description of how the diagnosis affects your child's behavior in the group, and what you would like them to do about it, if they are willing. Here are some examples:
  - "Rachel has learning disability affecting her handwriting. May she type her assignments?"
  - "When you are going to ask Jon a question, would you please say his name first to help him focus?"
  - "Elizabeth has a learning disability in reading. If you want her to read aloud, would you tell her before class what she will be reading, so she can look it over first?"
  - Don't be too demanding—private groups are not required to provide accommodations. If you have favors to ask, then ask, don't insist.
  - Don't give the adults too much information. Your child's teacher, leader, or coach may ask more questions later, if they aren't afraid of getting a lecture every time they see you.
  - Realize your child may need to drop a class if it does not work out.

3. Cohen, Cathie. "Raise Your Child's Social I.Q.: Building Social Skills at Home." Northern Virginia chapter of CHADD. Vienna, Virginia. March 27, 2008.

Helping a son pursue his interests

Eileen had been PTA president in her daughter's elementary school before her son Rob started school. When he started kindergarten, "turned south," and was diagnosed with Asperger Syndrome at age five, the school rallied behind the family to give them what Rob needed. But when he moved to middle school, he couldn't get the necessary services. So Eileen started homeschooling him two years ago. She said, "Rob is very articulate and verbal, but chooses not to speak in most social situations, so most folks who know him have not heard him speak."

Rob is very interested in fashion design. His mother is helping him pursue that interest, building on his passion, as Dr. Grandin recommends.[4] Eileen said,

> *I called Virginia Commonwealth University (VCU) School of Design. I wanted to show him there are schools where you can study fashion design. I was expecting to quietly wander the halls. But they gave him a full educational tour. One professor was so taken with him that he regularly invites him to events at the school. He is invited to sit in on classes.*

> *VCU has been wonderful. Rob is very interested in fabric and photography. Now he is taking a course in fabric dying there.*

Rob's favorite TV show is *America's Next Top Model*. Eileen says,

> *When this current obsession takes over his brain I have to wait before we can move on. One of the joys of homeschooling is having all day to get it done. Math is functional consumer math as opposed to boring problems on a page. History has to do with people rather than dates. I also love that we can gear the concepts to his interests.*

4. *Ibid.*

Different Kinds of Activities

Play groups for homeschoolers usually meet at playgrounds, although some meet in homes. They may have children of all ages, but usually the younger set. Typically a play group will advertise through homeschool newsletters, by e-mail or word of mouth, and have a set day and time. Playgroups are a good way to meet other children and find families you may want to invite over for a play date.

Clubs are organized around almost every imaginable interest: books, drama, chess, Lego® Robotics, horses, American Girl dolls. This can be another way to make friends, try a new activity, and get out of the house. Some parents organize these so their children can practice social skills. Some older children organize their own.

Homeschooled kids participate in many different *sports*: everything from children who compete at a national level to beginners learning the basics. For some special needs children, team sports are very difficult. Their learning problems can make it hard to succeed. Children with poor hand-eye coordination, with receptive language problems, problems with distractibility, or with reading social cues, may find solo sports more satisfying, such as horseback-riding, karate, or dance.

It may take a while to find a good sport. One mother reported, "We tried yoga. He hated it, and we tried other things he didn't like. What he likes best is using the therapy ball, doing pushups against wall, and playing basketball."

Martial arts may seem an unwise choice, at first glance: "You want my frustrated, socially unaware, or impulsive child to learn to kick and punch?" Studying martial arts can have many benefits, if you find a good instructor. There is great emphasis on concentration, attention to detail, and on following directions. It builds flexibility, muscle tone, balance, and kinesthetic awareness. In martial arts, the student is chiefly competing against herself: she cannot lose the game or be cut from her team. Your child may need longer to get promoted than some classmates, so choose a martial arts school that is not rushing students toward black belt. A good martial arts teacher teaches the students to respect others. Unlike many other sports, there is little throwing and catching. For those who need an extra second or two to figure out what to do with their arms and legs, practicing a karate routine on their own is great exercise.

In *homeschool co-ops*, families gather weekly or monthly for a day or half-day. Each parent contributes time, either by teaching, assisting, babysitting the teachers' small children, or other jobs. Co-ops may have physical education, music, drama, or other subjects that lend themselves to group activity. Some offer ongoing classes; others will have a class on a different topic at each meeting.

Homeschool classes are a more formal way that homeschoolers work together. Unlike co-ops, where work is shared among all parents, in group classes, teachers are paid. Classes are run by one teacher or a group of teachers teaching different subjects. Parents and other interested adults teach in their areas of expertise or interest. As the students get older, academic work becomes more specialized. It can be complicated for every parent to contribute equally to high school level classes, especially if they also have younger children to homeschool. A few classes can help.

As group classes evolve and grow, some groups see the need for more structure and more rules. Some evolve into umbrella schools, or occasionally into private or charter schools.[5] Others stay small and informal. Some groups fold as the leaders' children grow up.

Some local public and private school offer *part-time enrollment*; others do not. Some parents, though none I interviewed, enroll their students in public school for one or two classes that are hard to find elsewhere, like upper-level foreign language courses. Since this may lead to a school district pressuring you to enroll your child full-time, I would check with the Home School Legal Defense Association and with your state or provincial homeschool organizations to see how that has worked out for other parents in your area. Another complication of part-time enrollment is that many high schools use block scheduling, where classes meet every other day or so, which would make it hard to enroll in any other daytime activity. If you are considering part-time enrollment in a private school, observe a class and talk with the staff about your child's needs—they may not provide accommodations.

Community activities are another great way to get out of the house. My son was an apprentice re-enactor at a living history museum, a

5. Hill, Paul T. "How Home Schooling Will Change Public Education." Hoover Digest, 2000, No. 2. Accessed March 31, 2008. www. hoover.org/ publications/ digest/3483911. html.

volunteer at an adult day-care center, and a Boy Scout. Despite my years of homeschooling, I continue to be impressed by the variety of activities in which homeschooled children are involved. Folks I interviewed had children involved in YMCA, 4-H, Girl Scouts, gymnastics, baseball, recreation center classes, youth symphony, sports teams (as players and coaches), drama classes, summer theatre, and swimming.

An Anxious Kindergartner Blossoms into a Competitive Swimmer

Karen found her daughter Kari thrived with plenty of outside activity once they started homeschooling three years ago. She said:

There was lots of negative impact from having Kari in public school. We met with the school psychologist and counselor because Kari was suffering from anxiety, her sleep was erratic, there were few outlets for excess energy, and she was easily distracted. The school staff was nice, but since Kari was not a problem to the school, she got no help.

Her father and I decided homeschool couldn't be worse. Lots of friends saw a difference in Kari after she was homeschooled, which encouraged me to continue.

I was concerned because she's an only child, and I thought that socialization would be an issue. People warned me against homeschooling her; they thought it would be too much time together. As she gets older, it's become easier, because we can look at each other and say, "We need a break from each other!" Because I am able to find that balance and take care of myself, I have enough energy to find outlets for her.

We're out and about all the time. I make sure I stay connected via the computer and homeschool groups and local community newspapers.

And because Kari's self-esteem has gone up since homeschooling and her anxiety levels have gone down, her ability to attend has improved. She participates so much better in social events that it's been wonderful.

As far as homeschool group class and co-ops, yes, we go on field trips, and we're involved in a drama class. I'll get my connections there. She has taken art. That was a semester commitment. That has been a big, big blessing.

She's on a swim team. This has been a saving grace because she swims year round, and it is such an outlet for her. Kari swims on a national level. She started out at the YMCA and then at the local community pool. Because we saw her interest and love of that sport, we went ahead and had her assessed. They placed her on a competitive team. The swim team is absolutely not homeschooled. We had a few problems in terms of her attentiveness and ability to listen and follow directions, but we persevered and it's been fabulous.

I asked Karen if Kari could have competed at the national level in swimming if she was in still in public school.

No, she would not. In fact, that is one of the perks that we review with her in terms of public school versus homeschool. If there are major behavioral issues, we let her know that swimming is a time commitment and an energy commitment. Because it takes so much energy to do her [work at school], she would be exhausted after a public school experience and she would not be able to hold it together. Kari tends to melt down when she is overwhelmed.

She had an interest in gymnastics, and even in kindergarten—when it is just basically play—and she couldn't do it. It was like seeing a different child. My heart was breaking for her. I have no regrets of sending her to kindergarten, because we have that to compare to.

Homeschool Group or Community Group?

You will find different advantages to each. In community groups, you have to explain about homeschooling to non-homeschoolers. This can be awkward, since most of us with struggling learners do not have the homeschool poster child—plays violin concertos, fluent in three languages, gifted orator, taking three community college classes at age sixteen. We may feel defensive about our choice to homeschool. But we should not. The children in public and private schools are not all superstars, either.

On the other hand, the homeschooled families you meet may have less experience with special needs than their public school counterparts. In public schools, mainstreaming exposes many children to others with special needs. Depending on the severity of your child's learning problems, you may find yourself explaining about special needs to homeschoolers.

Many families I interviewed had children in both homeschooling and community activities. Selena in Pennsylvania explained that for her girls, both of whom have obsessive-compulsive disorder, and one of whom also is a high-functioning autistic, "to be in a group of kids who are special needs but all go to school has worked better than to be with a group of homeschoolers who are typical. My girls have been taking a special needs acting class, and all those kids go to school. The girls really enjoy that class." Other families had different experiences, as we will see next.

Choosing Activities

Homeschooling does not keep your child from having difficulty fitting in and being understood. Just like if you had kept your child in school, you can expect some group activities not to work out, for some children more than others. Denise in Florida said,

> *These seem to be more distracting than helpful for us so far. So why do I keep signing up for them? It's back to the guilt. I think they need the socialization, so I sign them up for a co-op, a sports program, or a dance class. The classes are sometimes fun, but usually they create a lot of stress because of the social issues that arise,*

because my children aren't obviously disabled. So I get strange looks that I allow my child to act like that. I have a lot more empathy for other parents, now. And then the kids start feeling rejected and lose interest, anyway.

Someone said to avoid outside activities your first year, and then to only add them in very gradually as the children display the maturity to warrant them. I think we rush our kids into outside activities far too soon. While a middle schooler might need an outside interest, your kindergartner probably doesn't.

Like Karen, whose story is in the last sidebar, many families I interviewed had good or excellent experiences in homeschooling activities, including homeschool classes in band, swimming, art classes, academic subjects like geography, book clubs, Bible studies, and field trips.

Explore both the homeschool activities and community activities in your area. Check with your local recreation department, the newspapers, and homeschool newsletters and local websites. Join listservs of local homeschoolers and groups for parents with a child with needs like yours. If there is no group specifically for her particular problem, you may find one for a similar issue, which can keep you informed about activities your child might appreciate.

Try activities out and see what is best for your particular child and her needs. Observe a class. Some will let your child try a free lesson. But if you sign up, I suggest you and your child agree to stick it out for a season, a six-week session, a month-long trial— whatever suits the program. Once you have made a commitment, I do not recommend letting your child quit after a week or two, unless you agree it is a complete, unredeemable disaster. It is unwise to let our children quit as soon as anything is uncomfortable. Sometimes children need time to adjust to new activities. My son was very changeable in his opinions, and sometimes wanted to quit an activity. I always said, "Okay, but we paid for this six-week session. We'll finish it, and then you can stop." By that time, he always wanted to continue.

Conclusion

Whatever you do, explore the possibilities beyond your front door. If you have had unsuccessful experiences, take a break, but don't write off an activity forever. Children grow. In a year or two, your child may be ready to try things you never imagined they would enjoy.

As a nine-year-old, my son was no fun to take on a hike. He would complain about how boring and tiring it was. Three years later, he visited a Boy Scout troop. His first hike with them was ten miles along the C&O Canal up to Harper's Ferry, West Virginia, and ended in a downpour. He loved it! He made friends in the troop and had kind, patient leaders, including his father. Since then, they have completed a twenty-mile hike, four week-long backpacking and canoeing trips, and more hikes and camping trips than I can count. In 2005, he became an Eagle Scout. Sometimes our children surprise us. What a privilege to watch them grow up.

Resources

Baker, Jed. *The Social Skills Picture Book: Teaching Play, Emotion, and Communication to Children With Autism.* Arlington, Texas: Future Horizons, 2003.

_____. *Social Skills Picture Book for High School and Beyond,* Arlington, Texas: Future Horizons, 2006.

Cohen, Cathi, L.C.S.W. *Raise Your Child's Social IQ: Stepping Stones to People Skills for Kids.* Washington, DC: Advantage, 2000.

Crary, Elizabeth. *Dealing with Feelings* series. Seattle: Parenting Press, 1992. Titles include, *I'm Proud, I'm Mad,* and *I'm Frustrated.*

Giler, Janet Z., Ph.D. *Socially ADDept: A Manual for Parents of Children with ADHD and/or Learning Disabilities.* Continuing Education Seminars, 2000.

Grandin, Temple, Ph.D., and Sean Barron. *Unwritten Rules of Social Relationships: Decoding Social Mysteries Through the Unique Perspectives of Autism.* Arlington, Texas: Future Horizons, 2005.

Gray, Carol. *Comic Strip Conversations.* Arlington, Texas: Future Horizons, 1994.

_____. *The New Social Story Book : Illustrated Edition*, Arlington, Texas: Future Horizons, 2000.

Joslin, Sesyle. *What Do You Say, Dear?* and *What Do You Do, Dear?* New York: HarperTrophy, 1986. Illustrated by Maurice Sendak, these two children's classic picture books humorously teach manners.

Lavoie, Richard, M.A., M.Ed. *It's So Much Work To Be Your Friend.* New York: Touchstone, 2005. Available in either book or DVD format from www.ricklavoie.com

Louv, Richard. *Last Child in the Woods: Saving Our Children From Nature-Deficit Disorder.* New York: Workman, 2008.

Mannix, Darlene and Tim Mannix. *Social Skills Activities for Special Children.* San Francisco: Jossey-Bass, 1993.

Nowicki, Stephen, Jr., Ph.D., and Marshall P. Duke, Ph.D. *Helping the Child Who Doesn't Fit in.* Atlanta: Peachtree Publishers, 1992.

Packer, Alex J., Ph.D. *How Rude! The Teenagers' Guide to Good Manners, Proper Behavior, and Not Grossing People Out.* Minneapolis: Free Spirit Publishing. 1997.

Rubin, Kenneth H., Ph.D. *The Friendship Factor: Helping Our Children Navigate Their Social World—And Why It Matters for Their Success and Happiness.* New York: Penguin, 2003.

Sande, Corlette. *The Young Peacemaker*. Wapwallopen, Pennsylvania: Shepherd Press, 2002. This curriculum includes twelve student activity books (comic books with questions and puzzles) and a teacher manual. This is a Bible-based curriculum, but families from any background should examine the website to see this approach to conflict resolution. For older teens, see Ken Sande's *The Peacemaker: Student Edition*, also from Shepherd Press. Both products available at peacemaker.net: click on "Resources," then "Young Peacemaker."

24

Helping Your Child Keep Going

Your child may be excited as you begin to homeschool, but as with any new project, when the newness wears off, sometimes our children get bored. We may become too set in our ways or too lax. In any case, the question is the same: how to keep going? How to revive our homeschool? In this chapter we will consider how to help our children keep going; in the next two chapters, we will discuss how to keep going ourselves.

In this chapter:
- Nurture a love of learning
- Dealing with disastrous days
- Building character, hope, and self-esteem

Nurture a Love of Learning

In a rut? Include activities that make learning fun:
- Get outdoors with your children. Explore a creek, the woods, a field, a mountain, the dirt in the backyard, a park, a garden.
- Make exercise a fun part of your school day. How many times can your child run around your house in five minutes? Graph how many push-ups he can do. Have him jump on a mini-trampoline

while practicing spelling or math facts. Take a short break mid-morning for basketball, soccer, or biking.

- Stop to enjoy creation: a beautiful sunset, a peculiar bug, sprouting fern fronds uncurling, frost crystals. Encourage your child to observe and notice the smell of hot chocolate, the crunch of an apple, a chorus of cicadas.

- Nurture curiosity. Ask questions, not as a teacher, but simply as a curious human. Has your child stumped you with his question? Tell him it was a good question, get out the dictionary, encyclopedia, or computer, and look up the answer. Better yet, teach him how to find it.

- Include art in your homeschool. Invest in some art supplies. Let your child try all kinds of media: paint, clay, charcoal, pencils. Place a few of his creations around the house.

- Music can enrich your homeschool, too. Sing together. Expose your children to a variety of music. Many musical groups and orchestras have inexpensive or free children's programs. Many homeschool groups have orchestras or bands. A recorder is an inexpensive first instrument you can teach at home from a book.

- One parent said, "Pets are good for kids. The cats been a blessing; they have a calming effect. They comfort the kids. Kids can be distracted by them and can learn responsibility from them."

Check yourself to make sure you are not contributing to your child's frustration unnecessarily. Are you making your child and yourself busier than you need to be? Review your goals and make sure your expectations are reasonable. Consider how you might incorporate your child's interests in his education. Your entire homeschool does not need to revolve around those interests, though it can.

Dealing With Disastrous Days

Like everyone, your child will have bad days, whether you homeschool or not. You will have days when your student seems to have forgotten everything, days he is frustrated, grumpy, or discouraged. So first, accept that you will have some. Accept that some days will be mediocre. Some days the work will be hard.

But what about the very bad days? When I spoke at the international conference of CHADD (Children and Adults with Attention Deficit/ Hyperactivity Disorder) in November 2007, my co-presenter Catherine Adams prepared a one-page "Homeschool Problem Solving Guide." Her last-resort solution for every problem was, "Take a break or a field trip!" It was funny, but it is also good advice. If you and the child need time apart to cool down, take it, if the child can be left alone safely. After some time apart, you might skip on to another subject, or try exercising, going to the library, a museum, or a nearby stream. Read aloud to the child. If possible, give him a task that he enjoys and can do well and independently, like making a drawing for a sick friend or brushing the dog. Don't assign work that you will have to supervise, instruct, or correct.

I am not saying to reward misbehavior with a fun activity or outing. If misbehavior and bad attitudes are spoiling the school day, they must be dealt with, whether it is the parent, the child, or both who are the problem. After issues have been discussed, apologies made, and the relationship restored, then sometimes a little holiday is just what parent and child both need. And some days we just grow weary and need a break.

As a parent, I have made too many mistakes to write a book on how to discipline children, but here are some basic tips. If you cannot divert a child from losing control,

- Don't lecture. When your child is melting down, he is in no shape to hear a lecture from you. Keep it short and simple.
- Don't get into arguments. Don't debate your decisions, rules, or reasoning.
- Don't be vindictive or nasty. If you are, apologize later.
- Deal with the issues promptly, but after everyone has calmed down.
- Enforce rules and principles you have established beforehand.
- Time-outs are helpful, about one minute per year the child has been alive. (A six-year-old has to be quiet for six minutes to be allowed out of time-out.) I set a timer, and if I heard yelling or complaining, I reset the timer and tell him I had to do so. If the child is too agitated to calm down, I would allow him to have a time out in his

bedroom, where there are distractions that can allow him to settle himself. This is not rewarding the meltdown, but only giving him a few minutes to calm enough so his conscience can begin to work and he can regain self-control.

- Dispassionately discuss the behavior problem with the child later, at bedtime or the next day.

Dealing with Meltdowns

Because our struggling learners deal with frustration daily, they are more prone to lose self-control. Children with autism spectrum disorders (ASD) have the additional frustrations of communication and social skills problems and may feel overwhelmed by sounds and sensations the rest of us can ignore. Parents of children with ASD provided the following tips for dealing with meltdowns:

- Recognize the preliminary symptoms, and allow him to go to a quiet place to relax and regain control.
- If he has a meltdown, sometimes I can get him in a tight hold and get him on couch, and give him a hard hug. If he lets me do that, I can rub his hair or head, and that calms him down. But this varies with the child! Distracting him can help sometimes. Sometimes I let him run it off.
- When my son melts down, my daughter and I learned if we ignore him, and then ask very casually, "What are you doing down there on the floor?" he would stand up, dust himself off, and say, "Oh, I don't know." We are not reinforcing his meltdowns.
- Leave him alone until he calms down!
- I give him time out in his room, then we discuss it. "What should you have done?" I make him give me feedback.

Building Character, Hope, and Self-Esteem

Are you discouraging your child without realizing it? Does your tone of voice communicate disgust, despair, or annoyance? You might tape record your voice. If turning the recorder on makes you suddenly sound kinder, leave it on until you forget it is on, then listen to how you sound. Maybe you are scowling or frowning as you teach. Try to "freeze your face," walk over to a mirror, and see what your children see, as Melinda L. Boring suggests in her book, *Heads Up Helping!* [1]

When the struggling learner finishes a task early, resist the urge to pile on extra work. It sounds absurd, but homeschoolers sometimes do. I have. We parents are so relieved that our child has reached a goal, we immediately turn our sights to the next goal. We tell him, "You finished early—good. Now you can do this, too." What a letdown! In our anxiety to help our child grow up, we respond to his success in a way that says, "What you achieved was insignificant, even though I have acted for weeks like it was important. There are a thousand more things to learn." Unless your child is doing work he wants more of, do not reward him for finishing early by giving him extra work.

How do we encourage our children? First, we praise them. Praise their progress. When we see no progress, we can still praise them for not giving up. Trying again and again is heroic. My son worked harder for his Cs in geometry than I did for my As, so I told him that I respected the way he did not quit. Have you ever struggled hard in a class, only to get a C, D, or F? A low grade is not much of a prize, considering the effort it costs sometimes. Is your child doggedly keeping on? Who will notice and praise them if you do not?

Your praise should be specific. It is easy to let our criticism be specific, ("You forgot to capitalize," "I cannot read this handwriting,") and our praise be vague ("Nice work," "Good job.") Tell your child what you like about their work. Perhaps they cannot capitalize, but they had an unusual insight, a creative idea, or a well-turned phrase. Look for something to praise.

Some teachers use the "three stars and a wish" approach to marking some assignments, which I learned from Writer's Workshop. (See chapter

1. Boring, Melinda L. Heads Up Helping! Teaching Tips and Techniques for Working with ADD, ADHD, and Other Children with Challenges. *Victoria, Canada: Trafford, 2002.*

19.) They put stars by three good elements of the work and one "wish," a suggestion for how to improve the next time. Writing teacher Diana L. Thomas once told of grading a paper so filled with errors of all kinds, that she was stymied for a while. Finally she wrote, "This paper has many correctly spelled words."[2] Start with whatever positive comments you can make. You can find something to praise, and encourage a discouraged learner.

In *Punished By Rewards*[3], Alfie Kohn recommends that praise be specific and urges that praise should never be overblown or insincere. Children recognize baloney. Don't gush over their work as if you are homeschooling a little genius. Even if you are, you do them no favors with extravagant praise. You will only teach him that either you are easy to fool, or the rest of the world should treat him that way. It will not.

Offer specific, brief, positive praise. Here is one test of whether you are gushing: how excited would you be if you were tutoring someone else's struggling child and he had produced this work?

A range of authors, including psychologists Drs. Robert Brooks, Sam Goldstein and Nancy Mather[4] and special educator Joyce Herzog,[5] recommend that we should offer more praise than criticism. For the teacher of a discouraged learner, it is a good goal. I am sure I never achieved it, and it is difficult to do without praising insincerely. But it is worth practicing and aiming for.

Kohn also points out that if we make rewards too big or important, children may learn only work to earn rewards. They will miss the joy of work well done. We want our children to read, not just because it earns them free pizza or ice cream or bowling, but for the pleasure of reading.

But if working on a basic academic skill like reading exhausts your child, an occasional small snack, treat, or pat on the back can help. Just as adults appreciate paychecks even when they love their work, so children appreciate rewards. Occasionally you might say, "If we get these four assignments done by noon, I will take you skating." Some parents told me their children responded well to token or point systems, earning that skating trip or other privilege by earning points for various kinds of good behavior through the week. (One parent recommended Dr. Russell Barkley's book for setting up a point system, *Taking Charge of ADHD: The Complete,*

2. Thomas, Diana L. "Writers Workshop." Herndon, Virginia, May 3, 2003.

3. Kohn, Alfie. Punished By Rewards: The Trouble With Gold Stars, Incentive Plans, As, Praise, and Other Bribes. New York: Houghton Mifflin, 1993.

4. Goldstein, Sam, Ph.D, and Nancy Mather, Ph.D., "Self-Esteem," with Robert Brooks, Ph.D. Overcoming Underachieving. New York: Wiley and Sons, 1998.

5. Herzog, Joyce. "Rx For Your Special Needs Child." Indiana Association of Home Educators Annual Convention. March 24, 2007. www.bestchristianconferences.com.

Authoritative Guide for Parents.[6]) When you offer incentives, make sure that your child has a reasonable chance of reaching the target, remembering that "Hope deferred makes the heart sick." [7]

More ways to build self-esteem:

- Give your child work to do: chores around the house or volunteering in the community. Helping with younger children can be especially helpful.
- Involve them in decisions. "Write me a paragraph describing a major character in this story. You can choose which one." "Which subject is hardest for you? We should do it when you are at your best. What time of day would that be?" When you are shopping for next year's history books, find out what they liked and did not like about the ones you used now. Ask them for ideas in solving family and homeschool problems when appropriate. Even when you cannot use their ideas, you can listen.
- Take them out and talk to them, one-on-one. Wayne Rice, in *Enjoy Your Middle Schooler,*[8] suggests going out occasionally, just one parent and one child, for a sandwich or other cheap date. The parent's goals should be to ask questions, listen, and not criticize or lecture. For thirty or sixty minutes, parents can practice for the day they will have an adult child they will want to be friends with.

  For a younger child, try to get a few minutes alone with him to play together and to listen to him. Doing this daily can be hard if you have several children, but try.
- Time alone together in the car is another good time to talk, if you remember not always to lecture.

Finally, build their self-esteem by helping them develop their gifts. This can take time with some children who mature slowly. Let them try different activities. My son tried soccer, swimming, karate, and two scouting programs before he found what he liked, and it was sometimes very frustrating, even then.

If you cannot tell what your child is good at yet, ask other adults who know him well. Sometimes we are so close to our child's problems and struggles, we can overlook his budding talents. It may be Legos®, an ability to ask good questions, it may be management, sales, writing, art, or music.

6. Barkley, Russell A., Ph.D. Taking Charge of ADHD: The Complete, Authoritative Guide for Parents. *New York: Guilford, 2000.*

7. Holy Bible: English Standard Version. *Wheaton: Crossway, 2003. Proverbs 13:12.*

8. Rice, Wayne. Enjoy Your Middle Schooler. *Grand Rapids: Zondervan, 1994.*

9. Raverat, Gwen. Period Piece: A Cambridge Childhood. *London: Faber and Faber, 1984. p. 273.*

When noted English composer Ralph Vaughan Williams was a young man, his family complained that he "would go on working at music when 'he was so hopelessly bad at it.'"[9] Your child's talents may not yet have blossomed, or they may be in an area so different from your talents that you have trouble seeing them.

In his lecture, "You Get More With Honey: Tools to Avoid Emotional Escalation While Working Toward Behavioral Goals," psychologist Dr. Mark Hurley urged parents that when they need to punish a child, not to take away the activity the child excels in. If your child struggles with school and only succeeds in soccer, don't pull him off the soccer team. It discourages him too much, and his coach probably won't have him back later, either, Hurley added.[10] Dr. Temple Grandin, a leading speaker and writer on autism, and autistic herself, agrees, saying, "Never take away something that could be the child's career, like musical instruments, arts, or computer programming. We've got to nurture the things that could turn into careers. … Talents are like fragile flowers. They can be stomped on and they've got to be nurtured."[11]

Herzog[12] and psychologists Goldstein, Mather, and Brooks[13] recommend spending at least half your time on your child's strengths. (The latter are not writing about homeschooling, but after-school time.) I never met this goal, but it underscores the need to build and encourage our child's gifts.

Finally, teach them how to deal with mistakes. When you discover you have made a mistake, let them hear you think out loud about how to deal with it. Let them hear you think of possible solutions, weigh the possible solutions, and choose one. When you stay calm, you are demonstrating how they ought to deal with their own mistakes. Some children get very anxious about mistakes, which makes it hard for them to think. Help them see that mistakes are common and that many can be fixed.

Some of us begin homeschooling to rescue our children's self-esteem and love of learning. Seeing our children blossom is one of the great joys of homeschooling. But it will not happen by accident. We must keep in mind that one of our chief goals is to encourage our children. In the last two chapters, we will consider how to keep ourselves going so we can help them flourish.

10. Hurley, Mark, Ph.D. "You Get More With Honey: Tools to Avoid Emotional Escalation While Working Toward Behavioral Goals." Children & Adults with Attention-Deficit/Hyperactivity Disorder 19th Annual International Conference, Arlington, Virginia. November 9, 2007.

11. Grandin, Temple, Ph.D. "My Experience with Autism." Distinguished Lecturer Series Lecture at the M.I.N.D. Institute, University of California at Davis. February 14, 2007. Accessed March 23, 2008. www.ucdmc.ucdavis.edu/mindinstitute/events/dls_recorded_events.html

12. Herzog. Op. cit.

13. Goldstein, et. al. Op. cit.

25

Support Groups

Teachers have a teacher's lounge to get time away from their students to work quietly, discuss problems, or just share a laugh. Homeschool parents find support for their efforts in others ways.

In this chapter:
- Family
- Churches and religious organizations
- Local homeschool support groups
- Finding other homeschoolers with struggling learners
- Online support groups
- State and national homeschool organizations

Family

Several homeschooling families I interviewed were well supported by their extended families. Homeschooler Selena reports that her mother, a retired opera singer, comes over weekly to give voice lessons and to assist with homeschooling Selena's two daughters, one of whom has high-functioning autism and obsessive-compulsive disorder. Anita, homeschooling a child with multiple disabilities, finds plenty of support from her extended family: social interactions for her son and help from her mother, who comes over one morning a week to assist. Other families said their families were supportive and their children enjoyed being with their cousins.

When I began homeschooling, my father, who had once taught government at a local university, volunteered to be my substitute teacher one afternoon a week, so I could run errands. But considering his interests and ability, soon we made him chairman of the history department of our homeschool. It was a win-win situation: my son had time with his grandfather studying a subject they both loved, I had one fewer subject to prepare for, had a little time to myself, and enjoyed seeing my father each week. He enjoyed teaching so much, he says he wishes he had been able to tutor all his grandchildren.

You may not have a trained teacher or a fellow homeschooler in your family who you can recruit to assist you, but look around your family. Can someone help, even it is simply coming over for an hour so you can run to the grocery store?

Churches and Religious Organizations

Several parents commented that they would be unable to homeschool without the support of their churches. Several are involved in church-based support groups, while others just appreciate finding supportive friendships.

Some parents told of the difficulties maintaining involvement in a religious group because of their children's special needs. One mother of an autistic son described her disappointment at being unable to attend church during periods when the child could not tolerate the Sunday school classroom. Now some places of worship are providing training for teachers and aides, so that both parents of special needs children can worship together, which can refresh and equip them for the week ahead. For a discussion of the valuable role of people with disabilities in churches, see Stephanie Hubach's book, *Same Lake, Different Boat: Coming Alongside People Touched By Disability.*[1]

1. Hubach, Stephanie. Same Lake, Different Boat: Coming Alongside People Touched By Disability. Philipsburg, New Jersey: P&R Publishing, 2006.

Local Homeschool Support Groups

Local support groups allow homeschooling parents to meet and exchange ideas and encouragement. Local homeschool support groups vary tremendously. Some share common religious beliefs. Some are united by a teaching approach, such as Charlotte Mason, unschooling, or classical. (See chapter 12 for a discussion of these teaching styles.) Groups can be large or small and meet weekly or monthly, in homes, churches, restaurants, or libraries. In addition to the parents' meetings, some support groups also run co-ops or classes, as described in chapter 23. Even in groups that plan no activities for children, your meeting other homeschoolers may lead to joint family outings or play dates for your children. These social times can energize you.

To find the right group, you may need to visit several. Even groups with the same beliefs and goals will be organized differently and be shaped by the different personalities there. More than half the parents interviewed for this book have been part of a local homeschool support group.

Within or beyond a homeschool support group, look for supportive people. Maryland homeschooler Ellen said, "Celebrate all the little achievements, and seek people who celebrate with you. Some say, 'Oh, great she's talking. So what? She should have been talking three years ago.' Forget those people. Find the people who say, 'Wow! This is great!' and gravitate towards them."

Homeschoolers love to help, and remember how hard it is to begin. But don't become a nuisance. Look for ways to encourage others, too. Ellen also said, thanks to Ellyn Davis' article on homeschool burnout, she has learned to avoid "energy vampires," people who exhaust you with their negativity or consuming neediness.[2]

And be patient when well-meaning people tell you all about their favorite teaching tips—especially if you have already used them and they didn't work for your child! In support groups, you might meet people who brag about their children, which can be hard to listen to when your child is far behind. Try not to be touchy. When I started homeschooling, I thought I would scream if one more person said, "What I love about homeschooling is that we're always done by noon." Very few people said this, but I was a

2. Davis, Ellyn. "*Homeschool Burnout.*" Homeschool Marketplace. *Accessed August 7, 2008. www. homeschool-marketplace. com/e-zines/journal jan1508 .html*

little touchy. When I found a friend who said their lessons ran late into the afternoon, I could have hugged her.

Some parents I interviewed said they face another problem with support groups and other contacts outside their immediate family. Children with emotional or learning problems are sometimes misunderstood by others. Pat, whose son has ADD/ADHD, Asperger Syndrome, and dyslexia, thought the hardest part of homeschooling was, "being in support group, but you're the only one like *that*." Another mother described a child at a playground taking something from her son, who exploded, hitting and screaming. Knowing her child was out of control and that she could not correct his behavior until he could listen, her first step was to try to calm him. She knew she was going to discipline him once he was calm enough to hear her, but she also knew that to the other parents nearby, it looked like she was rewarding an aggressive child with sympathy. When asked the greatest difficulty with homeschooling, a third mother said it was, "other people not understanding. If they can't see a physical handicap, they don't understand that there is a special need there."

To find homeschooling friends to encourage you, you do not have to find homeschoolers with their own struggling learners. It takes tact, kindness, and a little imagination on their part. One woman had a son two years younger than mine, but who probably read four years above grade level, while my son read about two years below his grade level. Our boys became friends, anyway, and so did we. She did not hide her children's accomplishments, but she didn't boast, and she offered intelligent sympathy with our struggles. One mother said when she gets discouraged with her daughter's behavior, "that's when I go upstairs and call one of my dear friends. Her child doesn't have ADD, but I'll say, 'This is what I'm going through, this is what's happening.' She'll say, 'I just went through that!' She normalizes it for me."

Sometimes when you are discouraged, these other adults can remind you of your child's strengths. They may encourage your child by praising one of his strengths. One mother recalled that when her daughter was told by an adult friend that the girl was patient, that transformed the girl. She began to think of herself as patient and act more patiently.

Find Other Homeschoolers With Struggling Learners

It is encouraging to talk with other parents of struggling learners, but they can be hard to find. It's not as if we wear nametags listing all our children's disabilities. We do not want to think of our children chiefly as "disabled" or ourselves as "parents of a child with [insert diagnosis here]." And some homeschoolers have not had their children's special needs diagnosed. Since you could offend someone by asking, "Excuse me, does your child have _____?", how can you find other homeschoolers with struggling learners? You can watch. You also can ask around in your local support group using less loaded terms. Instead of learning disabilities, attention deficit disorder, or hyperactive (which are all terms of diagnosis), you can talk about your child having "learning differences," "attention difficulties," or "high energy." Someone may say, "My daughter does, too," and you may have found someone to talk to.

Local support groups for homeschoolers with special needs children are rare, because these parents often do not have time to organize groups or keep them going. When they do start, these groups often include a range of special needs. While the members' children have different ages, abilities, and struggles, their bonds begin with a shared sense of struggle and eagerness to help our children thrive. Other groups may focus on one need. Near my home, for several years there was a group for homeschoolers with gifted and learning disabled children, and a new group is forming for those homeschooling children with Down Syndrome. In different parts of the country, several local groups have sprung up as offshoots of GIFTSNC (Giving and Getting Information for Special Needs Children), a support group begun in North Carolina.

If you want to start your own local group, GIFTSNC's Yahoo online group includes a file with advice on how to start. (Go to groups.yahoo. com, and search for GIFTSNC.) My advice on starting a group is, first, share the workload. In our local group, one mother moderates the Yahoo group, another arranges the room, another handles publicity, and several folks have brought snacks or found a speaker for us, sometimes their child's therapist. I also suggest you do not often change the meeting location or time, that you advertise using e-mail and through other homeschool groups newsletters. Finally, expect attendance to vary. Illness and fatigue can hurt attendance even more than the average homeschool group, because child care is harder to arrange for children with special needs.

If you join a support group, look for ways to help and encourage the leaders. Even a small task (copying the handouts, bringing snacks, lining up one speaker) can help the group keep going. It takes time and energy keep a group alive, but many hands make light work.

Online Support Groups

But what if you cannot find anyone within twenty miles of you homeschooling a child with difficulties like yours? Who can you talk to about your particular problems?

Online support groups may help. These groups may revolve around one particular special need (gluten-free diet, parents of children with Asperger Syndrome, and so on), or to homeschooling children with a particular special need, or to homeschooling in a particular region, or to homeschooling all sorts of special needs children.

I found most of the parents interviewed for this book by posting notes to online support group message boards. Online groups, also called listservs, message boards, or forums, operate through yahoo.com, aol.com, and other websites. The vendors of Sonlight Curriculum and the authors of *The Well-Trained Mind* each have forums for homeschoolers with special needs children, among their many forums. (See sonlight-curriculum.com and welltrainedmind.com.)

Online support groups have several advantages. As Sarita in Georgia said, "When you can't leave the house—your child is sick, or you just can't afford to go anywhere—you can go online and say, 'Okay, I've got this problem. How do I handle it?'" You can converse without waiting for a monthly meeting, and post a question or comment whenever you have five minutes. Within hours, you may have answers, comments, or moral support from anywhere in the country.

But here is the downside. Your post may sit unanswered, and if it does, you cannot tell if no one knows an answer, or if everyone is just busy. Occasionally groups without strict moderators may wander off-topic or get into arguments, but those with active moderators generally remain civil. (We should all thank the volunteers who serve as moderators of useful groups.) Another disadvantage of relying on online groups for support is that these friends usually live too far away to ever meet you for lunch, bring you a meal when you are sick, or take your child for an hour—which can happen with your friends from a local support group. Perhaps that is why most people I interviewed for this book have been in both local and online support groups.

For those unfamiliar with online groups, here's how they work. Membership is usually free. Most groups require you to join in order to post questions. When you post questions, they appear on the website. You can set your membership either to receive an e-mail every time anyone posts a message (which may flood your mailbox), a daily digest (one e-mail combining all the posts of the day), or no e-mail at all (meaning if you do not go back to the website, you do not know what's been posted). On some online groups, posts are visible only to other members, but in others anyone can read them, so do not include private identifying information such as your last name, address, or telephone number. Once members read your post, they can e-mail you privately *(off-list)*, or reply by posting to the group. You also can search the group's old posts *(archives)* to find if someone has asked your question before. Many groups have more than one moderator to share the work of seeing that the online conversation stays on the subject and civil.

A few warnings about online support groups. Realize that anyone can post *anything* on a message board. Moderators give guidelines, delete offensive material, and occasionally even bar members who are rude or break rules. But errors in fact and unwise opinions may stay in the archives forever. So be careful what you post. Do not post when you are angry. Be cautious. Sharing struggles can create a sense of instant intimacy, but you still are getting advice from strangers who might appall you if face to face. Remember also that no two children are alike, so you should not expect to find other parents with a child just like yours. Online support groups are a great resource if you use them wisely.

Local support groups for families dealing with particular disabilities let you meet parents and teachers who face the same struggles you do, even if few other members homeschool. Hospitals sometimes host support groups for various special needs. Several national patient advocacy organizations have local chapters that organize support groups. Check their websites, which often have links to state and local chapters.

A few patient advocacy group chapters have support groups specifically for homeschoolers, while others only have parent support groups, in which homeschoolers may be involved. Ask. Even if there are few or no homeschoolers in a support group, they still can encourage you and inform you about the latest research and treatment on a particular special need.

Even if your child is undiagnosed, you can learn useful tips and ways of thinking. For instance, if your child does not quite meet the criteria for a diagnosis of ADD/ADHD, but your child has some of those tendencies, you can learn strategies for helping them cope with schoolwork, family life, and preparation for independent living.

Local and National Homeschool Organizations

Though not designed specifically to help parents with struggling learners, your state, provincial and national homeschool organizations are good resources. Visit their websites to see what information they have about teaching special needs children. Ask for advice on finding consultants, testing, and meeting legal requirements. Look at your provincial or state organizations' annual convention: as homeschooling struggling learners becomes more popular, more and more conventions are offering a special needs track—a series of workshops. If you don't see one, ask for one. Also check conventions nearby, which may better suit your needs or schedule.

Conclusion

Homeschooling can be lonely at times, especially when you are teaching a struggling learner. But you are not alone. Local, state, and national homeschool groups, patient advocacy organizations, family, and online groups can provide the support you need to keep going. One parent's advice to beginners is, "I would encourage them to get support: When I started, I thought I could do it all. As my son gets older, I realized if I'm in for long haul, I've really got to set up a lot of support." In the next chapter, we will look at other ways to help yourself keep going as you homeschool.

26

Staying Sane: Balancing Health, Marriage, Family, and Homeschool

Homeschooling "has to become one of your main purposes in life. You do have to give up a lot of things to do it," said one parent I interviewed. But don't let the work of homeschooling occupy you constantly. When you homeschool struggling learners, you need to guard your sanity, health, marriage, and family.

In this chapter:
- Healthy parent
- Your spouse and homeschooling
- Healthy marriage
- Healthy family

Healthy Parent

I love learning and I love teaching. But I do not believe in teaching twenty-four hours a day, seven days a week. It isn't healthy, and it will burn parents out. Some of us have a tendency to make every moment educational, which we must resist. We need time to relax and laugh, and so do our children.

Healthy parents have interests beyond homeschool. They have hobbies, though they may not have much time for them while raising children. Perhaps they run a business from home or help with their spouse's business.

Maybe they volunteer at the library or a soup kitchen. Whatever their interests, they have a life apart from their children, and they will have something to do with themselves when their last child moves out.

> ### Taking care of yourself—
> ### advice from homeschoolers:
>
> Hannah in North Carolina:
>
> *It is important for moms to know that they shouldn't feel guilty about becoming frustrated with their children. We moms tend to beat ourselves up and these are difficult children. They're high energy. They lack a lot of self-control and it is hard. It is okay to acknowledge that it is tough and not feel guilty about not springing out of bed eagerly in the morning to homeschool this child. I learned that from experience.*
>
> Karen in Virginia:
>
> *We don't have energy to keep up with these kids, so I have explained to my daughter that I need a certain amount of time, usually twenty or thirty minutes a day, to take care of and to focus on myself. For me, I exercise just to reduce stress level and increase my ability to focus. I explain to her that if I can do that, if she can allow me to do that, then I can be a better mommy and a better teacher.*
>
> Michelle in Iowa:
>
> *Sometimes Mom is the one who needs the time out.*

Healthy parents have friends they like to spend time with. They don't spend all the time with friends talking about their children. Granted, nearly everyone with children wants to talk about them, but wise parents aim not to bore others, and try to notice when they do!

Healthy parents get out. If they don't have time or money for movies, theatre, kayaking, or backpacking anymore, they at least manage to take walks and escape into books. Homeschooler Angela recalled her pleasure when her children became old enough that she could walk down to the cul-de-sac, stand there, and enjoy the outdoors for a few minutes without them.

Good parents take care of their health. One mother I know made time for a weight-training class, which got her out of the house and improved her health. No money for a class? Can't get away? A mother of four gets up early and works on the treadmill while reading her book, and another mother with six children under the age of ten uses her treadmill while watching a morning news show, reminding herself of the world beyond her home-school. One mother plays softball, and another began taking karate with her son, and liked it so well she kept on when he dropped out.

Taking care of your health also means remembering to see your doctor and to eat well. This is an area where homeschooling and taking care of yourself overlap: by demonstrating healthy eating habits you reinforce what you are teaching about nutrition.

Good parents do not idolize their children. They don't make them the center of their lives. They don't live in a way that says to their children, "I'll be a failure if you don't learn to love reading/go to college/like Shakespeare/master calculus."

Good parents discipline their children. Their children know who is in charge—and it's not the kids! Wise parents train their children, making expectations very clear. They must firmly and calmly discipline them with the goal of raising self-disciplined, independent, caring adults. They teach their children to respect them. They respect the children, too, not domineering over them, belittling them, or disciplining in a fury. Parents must try to understand their children's limitations—for instance, the overwhelmed child may need to be calmed before his misbehavior can be corrected. When raising children with learning problems, it can be very hard to distinguish between when the child is lazy or tired, uncooperative or confused, won't obey or can't obey. We will get it wrong sometimes, but it is vital to keep trying. With human nature as it is, some days children may try to use their disabilities as an excuse for not trying or not helping out. While keeping their great struggles in mind, parents must focus on developing their children's character.

When asked how to advise beginners or how to cope with homeschooling a struggling learner, many parents I interviewed said to pray. These included many who said they were not homeschooling out of a religious conviction. But they recognized they needed guidance, patience, and strength for their work, and expressed confidence that God would guide and help them as they trusted him. These parents also believed that their children had been created as they were for a good purpose, and that there was an underlying, though unseen, plan to their lives and their children's lives.

Your Spouse and Homeschooling

In two-parent families, usually one does most of the homeschooling, while the other is the main wage earner. The homeschooling parent needs to include the working parent in the homeschool. The working parent doesn't have time for all the details, but can be a sounding board, advising and reflecting on decisions about goals, plans, and curriculum. The working parent should give his or her perspective: "Why don't you put aside [some subject], since this is so frustrating, and work on something else for a while?"

A working parent may help in different ways: teaching one subject, either one the other parent is least comfortable with, or the subject the working parent likes best. If time is limited, the working parent might only be the consultant on a course, tutoring in the evening when needed. Taking the child on a field trip, a hike, or a fishing trip can be a great help, too. On rare occasions, some working parents have had to come home early to help.

Todd Wilson, in an article in *The Virginia Home Educator*, offers great advice to mothers on how to get fathers involved in the homeschool. His secret? "Whenever your husband involves himself in any way—LET HIM. You see, most of the time when a husband tries to help out, he gets told that he did it wrong. … He makes a mental note never to do *that* again. And he doesn't."[1] Wilson says that simple appreciation will be effective, while criticism, correction, and even appeals for help will not.

1. Wilson, Todd. "Getting Your Husband Involved in Homeschooling," Virginia Home Educator. *Richmond: Home Educators Association of Virginia, Winter 2008.*

Getting a Break

I asked several parents, "How do you get breaks?" Here are five answers.

- *My husband traveled a lot, so I got few breaks. If I needed one when he was home, I'd say, "Honey, you got the kids," and he took over. I went to a coffee shop or bookstore for a couple hours.*

- *I work part time. Those are my breaks. My husband allows me to go on vacation by myself once a year.*

- *Breaks for me are not a problem. While my son plays with LEGOS®, I get some time to myself.*

- *My teen loves free time, so I can take a "Mom" break whenever I need it. I simply explain to him, that I'm tired or I don't feel well, and I need to "sit in my recliner, quietly." He will do a computer program or use a educational Playstation 2 game. I will read a magazine or one of my many books to relax.*

- *My husband and I have what we call Sanity Weekends. One of us leaves for a night, the other stays home with the kids. It could be a motel across the street or a trip up to the mountains, but there are no barking dogs or ringing phones or laundry that needs to be sorted—or home school plans to be made! We are polar opposites, and so his idea of sanity is different from mine. And we can't leave the kids every six weeks. He wants to be alone and contemplate life, and I want human contact. So we need separate breaks. And our son is old enough he can stay alone for a couple hours when we are going places together.*

Whether male or female, as you aim to involve your spouse, do it thoughtfully. Don't overwhelm them with information. One father with ADD/ADHD told me how he loves his wife, but after all these years, she still hasn't grasped that he finds it impossible to follow the long, detailed reports she gives him at the end of the day. He pointed out that he has the same trouble with detailed reports at work, but his subordinates have learned that he wants a five-minute summary.

And it doesn't take an ADD/ADHD diagnosis to want the short summary. Personalities vary. I always want to give too many details, while my husband just wants the main points. That's good for me, forcing me to think out what the main points are.

Another way to approach your spouse thoughtfully is by watching your timing. I know not to bring up problems until after dinner. None of us likes to be given a problem at bedtime. If your spouse travels, realize that most people are preoccupied a day or two before and after a trip. So if I have anything important to discuss, I don't do it while my husband is already on the runway mentally, preparing for take-off. Know your spouse's style and be kind as you tell him or her about your homeschool day, decisions, and frustrations.

Healthy Marriage

In a two-parent family, homeschooling can become the main topic of conversation. But for the sake of the family and the children, parents must make a priority of their marriage.

To keep a marriage healthy, couples need to spend time together when they are not discussing school. Regular date nights are important, even if all you do is go to the hardware store together and stop for ice cream on the way home. My husband and I feel that if we don't take the kids and don't talk about them more than half the time, it counts as a date. If money is tight, take a walk together after dinner. Make the kids spend time alone in their room for an hour on Sunday afternoons. Do whatever it takes to get time to yourselves. You have to work hard not to drift apart and you must work to keep romance in any marriage.

Healthy Family

Another reason not to teach twenty-four/seven is for the sake of your family. You need time to enjoy your children. Take one child out, just the two of you, for a donut, for a walk, making cookies together (only if you both enjoy it—I only cook with children when I am sure I am in a really good mood!), or a simple outing, but one with a difference. Your main goal for the time is to listen and converse, not to criticize or advise. Ask questions and try to learn more about your child. Let him tell you about something important to him.

If you also have other children, there are two pitfalls to avoid. Some parents become so absorbed in the problems of one child they neglect the needs of another. Naturally, if you have one child with severe needs, those needs are your focus. But your other child might need special attention, too. If you can only afford therapy for one child, you will want the needier child to benefit. But talk to the therapist, or find another who will give a family discount or offer a sliding rate scale. You may need to divide your planning and research time to attend to the special needs of the other struggling learners in the family.

The second pitfall is to feel guilty for not dividing your time evenly among your children. As Melinda Boring explains to her children, "Being fair means giving you what you need when you need it."[2] In "The Myth of Equal Time," Carol Barnier describes her surprise when a parent with a child with serious multiple disabilities said that giving equal time to all her children is neither realistic nor desirable. In her article, Carol recounts the many good things that she saw her other children learning from Carol's having to give extra attention to the child with the greatest needs.[3] So don't focus all your attention on your neediest child, but don't feel you must divide your time and energy equally.

Are you too busy running to libraries, appointments, lessons, and practices, to eat together? Cut out some activities and make a priority of having your family eat supper together most nights. It keeps everyone saner, they will eat healthier food, they can practice communication and social skills, and it knits you together as a family.

2. Boring, Melinda L. Heads Up Now catalog. 1308 Mulford Road, Columbus, Ohio 43212. www.headsupnow.com.

3. Barnier, Carol. "The Myth of Equal Time." Accessed March 22, 2008. www.crosswalk.com/homeschool/11552735/page1/ Originally published in the July/Aug '07 issue of Home School Enrichment Magazine. www.HomeSchoolEnrichment.com

And as you work through your busy days, make time for laughter and fun. Don't correct all the time. Let your seven-year-old read silly jokes to you. Do your children like slapstick? Rent an old Buster Keaton movie. Did it snow last night? How about an hour of sledding before school, followed by hot chocolate and a good read-aloud book? If it's the first gorgeous day of summer, can you take the afternoon off for a picnic or a hike? When my son was young, sometimes I would save a little treat from the dollar store as a surprise after a long day. Other times I wrote notes saying "I love you" or telling him something I appreciate about him, and slip them where he would find them. Sometimes he wrote us notes, too.

Laughter cannot be scheduled. But when we make a mistake, if we can laugh at it, we help our children learn not to take themselves to seriously, either. As they grow in maturity and self-esteem, they can laugh at their own mistakes, and we can laugh with them. C.S. Lewis said that no people find each other more absurd than lovers.[4] Healthy families can enjoy each other's absurdities, too, without wounding each other. "A cheerful heart is good medicine."[5] Enjoy your family as you homeschool.

Conclusion

Homeschooling parents need to take care of themselves, their marriages, and their families if they want to succeed. Homeschooling a struggling learner may have sounded impossible at first, but many families have found it worthwhile. These families are not part of a well-known movement; they work quietly and celebrate small successes. What makes these parents keep going? Seeing their children learn and improve, reducing stress, and knowing they are providing the flexible, customized education that suits their children best. They have seen children blossom, gifts develop, and family ties deepen. When you commit time and thoughtful effort, you may find, as I did, that it is the best thing you can do for your struggling learner.

4. Lewis, C.S. The Great Divorce. New York: Macmillan, 1970. p. 115

5. Holy Bible: English Standard Version. Wheaton: Crossway, 2003. Proverbs 17:22.

Resources

Baskin, Amy, and Heather Fawcett. *More Than A Mom: Living A Full And Balanced Life When Your Child Has Special Needs.* Bethesda, Maryland: Woodbine House, 2006.

Hart, Betsy. *It Takes a Parent: How the Culture of Pushover Parenting Is Hurting Our Kids—and What to Do About It.* New York: Putnam, 2005.

Leman, Kevin, MD. *Bringing Up Kids Without Tearing Them Down.* Nashville, Tennessee: Thomas Nelson, 1995.

Marshak, Laura E., Ph.D., and Fran Pollock Prezant, M.Ed. *Married with Special-Needs Children.* Bethesda, Maryland: Woodbine House, 2007.

Index

About the Author

Kathy Kuhl teaches, writes, consults, and speaks, helping parents teach their children at home. She began working with exceptional children when she was fourteen. A graduate of William and Mary, she earned teaching certificates in English and mathematics. She has taught two-year-olds, junior high math students, adults, and homeschooled her son for grades four through twelve. She now teaches homeschool group classes in English and mathematics in northern Virginia. She speaks to homeschool conventions, patient advocacy organizations, and other groups. You may contact her though info@LearnDifferently.com

To order copies of this book, learn more about helping children learn, or see Kathy's speaking schedule, visit www.LearnDifferently.com

20476800R00214

Made in the USA
Lexington, KY
05 February 2013